EVERY MAN FOR HIMSELF

HOPKINS MOORHOUSE

Every Man for Himself

Hopkins Moorhouse

© 1st World Library, 2007
PO Box 2211
Fairfield, IA 52556
www.1stworldlibrary.com
First Edition

LCCN: 2007930798

Softcover ISBN: 978-1-4218-4841-9
Hardcover ISBN: 978-1-4218-4744-3
eBook ISBN: 978-1-4218-4938-6

Purchase *"Every Man for Himself"*
as a traditional bound book at:
www.1stWorldLibrary.com/purchase.asp?ISBN=978-1-4218-4841-9

1st World Library is a literary, educational organization
dedicated to:

- Creating a free internet library of downloadable ebooks

- Hosting writing competitions and offering book publishing
scholarships.

Interested in more 1st World Library books? contact:
literacy@1stworldlibrary.com
Check us out at: www.1stworldlibrary.com

1st World Library Literary Society

Giving Back to the World

"If you want to work on the core problem, it's early school literacy."

- James Barksdale, former CEO of Netscape

"No skill is more crucial to the future of a child, or to a democratic and prosperous society, than literacy."

- Los Angeles Times

"Literacy... means far more than learning how to read and write... The aim is to transmit... knowledge and promote social participation."

- UNESCO

"Literacy is not a luxury, it is a right and a responsibility. If our world is to meet the challenges of the twenty-first century we must harness the energy and creativity of all our citizens."

- President Bill Clinton

"Parents should be encouraged to read to their children, and teachers should be equipped with all available techniques for teaching literacy, so the varying needs and capacities of individual kids can be taken into account."

- Hugh Mackay

To My Mother

FOREWORD

Although prefaces are not the fashion in these accelerated times, some word of warning is due those who had the patience to read "Deep Furrows." It seems but fair to point out that whereas "Deep Furrows" was historical and its "characters" actual people taking prominent part in current events, the present pages are purely fictitious and the characters therein not even composite portraits of living personages.

Similarly the story events are pure invention and as fittingly might have been staged in any other of the nine provinces. The author humbly craves indulgence if he has in any way exceeded the license allowed him in spinning the incidents necessary for a novel of this type while seeking verisimilitude in settings with which he is familiar.

—H. M.

Winnipeg, February, 1920.

CONTENTS

CHAPTER I

FOG

Except for the lone policeman who paused beneath the arc light at the Front Street intersection to make an entry in his patrol book, Bay Street was deserted. The fog which had come crawling in from the lake had filled the lower streets and was feeling its way steadily through the sleeping city, blurring the street lights. Its clammy touch darkened the stone facades of tall, silent buildings and left tiny wet beads on iron railing and grill work. Down towards the waterfront a yard-engine coughed and clanked about in the mist somewhere, noisily kicking together a string of box-cars, while at regular intervals the fog-horn over at the Eastern Gap bellowed mournfully into the night.

After tucking away his book and rebuttoning his tunic the policeman lingered on the corner for a moment in the manner of one who has nothing to do and no place to go. He was preparing to saunter on when footfalls began to echo in the emptiness of the street and presently the figure of a young man grew out of the gray vapor—a young man who was swinging down towards the docks with the easy stride of an athlete. As he came within the restricted range of the arc light it was to be seen that his panama hat was tilted to the back of his head and that he was holding a silk handkerchief to one eye as if a cinder had blown into it.

"Good-night, Officer," he nodded as he passed without halting his stride. "Some fog, eh?"

"'Mornin', sir," returned the dim sentinel of the Law with a respectful salute as he grinned recognition. "Faith, an' 't is, sir."

High up in the City Hall tower at the head of the street Big Ben boomed two ponderous notes which flung eerily across the city.

Already the young man had faded into the thickening fog. He was in no mood to talk to inquisitive policemen, no matter how friendly or lonesome. It was his own business entirely if concealed beneath the silk handkerchief was the most elaborate black eye which had come into his possession since Varsity won the rugby championship some months before. If his face ached and his knuckles smarted where the skin had been knocked off, that was his own business also. And when the judgment of calmer moments has convinced a respectable young gentleman of spirit that there is nobody but himself to blame for what has happened he is inclined to solitary communion while taking the measure of his self-dissatisfaction.

It was indeed the end of a very imperfect day for Mr. Philip Kendrick. As he descended the stairs to the Canoe Club his thoughts were troubled. At that hour there was nobody about, but he let himself in with a special key which he carried for such contingencies. He found the suitcase undisturbed where he had left it and soon had his canoe in the water. A moment later he was driving into the thick wall of fog with strong, practiced strokes, heading straight across the bay for Centre Island.

Hopkins Moorhouse

The fog gave him little concern. This land-locked Toronto Bay he knew like a well-marked passage in a favorite book and at two o'clock in the morning it was not necessary to nose along cautiously, listening for the approach of water craft. Away to the right the lights of the amusement park on Hanlan's Point had gone out long ago, before the fog settled down like a wet blanket. The ferries had stopped running for the night. Even the "belt line boat," *Lulu*,—last hope of bibulous or belated Islanders—was back in her slip, funnel cold, lights out. The whole deserted waterfront lay wrapped in the shroud of the fog, lulled by the lap of water against pilings and the faint creakings of small craft at their moorings.

As the solitary canoe poked out for the open bay these minor sounds fell behind and were replaced by the steady purl of water under the bow. It filled with pleasing monotone the interludes between the fussing of the yard-engine back on the railway trackage and the blatancy of the foghorn at the Eastern Gap, every half minute bawling its warning into the open lake beyond.

There was nobody over at the big summer residence on Centre Island except Mrs. Parlby, the housekeeper, and her husband who acted as gardener. The place belonged to Kendrick's uncle, the Honorable Milton Waring, and it was usual for them to open the big house about the end of May. This year, however, his aunt and uncle had chosen to spend the summer at Sparrow Lake and for the past week they had been up at a rented cottage in the woods, leaving Phil behind in charge of the Island residence.

In response to a wire from his uncle, requesting him to join them at once and bring along certain articles which had been overlooked, he had packed his suitcase and paddled across to the city in the morning, intending to take the train for

Sparrow Lake. A chance meeting with an old classmate, however, had resulted in a sudden decision to delay his departure for another twenty-four hours in favor of a good time with Billy Thorpe.

As if in punishment, things had seemed to go wrong with him all day. In the afternoon the Rochester baseball team had knocked three Toronto pitchers out of the box, a blow-up which had cost the loyal Mr. Kendrick twenty-five dollars and a loss of reputation as an authority on International League standings. Then in the evening, in the crowd out at The Beach, somebody had taken hold of his silk ribbon fob and gently removed the gold watch which his aunt had given him on his birthday. Later still—!

It was the left eye, so swollen now that it was closed to a mere slit. There was no optical delusion about its nomenclature and in diameter and chromatic depth it was at the head of its class; in fact, it gave promise of being by daylight in a class by itself. It was the sort of decoration which could be relied upon implicitly to fire the imagination of misguided acquaintances through several merry weeks of green and yellow recuperation. And withal it cast a reflection upon the fistic prowess of young Mr. Kendrick which was entirely unjust, it being the product of what is known as a "lucky punch"—for the other fellow.

No, it was not in the result of the fight that dissatisfaction lay, but in the cause. McCorquodale's remarks about the Honorable Milton Waring had been addressed to McCorquodale's two companions; there had been no intent to insult the Honorable Milton Waring's nephew who sat at the next table in the restaurant, none of the three worthies being aware that they were within earshot of a hypersensitive member of the honorable gentleman's family. That being so, it had been distinctly foolish for the aforesaid nephew to walk over to the other table and demand an apology. He should have finished his coffee and cigarette and strolled out. Or, if he had deemed it imperative to participate in the political discussion, why in the mischief hadn't he just stepped across, proffered his cigarette-case and made a joke of the situation?

Of a truth the expression upon this fellow McCorquodale's homely, good-humored face when Kendrick revealed his identity had been sufficiently quizzical. He had grinned widely as he waved the indignant young man to a seat at the table and even then the situation would have adjusted itself had it been left to the principals. But McCorquodale's companions were a pair of flashily dressed young "sports" who, thinking they saw a chance for some fun at Kendrick's expense, had proceeded to tread upon Mr. McCorquodale's professional pride—McCorquodale, one time known to ringside patrons as "Iron Man" McCorquodale, one time near middle-weight champion.

"Y'see, it's this way," the ex-pugilist had explained earnestly. "I aint said nothin' about y'r uncle as aint public anyways. It's in the papers off an' on, see? An' now another election's comin' down the pike, y'll have to be gittin' used to all kinds o' spiels. Fac's is fac's, kid, an' when I says the Hon. Milt aint no sweet-scented geranium but's out fer all the simoleons he can pick off the little old Mazuma Tree,—why, I on'y says what I reads an' hears, believe me. You bein' his nephew aint changin' public opinion none. See?"

Kendrick's anger at this brazenness had prevented him from thinking clearly. He was getting "touchy" about his uncle's political record of late and had had occasion to defend it with some heat during certain discussions among friends; there had been several newspaper attacks which he had resented greatly also. His uncle's reputation as a public man he had been

Quixotic enough to take to heart as a personal matter of family honor and, as everyone knows, family honor is a thing to uphold. He had demanded that McCorquodale retract his statement. McCorquodale had refused flatly to do so.

One of the two grinning "sports" knew a place where they could settle it undisturbed—just around the corner in the basement of a pool-room. It had been a brisk little mix-up while it lasted; but it had not taken the ex-pugilist long to discover that he was facing the best amateur boxer Varsity had produced in a number of years and right in the middle of it he had put on his coat deliberately, to the overwhelming disappointment of his two friends.

"Nix, you guys!" he had grunted, breathing heavily. "I knows when I'm up against it. Y'see, I got a date with a Jane to-morra an' I aint hankerin' to lose me way with no mussed map. Not on y'r tintype!"

Whereupon the "Iron Man" had proceeded to demonstrate his malleability by assuring Mr. Kendrick that he was ready to agree that the sun rose in the south and made a daily trip straight north to escape the heat, if Mr. Kendrick said so. His anxiety to make friends had been positively funny; but there had been a sincerity in his handshake that somehow had seemed to rob the apology of its satisfaction. And when McCorquodale had proffered a broken cigar Kendrick had accepted it with an uneasy feeling that he had made somewhat of a fool of himself; for Phil was no prig and he found that McCorquodale was a pretty good sort with a certain whimsicality that was not to be denied.

He rested his paddle for a moment and floated in the dark, listening. As soon as he got home he would go to the refrigerator for a piece of raw beefsteak for his swollen eye. Darn that eye anyway! He would have to hibernate up in the woods till it became more presentable. Far behind him in the mist somewhere the yard-engine was still coughing; across the water came a subdued squeal of protesting flanges, followed by the distant bang of shunted box-cars. He listened for any sound of the harbor patrol boat; but even had he bothered to show a light it would have been obliterated in the fog, which was the worst Kendrick ever had experienced. A raw beefsteak poultice—He fancied the fog-horn was a little louder; he would need to keep more to the left or he would find himself hitting Mug's Landing, west of Island Park, or wind up away over at the Point somewhere.

He resumed his paddling. This matter of his uncle—Was it possible that in pursuit of political ambitions his uncle was forgetting the principles for which he professed to stand as a public man? Was it just possible that this fellow, McCorquodale, knew what he was talking about? Wasn't it men of that stamp who became the tools for corrupt practices—the boodlers, the heelers who did the actual ballot-stuffing, the personating at the polls, the bribing? Did McCorquodale know of what he spoke?

The thought brought with it a sense of disloyalty to his uncle; but the young man forced himself to face the idea seriously. He was beginning to realize that there were many things about which he was woefully ignorant—practical things entirely outside academic curriculums. For twenty-two years he had eaten his meals regularly and lived a life uncolored by any event more significant than his recent graduation from 'Varsity with honors. That he had captained the football team to victory the fall before was nothing extraordinary; many another fellow with equally broad shoulders and an equally well balanced head upon them had done the same thing before him. Financial worries had never intruded upon his good times, while social standing was something which he had come to accept as a matter of course. Only of late had he begun to analyze things for himself and it had been something of a shock to discover that a college education was just a beginning—that beyond the campus of his alma mater spread a workaday world which scoffed at dead languages and went in for a living wage, which turned from isoceles triangles and algebraic conundrums to solve the essential problems of food and clothing and shingled roofs. It was a new viewpoint which planted doubts where what he had supposed to be certainties had been wont to blossom.

The Honorable Milton Waring's very position as a cabinet minister in the government of the day always had seemed to carry its own credentials. As a youth Phil had thrilled with pride on occasions of public demonstration in his uncle's honor and there had been times of speech-making when the Honorable Milton's eloquence had swayed his audience to unrestrained applause. To the unsophisticated eyes of youth a shiny silk hat, a long-tailed frock coat, a gold-headed cane, a diamond ring and a prominent place upon the platform had been indicative of the top rungs of Fame and Success and Honor among men. The goings and comings of Society's votaries, the bright lights of the big Waring residence in Rosedale, the orchestras and bands and public processions and cheering and flags and bunting—these things had contributed to the awe with which Phil had regarded the Honorable Milton Waring in the days of boyhood impressions. The mere fact that his uncle received the acclamations of the people and held high public office by their gift had seemed to invest the Honorable Milton with all the attributes of an honorable gentleman of distinction.

Such early impressions are tenacious of place. Yet with maturer years had come certain doubts that thrust their shadows across moments of serious thought. Phil Kendrick had begun to think for himself and his study of political history had awakened him to the knowledge that there was a very "practical" side to politics as they existed throughout the country just then—that successful politicians too often were men who regarded the whole thing as a game wherein the end justified the means, the end being to carry elections. Was his uncle of this ilk? It had been hinted. There were those who said that the Honorable Milton Waring knew much about assembling political machinery around election time and oiling it for a smooth run. And such rumors aroused thoughts which Phil had been very loath to entertain.

After all, though, did he really know his uncle? Between them there had never been any very close bond of sympathy—such, for instance, as always had existed between Phil and his aunt. His uncle's share in the growing lad's up-bringing had been of the superficial sort—a pat on the back, a "run along now, my boy; I'm busy." Always it had been Aunt Dolly to whom he had taken his childish difficulties for sympathetic adjustment. It had been that way from the first when the sudden loss of both father and mother had thrown him upon Aunt Dolly's care. His own mother could not have meant more to him and Kendrick's smile was very gentle as he thought of his aunt. First and last, her happiness—

Ah, but was she happy? That was the question. She pretended to be, of course; but how much of it was mere pretence? Beneath her smiles Phil had sensed of late a vague unrest, disappointment—he hardly knew what to call it, so illusive it was. She had laughed at him fondly and called him "a foolish boy" when he had ventured to ask her if anything was wrong. After that she had been careful that he did not surprise any look upon her face but one of cheerfulness.

The possibility that in some way his uncle was the source of that subtle change in Aunt Dolly had disturbed Phil's peace of mind not a little. In his presence she had been the same gentle, smiling, thoughtful Aunt Dolly that she had always been; but once or twice he had read fleeting anxiety in the glance with which she had followed her husband's departure from the room. Her love for the Honorable Milton was unqualified, Phil knew. It was, in fact, the directing force of Aunt Dolly's whole life. It had enabled her to overcome her innate dislike for the everlasting round of social trivialities and assume her place as a society leader with a brilliance and tact which had earned the commendation of even her exacting husband. What was going wrong in the Waring household? Or was it all imagination and Aunt Dolly's look of concern sum-totalled by the weather in relation to a change to lighter flannels?

Certainly when it came to considering his uncle's political record there was always the Rives case to fall back upon, to cast a halo about the Honorable Milton's head. The Rives case had provided a sensational aftermath to a strenuous election campaign which had resulted in the complete overthrow of the former government. The "Honorable" Harrington Rives with his large head and bushy shock of black curls had been a picturesque figure on the rostrums of the country districts. He took a good photo—and knew it! It was displayed in every conceivable pose in the newspapers and fought the weather on the side of many a livery barn long after the "Grand Rally" with its crop of cheer-strained throats was a thing of the past. His ability as a stump speaker and his hail-fellow-well-met-and-how's-the-baby way of mixing with the crowd had popularized him to the bamboozlement of his admirers. So that in election forecasts his seat in the Legislature always had headed the list at party headquarters, while in the opposition camp it had been chalked up as "election conceded."

But as is the law of it, there cometh a day when the evil a man doeth findeth him out. Whispers had stolen abroad in the land and the rumors had drawn men together in scattered groups. Rivulets of resentment had run together in widening pools of public opinion till the mysterious forces which slowly arouse the "Great Common People" had broken loose suddenly in one of those periodic reform waves which sweep everything before them. And into the arena with shining sword drawn had stepped a brilliant lawyer named Waring to pick up the gauge of battle against Rives and his corrupt associates, with Rives himself as his individual opponent.

The fight in Rives' constituency had gone to bitter lengths. The government forces had poured money into the campaign and under the practiced hand of Harrington Rives the "Machine" had gone to indiscreet lengths to defeat Waring. Bribery and corruption, which for a long time had characterized the administration's political organization, had become more open and Rives' opponent quietly had gathered the irrefutable evidence which ended in the arrest of Rives and several of his henchmen on the eve of the election. The exposure had been so complete and far-reaching—actual misappropriation of public funds in Rives' case—that the reform forces had made a clean sweep amid great public rejoicing.

It would require a short memory indeed to forget all this, thought Kendrick. Remembrance of the Rives case, which he had taken the trouble once to look up in the old newspaper files, never failed to re-establish his faith in his uncle and it was with a sweep of irritation now that he dug in his paddle—and veered sharply to the left as the rustle of reeds against the canoe warned him that he was close inshore somewhere. Mechanically he tried to peer through the dark. This ought to be the sandbar to the left of the Island Park ferry landing if he had not gone out of his reckoning. He waited for the fog-horn that presently bellowed loudly off to the left. If this were the sandbar he would have to skirt it east to the cut that ran in beside the Yacht Club.

A moment's paddling convinced him that he had guessed correctly. Something scraped alongside—a yacht, moored in the channel. He turned to the right and presently was gratified to find himself in quieter water. A moment later he was safely within the inner channel that followed the park embankment and led east past private boathouses.

From the canal short streets here cut south across the island to the lakefront, where many fine residences of the wealthy faced open water. The steady rhythm of the waves against the breakwater reached him in sharp contrast to the brooding stillness of the channel water.

Kendrick was almost home now. The Waring boathouse was within a stonesthrow. He edged the canoe forward gently, close to the bank, feeling his way toward the familiar landing.

And there was not one thing to prepare him for what immediately followed. A voice which seemed to be almost at his elbow spoke to him out of the darkness in low hurried tones—a woman's voice! At the same time he felt the bow of the canoe pulled in against the bank. Before he could recover sufficiently from his surprise to speak she had stepped aboard and he could hear her adjusting a cushion beneath her knees. Then came her tense whispered warning:

"Stick right here and don't talk. We haven't time to get away, but they can't see us. Sh! Here they come!"

CHAPTER II

BLIND MAN'S BUFF

With difficulty Phil Kendrick restrained a desire to laugh outright. The totally unexpected situation in which he found himself paralyzed his speech and by the time he had recovered from the first shock of it a further development held him silent. With senses sharpened he listened in the dark to approaching footsteps and a murmur of voices, his wonder growing as he recognized the unmistakable accents of Stinson, his uncle's personal servant—Stinson who, by all the rules of valet service, should be up at Sparrow Lake at that very moment with the Honorable Milton Waring.

A key was being fitted into the padlock of the Waring boathouse. The planking creaked as the strangers tip-toed inside. There appeared to be several of them. A sloshing of water as they boarded the big launch, then the first fitful rustlings of the engine as it was turned over. Soon its loud staccatto rose above the wail of the foghorn.

Had the house been robbed? Phil dismissed this idea at once. No valuables likely to invite burglary were kept at the Island residence, even had Stinson's long and faithful service not placed him beyond suspicion. Probably the valet had slipped away on a little holiday and had been entertaining a few of his friends. With paddle shoved into the mud to hold the canoe steady against the embankment so that it would not capsize in the wash of the launch, Kendrick decided to sit still and await developments.

The launch passed presently, so close to them that he held his breath. One of the occupants was talking in low tones. Somebody laughed and said: "That's a good one, Nickleby." A third voice spoke in gruff admonition: "Shut up, you fellows! No names, please." After that—silence, except for the slow chug of the engine and the purl of water, diminishing. They were gone.

A breath of evident relief came from the unknown passenger in the canoe.

"Pretty close, that," she whispered. "I guess we can go now, but it would be better not to talk till we get out on the bay."

Without a word Kendrick shoved off with his paddle and turned the nose of the canoe for the Yacht Club channel. The launch had gone straight down the main canal to the ferry pier before heading out into the bay and all sound of it presently was lost. He strained his eyes to catch a glimpse of his mysterious companion, forgetting for the moment that even had it been broad daylight the fog would have concealed her.

He tried to decide what was the best thing to do. What sort of a game was this that he had stumbled upon? What was this woman doing over at the Island at 2.30 a.m. in weather like this? Who was she? Why was she spying upon Stinson's little party, if that was what she had been up to? It was a situation with which any young man of zest and imagination might find interest in dallying. How should he begin?

"Pass me a paddle, Joe. It's all right to talk now." She gave a little laugh of satisfaction and he noted that her voice was contralto and well modulated. "This has been the best night's work yet. Did you think I was never coming?"

Kendrick cleared his throat.

"Excuse me, madam, but there appears to be some mistake." He could hear her startled gasp. "It is evident that you have got into the wrong canoe in the dark. I am neither Joseph nor any of his brethren; so he must be waiting for you still. Do you want me to turn back?"

"Wh-why,—who are you?" she managed to gasp in an alarmed voice.

"The same to you, madam, and many of them," laughed Kendrick easily. "There's no occasion to feel frightened as I have just had a meal. Anyone is liable to lose the way in a fog like this and I will count it a privilege to help you locate Joe. He must be somewhere about if he was waiting for you."

"Who are you?" she repeated more evenly.

"The owner of this canoe which you have commandeered so successfully. Please pardon me for pointing out that it is your lead, madam. I would be glad to have you begin by telling me who was in that launch? Why all the excitement? Where do you want to go now?"

"You are inquisitive enough to be a detective. Are you?"

"In that case would I need to ask where we were going?" countered Kendrick. "I believe you said this had been the best haul yet. Whose house was it this time?"

She remained silent. When she spoke again Kendrick fancied a nervous note in her voice.

"Will you please explain how you happened to be waiting for me at that particular spot?"

"Bless your heart, madam, I wasn't waiting for you! I happen to live nearby and was getting ready to step ashore when you grabbed my canoe and ordered me to keep quiet. I did so. Here we are."

"Your discretion was commendable," she approved. "It certainly is most extraordinary. I don't see where on earth—I guess my escort has taken French leave." She tried to laugh carelessly, but she could not hide the fact that she was greatly disturbed. "Will you paddle me across to the city?"

"And leave poor Joe out in the cold gray fog? Don't you think it would be better to turn back and give a holler or two?"

"Never mind him. He has gone home already very likely. I will pay you one dollar to paddle me over. Is that satisfactory?"

"It all depends. Supposing I refuse?"

"Then I would have to ask you to step into the water and swim to shore while I do my own paddling and keep down expenses."

"Presupposing, of course, that you own the canoe."

"It is too bad it is so dark," she retorted impatiently, "or you would know that a revolver is pointed straight at you this very moment."

Kendrick laughed in pure enjoyment of the situation.

"My dear young lady,"—he had decided that she was young and he wondered if she were pretty—"you force me to the conclusion that either you are bluffing outrageously or you are a desperate character! Please don't be frightened. I'm neither Steve Brodie, the Bridge Jumper, nor the famous Jack Dalton, and in this age of safety razors Bluebeards are *extra muros*. This isn't the opening spasm of some blood-and-thunder novel, you know. We're right here on Toronto Bay where one can get into trouble for not showing a light after dark. Will you oblige me by unhooking the lamp at the bow there and passing it back to me so that I can light up. I promise then to start earning that dollar without further delay."

He heard her fumbling with it. There was a splash in the water, a little cry of well feigned dismay.

"Oh, how careless of me! It—slipped out of my hand."

Phil grinned cheerfully as he began to dip his paddle, interest quickened. It was a neat sidestepping of his inconsiderate attempt to scrutinize her. She had taken the first trick.

"You do yourself an injustice, madam. Are you usually so careful when you are careless?"

"You have not told me your name yet," she reminded him, apparently more at ease now that she knew he intended to paddle her across the bay.

"My name? It's an Indian name—Watha—Hy. A. Watha, at your service, and I am very fond of canoeing. What's yours?"

"You need hardly ask that, Mr. Hiawatha, when you knew

my sister, Minnie, so well," she laughed. "I am *Mary* Ha-ha!"

"You don't say!" chuckled Kendrick in appreciation. "The original little Merry Ha-Ha, eh?—Little Laughing-Gas!"

"If you are Hiawatha, why are you using a paddle?" she pursued. "I always understood from the Poet that all you had to do was to guide your canoe with your thoughts."

"Not when they're travelling in a circle. But this looks more like 'Blind Man's Buff' than 'Ring-Around-A-Rosy,' don't you think? Or are you trying to play 'Tag' with me? Well, you're 'It' anyway," he said, dropping all hint of banter in his tone. "I'd advise you to meet a few straight questions with straight answers. First, who is this Joe person you were expecting to do the canoeing for you?"

"My husband."

"And the people in the launch?"

"How should I know who they were? By what right do you ask me that?" she demanded.

"The circumstances are somewhat unusual, madam, you must admit," Kendrick reminded her sharply. "Do you wish me to play safe by handing you over to the police?"

"Police? My Good Gracious me! What crime have I committed?"

"That would be a matter for official enquiry. It may be that you and your husband are in the habit of wandering about the Island in a thick fog at two o'clock in the morning—picking daisies for the sick kiddies over at the Children's Home, I presume—but, to be perfectly frank with you, I doubt it. Besides, there is the little matter of the launch."

"Why are you so interested in that launch?"

"Because I happen to be the nephew of my uncle who happens to own it and to have left it in my charge during his absence," said Kendrick deliberately. "I'm laying the cards face up, madam. The launch is the property of Honorable Milton Waring, of whom you may have heard. Undoubtedly it has been stolen."

He was not prepared for the laughter with which his unknown passenger greeted this bold announcement. He knew she was trying to smother her mirth, but it finally broke all bounds. A very musical laugh it was, very pleasant to hear.

"Oh, please forgive me," she gasped finally. "It is very rude of me, I know; but—you said you were the Honorable Milt's nephew—" Again she laughed in spite of herself.

"You know my uncle?" he asked eagerly.

"I read the papers," she said evasively. "Everybody knows a public man."

"I'm laying the cards face up, madam," repeated Kendrick solemnly. "My name is Kendrick—Philip Kendrick. I was on my way home when you—well, shanghaied me. Won't you meet me half way by equal frankness, so that we may avoid—well, any unpleasantness?"

"You mean—?" She had stopped laughing.

"That unless you answer legitimate questions I shall be

forced to hand you over to the police."

"I warn you that you would regret it," she said quietly.

"Very much," agreed Kendrick readily. "I would be sorry to cause you any inconvenience; but surely you see how impossible it is for me to avoid being inquisitive under the circumstances. Are you going to be frank with me or not?"

She did not answer him immediately and he smiled to himself as he paddled in silence. For, if the truth must be told, Mr. Philip Kendrick was enjoying himself immensely. He had only the sound of her voice from which to draw deductions; but the cultured tones of it and the lilt of her low laughter bespoke an education and refinement with which he failed to reconcile the idea that she was a lady burglar. Yet—

He stopped paddling to listen intently. Several times now he had thought he heard a sound off in the darkness behind him. It came again—a slight hollow sound, as of a paddle scraping against a canoe. They were being followed. Had the girl heard it, too? He waited for the wail of the fog-horn to die away—and found her speaking.

"—frank with you, Mr. Kendrick," she was saying. "The circumstances are less extraordinary than they appear to you. My—husband and I were at a party at a friend's house on the Island. We paddled over in a canoe and Joe went ahead of me to locate it. In the dark I must have missed the spot where he was waiting for me and when you came along so silently and so close to the bank I naturally thought it was Joe. Ridiculously simple, you see."

"You have forgotten the launch," prompted Kendrick severely.

"I know nothing about the launch," she denied with resentment. "When I heard those people coming I thought it was some of the guests from the party who had said they would race us home. Will you please paddle on, Mr. Kendrick. It is damp and chilly in this fog and I am naturally in a hurry to get home."

He laughed with skepticism, but plied his paddle again. He was not as concerned about the launch as he pretended, of course; at the worst it probably meant that Stinson had been entertaining some of his friends on the sly. He had no intention of handing his mysterious passenger to the police. But was he to let her laugh at him and disappear unchallenged into the fog out of which she had come?

Phil Kendrick's experience with the opposite sex was very limited, he had to confess. He had been too completely absorbed in athletics to afford girls more than passing attention. Those of his social set—those he had met—had failed to impress him. One or two of them were attractive enough in a general way, he realized; some were amusing to him and some very very tedious. It was a new experience to find himself actually interested in a girl—or rather, her voice! He wished he could get a look at her till he remembered the poor showing he would make with his blackened eye. Then he was thankful for the darkness.

Phil planned to land her at the Queen City Yacht Club at the foot of York St., or at the Canoe Club; either would provide an easy landing. They must be well across the bay now; but it was hard to say just where they would come in. Ordinarily he could have steered by the illuminated dial of the City Hall clock and the spire of St. James'; but the fog obliterated all landmarks.

They were both very damp from exposure to the mist, but it

is doubtful if either of them was aware of it. He made several further attempts to discover her identity without avail; at every turn she evaded him skillfully and it was beginning to look as if she would step ashore and vanish into the fog without leaving behind her a single clue for him to follow. This illusiveness was an added spur to his desire to know this girl. He did not believe that she was a married woman at all. It was a conclusion which seemed to be justified by her elaborate precautions to make him think otherwise. Because of some foolish notion of the conventions she intended to go as she had come, taking advantage of the fog to write down the night's adventure in a book which must be closed to him for all time and forgotten.

Deliberately Phil held back the canoe. They were within a few strokes of the landing now.

"Listen to me very carefully," he began. "I am going to ask you for the last time to tell me your name or the name of some friend whom I can get to introduce me to you properly. Isn't that fair? I have told you the truth about myself and will hand you my card to prove it. You must play equally fair with me or—"

"Or what?" she demanded haughtily as he hesitated.

"Or—well, take the consequences," he finished lamely.

"Which are—? Be explicit, Mr. Kendrick."

"Well, I might turn around and paddle you back to the Island and leave you there, for one thing. The circumstances are not such as entitle you to the consideration I have shown you. For all I know, you may be an ordinary crook. Think it over, madam. Is there any reason why I should not call you 'kiddo' and help myself to a kiss? Is there?"

"Yes—the fact that Philip Kendrick is a gentleman. I dare you to prove it otherwise!"

"It is kind of you. If you are so sure of it, why won't you give me a chance? Come on, be a sport. I will promise anything you wish to meet you legitimately, and I really would regret it very much if I thought—"

"I have told you already that it is impossible," she interrupted coldly. "I always understood it was a woman's prerogative to choose her acquaintances. I am grateful for your services tonight, of course; but beyond that—The fact is, I do not care to know you, Mr. Kendrick. Please put me ashore and say good-bye."

A cold fire of resentment burned in Kendrick's eyes as he drove the canoe to the landing with a few skillful strokes. Why had he been so foolish as to tell her his real name? Why didn't she want to know him? Without a word he caught the canoe in one hand and stepped out. He felt along the gunwale to the bow and fastened the painter to an iron ring in the planking, then handed her out safely. He retained his grasp of her hand.

"A moment ago you dared me to kiss you," he said gravely. "I am not in the habit of taking dares from anybody."

"Let go my hand at once, sir. You know very well you cannot so far forget yourself as to take such a liberty. I dare you to prove yourself no gentleman."

"I warn you—!"

"I dare you!"

"Very well! On your own head be it, then! The boatman is

worthy of his hire," he paraphrased and laughingly he seized her in his arms and kissed her.

The next instant he received a resounding slap in the face. It had young muscles and indignation behind it and it found him unprepared. He started back automatically, tripped, lost his balance and fell into the water.

"Oh, you—you miserable—*fresh Aleck*!" came her mortified cry.

She lingered only long enough to make sure that he could swim. As he drew himself out of the water the sound of her running feet died out on the pier.

With chattering teeth Kendrick cast loose, seized his paddle and drove it deep into the water. Ye gods, what a fool! Very angry at himself, he set out across the bay once more, guided by the derisive bawling of the fog-horn at the Eastern Gap.

Hopkins Moorhouse

CHAPTER III

"NO MATTER WHAT HAPPENS"

At no time had it been Phil Kendrick's habit to entertain an inflated opinion of his own importance. On occasion he had ridden around the gridiron on the shoulders of idolatrous students; but his modesty had been one of the factors underlying his popularity. Despising conceit in others, he was too prone, perhaps, to take himself to task for those little mistakes which every young man is liable to make from time to time.

It is safe to say, however, that never in all his life had he arraigned himself upon the carpet of his own condemnation so severely as now while paddling across the bay for the second time within the hour. If the McCorquodale incident earlier in the evening had lowered his opinion of his own judgment he was now ready to concede that he had no judgment whatsoever. It was of little use to tell himself that it served her right, or that she had dared him deliberately to do what he had done. That did not alter the fact that if he ever met her again—it was not likely that he would, of course, but if he did,—somewhere, sometime—he had erected a barrier to her good will which would preclude all hope of her friendship. His status in her sight was that of a "miserable fresh Aleck!"

Thus, as a relief to his feelings and in part to keep warm by exertion, did Phil come home through the fog at headlong pace in a high state of discontent, a veritable bear with a sore head. As he lifted the canoe to its place in the boathouse something pricked his finger, and by the light of a match he found a dollar bill pinned to one of the canoe cushions with a tiny brooch. His hire!—the only reward he had had any right to expect! The sight of these souvenirs did not tend to restore his peace of mind, and there was little mirth in the short laugh which he bestowed upon them as he thrust them into his pocket; yet it is interesting that he looked upon them as souvenirs, even while deciding to dismiss the whole matter permanently from his thoughts.

The launch was not back yet, he noted. Well, Stinson could go to the devil with it for all he cared! He slammed the boathouse door and strode up the side-street, this mood carrying as far as the picket gate. His hand was on the latch before he realized that the library windows were blurring through the fog with light.

Had the servants all gone crazy to-night? He went around to the front of the house, and with his face between the slats of the verandah railing, peered through the French windows. Muttering astonishment, he climbed over the railing, fitted his latch-key noiselessly and swung open the double glass doors that gave direct entrance to the room. The slight sound of his entry passed unnoticed by the Honorable Milton Waring, who continued to lean over his desk completely absorbed in a litter of papers.

But for the heavy odor of stale cigar smoke it would have been easy to suppose that the fog without had crept into the library. The air was blue. Phil's glance swept the disordered room. Three empty whisky glasses stood on the library table. The butts of cigars and innumerable cork-tipped cigarettes lay smothered in gray ashes that spilled untidily in sundry ash-trays. There was a char of burned paper in the open grate where a few coals still glowed redly. The desk was covered with packets of folded papers, held together by rubber bands, and loose sheets upon which much figuring had been done with the blue pencil which his uncle favored. A stock certificate or two peeped from a closed account book.

Phil looked again at the bowed figure, struck by a laxity of manner that was foreign to the Honorable Milton Waring. His thick iron-gray hair, usually so carefully brushed, was rumpled on end where his fingers had plowed and held his head while he figured with the other hand. He had removed his collar and tossed it aside impatiently; it lay on the floor behind the chair, leaving the tie still hanging loosely around the neck, the end of it twisted over one shoulder. The door in front of which the intruder stood was outside the older man's line of vision; but Phil could see a flushed cheek, and there was an air of dejection in his uncle's attitude quite out of keeping with customary poise.

The subject of these observations reached abruptly for the decanter on the desk and poured himself a stiff drink of Scotch whisky. The neck tinkled a little tattoo against the glass. He swallowed the liquor neat and shook his head in a spasmodic grimace. The sigh with which he settled back in his chair was one of utter weariness.

Phil gave a slight cough to announce his presence.

"Pardon me, Uncle Milt, if I'm intruding, but I didn't know you were in town—Why, what's wrong?" he ended quickly; for his uncle had sprung from his chair and was clinging to the edge of the desk for support while he stared as if he were gazing at an apparition.

In truth, quite aside from his quiet entry, the young man's appearance was startling enough. His facial disfigurement achieved a bizarre effect which the condition of his clothes served to heighten. The once jaunty panama hat hung shapelessly about his ears and from beneath it a plaster of blond hair slanted across his forehead rakishly. His collar was a soggy mess, from which depended a dark red string in sorry travesty of a flowing tie. His shirt was soiled with mud, his coat and trousers full of wrinkles.

"For heaven's sake, boy! What's happened? Train wreck?" He dropped back into his chair, eyeing his nephew in amazement. "Why aren't you at Sparrow Lake with your aunt? Get my wire? Eh? They told me you left this morning—" His voice was hoarse and it trailed away as if the situation embarrassed him and he was not quite sure how to handle it. He stared uncertainly, drumming nervously with his fingers.

Phil nodded as he sat down in the nearest chair and stared back. The surprise of finding his uncle there was overridden by the new discovery of his evident diffidence, his flushed face, a lack of that self-contained bearing which always had marked him as a man of large affairs. It was his uncle's strict rule, he recalled, never to take a second drink; it was an axiom of the Honorable Milton's that the second drink drew the cork on indiscretion and eventual inebriety. That something had happened which must have disturbed him greatly to make him break this rule was a deduction as simple as the evidence that he had broken it.

"What about you, Uncle Milt?" suggested Kendrick after a brief explanation of his change of plans—a recital which carefully avoided mention of McCorquodale or the mysterious woman of the fog. "If I had known that Aunt Dolly was going to be alone I wouldn't have let Thorpe persuade me to stay over a day."

"I was called in unexpectedly—important business—" He pushed uneasily at the papers on the desk. "Have a cigar, Philip?" He passed the humidor as he spoke, then scratched a match and held it to his nephew's selection with careful courtesy. He shook his head in smiling disapproval of the swollen eye. "Bad business, young man! Bad business! A fine flower of folly you have there, eh? Don't grow 'm like that at the Ladies' Aid meeting at the First Baptist Church, do they?" He settled back in his chair, chortling.

Phil smiled as he tossed aside his hat.

"Blame it on the fog, Uncle Milt. I was foolish enough to trip over something in the dark and take a header down the Canoe Club stairs into the water," he explained mendaciously. "Me for the woods to-morrow without fail. I guess I got off easy at that, for you can't see your hand in front of your face out on the bay to-night. Stinson almost ran me down with the launch—missed me by a couple of feet and that's all."

"Stinson? Stinson, d'you say? Don't mean *our* Stinson—in— *our* launch? Not our Stinson in our very own launch, Phil'p? You s'prise me greatly. In the dark like that—How do you know?" he challenged.

Kendrick smiled at the transparency of this attempt.

"I recognized his voice for one thing. Stinson was speeding the parting guests—the three who drank out of the glasses yonder. Pshaw, you know as well as I do that you sent me that wire to clear the way for this little affair to-night, and you're wishing right now that I was at the bottom of the lake! But it's all right, Uncle Milt."

His uncle did not laugh. Instead he eyed the younger man from beneath heavy brows that met in a scowl.

"Sherlock Holmes, eh? When'd you start emulating Sherlock Holmes?" he growled. "Been a meeting here—yes—business. What of it?"

"Nothing at all, if you say so. Only don't make the mistake of thinking I'm still a mere kid, Uncle Milt. I'd hate to think there was any other reason why you have never admitted me to your confidence. Did it ever occur to you that perhaps I might—well, sort of dig in and help you in some way? You and Aunt Dolly have been mighty good to me and I kind of feel—Well, you know what I mean," he finished diffidently.

The Honorable Milton Waring's brows unbent. His gaze wandered automatically to the pile of papers on the desk and for a moment he was silent.

"There is nothing you can do, Phil—Phill*up*,—to help," he said at last, shaking his head slowly, while the tired lines deepened about his eyes. "I—thanks all same."

Kendrick hunched his chair nearer and laid a hand on the other's knee.

"You're in trouble of some kind," he said earnestly. "Please don't try to deny it, Uncle Milt. I promised Billy Thorpe I'd join him next week on a fishing trip, but that's all off if I can be of any use to you. That special course in engineering next fall—that's all off, too, if you need me. It's my duty to help and it's your duty to let me. We both owe it to Aunt Dolly, don't we?"

A look of apprehension sprang into the tired eyes. He waved his hand swiftly towards the empty glasses.

Hopkins Moorhouse

"Your aunt—she must know nothing of—all this. I warn you now, Phil'p,—not a word. No use causing her needless worry. Her social duties, understand,—These business affairs—" His voice trailed again and he looked anxiously for his nephew's acquiescence.

"That goes as a matter of course," nodded Kendrick. "So far as I am concerned, this little chat with you has never taken place and there's been nobody here except the servants—so far as I am concerned. But is there any danger of anybody— What would be the object of anybody spying on this particular little seance—?" He paused at the quick consternation which the suggestion aroused.

"What do you mean, Philip?" demanded the Honorable Milton sharply. He sat up more alertly. "Why do you ask such a foolish question? Are you talking at random or—?"

"Very much at random," assured Kendrick hastily. "I was just wondering. Because—Well, it would be the only way anybody who happened to be interested would find out about your meeting, wouldn't it? I don't intend to talk about it, as I said before. I thought perhaps if it had anything to do with the political situation, for instance,—detectives, you know— around election time. I don't pretend to know very much about these things, of course."

"You are fortunate," grunted the Honorable Milton, dryly. "Seems to me you are allowing your imagination to run away with you, young man. Advise you to curb it."

Phil took a long pull at his cigar and studied his uncle keenly as he blew the smoke into the air.

"Do you want to know how I really got this beauty spot— this 'flower of folly' as you called it?" he asked unexpectedly.

"I had a little argument with a fellow to-night who insisted that you were—he retracted it, of course—were a political grafter!"

The smile with which the Honorable Milton Waring had welcomed the promised change of subject faded slowly. He wagged his head in reproof.

"Very foolish of you, Philip—to take any notice of that sort of thing. Let 'em talk!" Yet he looked at this nephew of his with a new interest. "Grafter, eh? Didn't believe it, eh?"

"Anyone who looks up your political record, Uncle Milt, must respect you," said Phil seriously. "These newspapers that are so fond of handing out roasts seem to overlook the fact that you were the man mainly responsible for kicking out Rives and his crowd and cleaning up the whole rotten administration. It makes me mad. And some of them have got the nerve to hint that the present Government—"

"Don't let's get into any political discussion, Philip," interrupted his uncle, holding up his hand in protest. "Please. I'm too tired for that. I'm sick of it, d'you hear? Politics! Politics! The same miserable tactics of misrepresentation! The same petty motives that have bedeviled public life for the past—Damn them!"

He heaved himself abruptly from his chair and began to pace the room restlessly while Kendrick watched him, surprised by the unexpected vehemence of the outburst. After a turn or two he stopped directly in front of his nephew, and in his eyes was a strange look.

"There are many things, my boy, which you cannot be expected to understand without a lot of explanation," he said more quietly. "I cannot go into any of these things now. If you ever accept a public office in later life try to look upon it as a sacred trust to be fulfilled according to the dictates of conscience. Then you will begin to understand what is meant by 'burden of effort' and 'the heat of the day.' I want you to believe that even one man against a pack of wolves can put up at least some kind of a fight, even though he knows that sooner or later he is doomed to go down. I have tried conscientiously to do what I thought was my duty. Do you believe that?"

"Certainly," nodded Kendrick without hesitation.

"Thank you, Philip. No matter what happens I want you to continue to believe that."

"Look here, Uncle Milt, if anybody is trying to put anything over on you, why not let me in on the scrap?" urged Phil eagerly. "I meant what I said a moment ago. What is it? What's the matter? Finances? Let me help. I'll write you a cheque for what I have in the bank and we can raise something on my Parkview property—"

The Honorable Milton tossed his head in a chuckle of amusement.

"How much have you got?" he smiled.

"About two thousand in the bank, another couple of thousand in negotiable securities—oh, about ten thousand, roughly, including the real-estate. We could sell that. I'll look after it first thing after breakfast."

"Ten thousand dollars is neither here nor there, Philip," said his uncle, shaking his head slowly. "I could raise such a sum by the mere request. Perhaps if it were five times the amount—Just the same I am grateful for your offer, my boy."

"Fifty thousand dollars!" murmured Phil. "It's a lot of money when you haven't got it."

The Honorable Milton glanced at the clock on the mantel and gave an exclamation.

"It's time you and I were in bed. I hear Stinson just coming in. Everything's all right. I'm going to turn in now."

At the foot of the stairs he paused to lay a hand on his nephew's shoulder and there was unwonted gentleness in his manner.

"Good-night, Philip. And thank you for the—the 'flower of folly,'" he said awkwardly.

For a moment Kendrick stood watching the Honorable Milton Waring as he mounted the stairs slowly, a heavy hand upon the banister rail. The gray head was bowed. There was an air of dejection in the whole figure as of one who tastes the bitterness of defeat.

CHAPTER IV

THE LISTENING STENOGRAPHER

When Phil opened his eyes on the morning sunshine—both eyes—he was gratified to note a slight improvement in the blackened orb. Before retiring he had sent the newly returned Stinson around to the front of the house to bring in the suitcase left by the verandah and had instructed the valet to bring a piece of raw beefsteak to his room. Nevertheless, as he studied his appearance in the mirror with some anxiety he was glad that he was going to Sparrow Lake and thence to North Bay as fast as he could get there. Thorpe would soon tire of making witty remarks, and the fish would not care whether he had a black eye or not.

As he dressed leisurely Kendrick's mind reverted soberly to the events of the past twenty-four hours. Reviewing in detail the interview with his uncle, there grew out of his confusion of thought an odd sense of disquiet. Close questioning of Stinson had yielded the information which his uncle had not seen fit to volunteer in regard to last night's clandestine visitors at the Island residence—Nickleby, President of the Interprovincial Loan & Savings Company; Alderson, of the Alderson Construction Company; Blatchford Ferguson, the lawyer. If, as the Honorable Milton had intimated, it had been a business meeting merely, they must be planning a raid on the stock market to account for all the secrecy with which the meeting had been shrouded. His uncle, Phil knew, had invested heavily in mining stocks, and J. Cuthbert Nickleby was the man who had been most closely associated with him in these private investments, while for some time now Ferguson had been favored with Waring's legal patronage in such deals as had come to Kendrick's notice. As for Alderson, he was a comparative stranger to Phil—a contractor who had risen rapidly during the real-estate boom, and who very reasonably might be taking a flyer on the market.

It must be something of this sort, and in the face of his uncle's evident desire for him to mind his own business Phil was inclined to let it go at that. It was scarcely to be expected that his uncle would break the custom of years in a sudden burst of confidence just because his nephew happened to surprise him in one of his difficult situations. His life was full of such difficult situations, no doubt,—had been for years—and the Honorable Milton was accustomed to relying upon himself to surmount them as he saw fit.

Far from feeling any resentment of his uncle's refusal of his boyish offer of assistance, therefore, Phil now regarded the offer itself as somewhat ridiculous from his uncle's standpoint. To one of such large connections ten thousand dollars was the same as a hundred-dollar bill to the average man. Yet his uncle had thanked him for his good intentions and tactfully had made him feel that the appreciation was sincere. At no time had the two been in closer sympathy than during this unexpected interview. His uncle was not given to sentiment. Perhaps the liquor—

Phil paused in the act of lacing his boot to frown out the window. The Honorable Milton Waring undoubtedly was greatly worried about something—financial affairs maybe. Or was that only one side of it, incidental to something not so simple of adjustment? The searching look, the solemnity of the words which had followed that sudden outburst against political conditions of the day, that reference to one man fighting a pack of wolves—what about that? No matter what happened he wanted his nephew to continue believing that he had tried to do his duty.

No matter what happened! It was this remark, more than any other, which fostered Kendrick's disquietude. Something was liable to happen, then?—something calling for a blind exercise of faith in his uncle; something which on the surface might seem to question his—his what? Integrity? Political honor? Social standing? Or was it merely an emphasis of speech with no special significance? Phil shifted uneasily on the chair as he thought of his aunt's position if some catastrophe befell his uncle. If any trouble of that kind were likely to develop, surely his uncle would have told him. Well, there was no use in getting himself all worked up over nothing.

He began to whistle softly as he rummaged among his ties. Then his thoughts switched to the girl with whom he had talked in the fog. If he had only known then what he knew now! She had been spying upon the Waring residence, upon this secret meeting with the Honorable Milton. That much seemed certain. But why was she interested in what had transpired? Who was she? And what had transpired? It was lack of this information which made it difficult to analyze the situation intelligently.

Had he done right in withholding from his uncle the fact of his unusual encounter with this girl? He imagined the laugh with which the Honorable Milton would be likely to greet relation of the incident. If it were true that there was no use in sending a boy on a man's errand, what about a woman on a spying expedition in a thick fog at two o'clock in the morning? Perhaps her story of the party at a friend's house was true, after all. Perhaps she and this "Joe" were a pair of sneak thieves—!

But he *knew* she wasn't, just as he knew that she was a girl of education and refinement. A tantalizing thing to meet a disembodied voice like that, a low laugh, a mystery! The lady might have a face like a dried prune! (Only he knew that she hadn't!) Voices were not to be relied upon. Take that "hello-girl," for instance; she had had the softest lilting voice over the wire, then when he got a look at her she hadn't been a day under forty-five and her face—! Certainly it hadn't been the fairest that e'er the sun shone on! (Only in this case he knew it must be different!) He was a hopeless fool if ever there was one! The best thing he could do was to forget the whole affair and with this sensible decision he reached into his pocket for the souvenirs, and spent some time in re-examining the little hand-painted shirt-waist pin with which she had fastened his pay to the canoe cushion!

Phil breakfasted alone. Although the sun had climbed high enough to dispel the fog his uncle still slept the heavy sleep of utter exhaustion. Without disturbing him, therefore, Kendrick had Stinson run the launch over to the city half an hour later. As a concession to the possibility of there being a serious side to the espionage of the girl and her accomplice, he had decided to advise his uncle's lawyer of the adventure; Ferguson then could assume responsibility for the consequences, using his own judgment as to its significance. Also Phil intended to have a chat with President Wade, of the Canadian Lake Shores Railway, if he happened to be in the city; Ben Wade was an old boyhood friend of the Warings and Phil knew that he could talk to him freely without fear of his confidences being abused.

At the docks almost the first person Kendrick encountered was Chic White. Chic was the more or less renowned sporting editor of the *Morning Recorder* and he had a most abominable habit of going through the motions of spitting every little while as he talked, more a matter of nervous habit than saliva. He spat dryly three times as he stared at the approaching Kendrick and greeted the erstwhile captain of the 'Varsity rugby champions with a grin that bared two rows of teeth.

"Ye gods! What a fall was there, my countrymen! Wow! Who slipped you the haymaker, Ken?"

"Stick to the quotation, Chic," laughed Phil good-naturedly, barely pausing in his stride. "Got it in the fog last night— Canoe Club stairs in the dark. I had a pretty bad fall."

"So did Humpty-Dumpty!" Mr. White's grin widened, and with a deliberate wink and a final spit he waved his hand and walked off, laughing loudly.

The owner of the black eye went his way, face set in abnormally forbidding lines. People smiled as they passed him on the street. He would have given a ten-dollar bill to have met the redoubtable Mr. McCorquodale around the next corner. He thought of buying one of those pink shields; it would not hide it all, but it might help. He tried tying his handkerchief over his eye as a bandage, but felt so foolish that he tore it off and laughed at himself.

The office of Blatchford Ferguson, barrister, etc., in the Broker's Bank Building, was laid out along somewhat unconventional lines. Of course the public entrance from the corridor gave admission to an outer office where two or three stenographers operated their typewriters under the eye of a law student, while just inside the railing of the entranceway sat a pompadoured office boy who occupied himself variously with an old-fashioned letter-press alongside the vault, with sharpening lead-pencils, chewing gum and guarding the gate in the railing. But the partitions which enclosed this general office were built solid from floor to ceiling and the only sign of an inner presence was a door directly behind the youthful sentry, the ground glass of which bore the single word, "Secretary," in neat gold and black lettering.

The Secretary's office had a private entrance from the public corridor of the building and an inside door, lettered "Loans and Investments." On through this office was still another door, inscribed "Insurance Department," while beyond this second sanctum was a third door which led into the *sanctum sanctorum* with its unexpected exit upon a narrow back hallway and a dusty flight of stairs by which it was possible without undue publicity to reach the street or, rather, the back lane where carters made deliveries.

At times this carefully planned office arrangement was found to be highly convenient, no less by the confidential Mr. Ferguson than by certain of his clients. For although Blatchford Ferguson, barrister, etc., really could—and did— go barristering about the courts quite legitimately, he also carried on a substantial business in et ceteras. Thus, he could talk to an insurance prospect in a private office provided with insurance files and hung with insurance company calendars; or he could talk to a possible investor in a private office which had just the right financial atmosphere to foster confidence. Buying, selling, borrowing, lending, advising— nothing that could be "farmed out" on a split commission was beneath the notice of Blatch Ferguson, who would have negotiated a deal for a carload of Russian whiskers could he have found a responsible master barber to make the contract with a mattress factory which had the price!

As he shook hands with Conway, the young student who

presided over the outer office, Kendrick was conscious that the office boy and the stenographers behind him were enjoying the mild sensation which his black eye inspired. Even Conway was grinning like an idiotic cat from Cheshire. The two had known each other, somewhat casually, at the university.

"I bumped into the parallel bars during a game of volley ball at the gym the other night," he explained gravely. "Is Ferguson in?"

Conway told him to walk right through. Miss Williams would take in his card. Thus it came about that Phil, unescorted, passed through the gate in the railing and on through the door to the secretary's office. As he closed this door behind him he paused for a moment in some uncertainty at finding the secretary's office deserted. Her hat and coat were hanging in place, however, and a half finished letter was in her typewriter; so he ventured through to the open doorway beyond, thinking she might have stepped into the adjoining office.

She had. She had gone right through it and through the second office of the suite also. The young lady was visible through the vista of open doorways and she was so absorbed in her own activities that she was quite oblivious of his presence. For she was kneeling with her ear to the keyhole of the farthest door of all, the one which led into the *sanctum sanctorum* of her employer, and there was no doubt whatever that she was listening with all her might.

Not a little astonished, Kendrick watched her. Then at his slight cough the girl straightened quickly and stared at him with widened eyes. In answer to his beckoning finger she came towards him slowly, her color mounting swiftly. When she had shut the last door behind her she faced him with an air of defiance.

Kendrick gazed at her in speechless admiration of the picture she made as she stood there, symmetrical figure gracefully erect, her head held high with its elaborate coiffure of brown hair, her dark blue eyes flashing resentment. The creamy column of her well shaped neck, the firm chin, the almost classic perfection of her features, the rich red of her cheeks—wherever did Ferguson go for his secretaries? She was plainly dressed in some dark material with white collar and cuffs; but the sensible office dress served only to heighten the pleasing effect. There was only one jarring note—the fact that she was chewing gum, chewing it rapidly as if to relieve nervous tension.

"Well! Hope you'll know me next time you see me! Get it off your chest please! Whatcha goin' to do about it?"

Kendrick smiled slowly at the incongruity of the speech, even while thankful that her voice at least was not in harsh discord with her appearance, but well modulated.

"I beg your pardon," he apologized, realizing all at once that he had been guilty of staring somewhat longer than was warranted even by the unusual circumstances. "I am very short-sighted and there are times when I cannot distinguish objects at a greater distance than a very few feet. This morning my eyes are exceptionally bad."

She glanced at him quickly as if searching for indications of mockery which were lacking in the courteous tones of his voice.

"If you will be good enough to take in my card—?" he suggested, extending it.

She hesitated, then laid down her notebook and accepted the card without speaking. Ferguson coming to meet him at the door with extended hand, stopped short and stared.

"It's a peach, Phil! I must admit it's a peach!"

"A Lombard plum, you mean, Blatch. How'd I get it? Why, you see,—I had the misfortune to step on a wayward banana skin—Oh, well, if you really must know, I tried to help an old lady pick up some bundles she'd dropped and she hit me with her umbrella, thinking I was going to grab them and run."

"Come right in. Come right in," chuckled Ferguson. "Here, have a cigar?"

"Thanks, but I'm only staying a jiff. Got to make another call and it's nearly noon now. Would you mind if I leave the door open? The smoke's pretty thick."

"Hit you with an umbrella, eh?" chortled the lawyer with jovial skepticism as he tilted back in his swivel chair. "Deduction: It had a knob on the end of it! Sentence: Thirty days in the woods!" and Mr. Ferguson stroked his nose while he permitted his shoulders to shake in appreciation of his own pleasantry. Mr. Ferguson's nose was fleshy and its color was red.

"On my way there now—going fishing down the French River with an old schoolmate," grinned Phil. "Say, there was a meeting over at my uncle's on the Island last night, Blatch," he added briskly. "I believe you were there. Will you tell me what took place?"

Ferguson sat up. He ran his fingers over his head in a habitual gesture which long since had worn a bald streak along the top. He leaned back again in his chair, the tips of his fingers pressed together, and for a moment scowled thoughtfully at the wall.

"You're getting into deep water, boy," he warned at last slowly. "I don't know where the mischief you got that information; but I'll have to refer you to the Chief himself for your answer. Why, what do you want to know for?"

"Oh, nothing in particular, except—it was very foggy, you remember?—a pretty good night for concealment, if anybody happened to be interested in spying on you people over there. You know more about that than I do."

Mr. Ferguson played a good game of poker; he prided himself upon his self-control. But the seriousness of his manner indicated that he was startled.

"Just what do you mean by that, Phil? You've come here to tell me something. What is it?"

So Kendrick told him, omitting nothing except the fact that the girl had dared him to kiss her, and that when he had done so he had gone in for an involuntary swim.

"And you let that woman go home alone at that hour of the morning? You are neglectful both of your opportunities and your etiquette!" but although the lawyer's tone was light he was very serious as he pursed his lips and scowled.

"Don't go blaming me, Blatch. As soon as I helped her ashore she ran off and the fog was so thick you couldn't see anybody within a couple of feet of you. I tried my best to find out who she was; but she ducked. Besides, how was I to know the thing mattered? I didn't know Uncle Milt was in town even—not at the time."

"I didn't say it mattered, Phil," said Ferguson hastily. He laughed at the idea. "Whatever put it into your head to think this—er—lady was spying on a—an ordinary business meeting? Supposing she was—why, what earthly good would it do her?"

"Search me, Blatch. Thought I'd better tell you about it anyway."

"Quite right, of course. Hm—just so. She got away without leaving a single clue, eh? Not that it matters in the least, but—You did right in reporting it. Thanks."

"Would you mind telling me if you had anybody in the office here with you just before I came in? Or were you using the telephone?"

"Why," hesitated Ferguson in some surprise, "I was called on the 'phone by an old newspaper acquaintance—yes. Perhaps you know him—Hughey Podmore? He got a job recently as President Wade's private secretary—Canadian Lake Shores Railway. We used to work on the same paper long ago. Why?"

"Oh, nothing—just my idle curiosity. Say, there's something you can do for me, like a good fellow, before I go. Give me a knock-down to the lady outside, will you? Didn't know you owned a peach orchard, Blatch? Who is she?"

Ferguson chuckled as he pressed a button.

"Name's Margaret Williams. My regular stenographer was taken sick suddenly the other day and she sent around this friend of hers to substitute. She's a dandy good worker, too. But you're too late, my boy. She's leaving soon to marry a fellow at Buffalo—er—Miss Williams, allow me to present

Mr. Philip Kendrick."

Her bow was very formal and as, at her employer's request, she escorted him to the private exit at her own end of the office, her manner was equally cold.

"I hope you bear me no ill will, Miss Williams," smiled Phil. "I assure you I have done nothing to merit it."

"That is for me to judge," she retorted calmly. "Please go. I do not care to know you, Mr. Kendrick."

Phil turned quickly. It was the second time within twelve hours that a girl had told him that—in those very words, with that same disdainful tone. Why, if he were to shut his eyes he felt sure he could imagine it to be the very voice inflection used by his Fog Lady when delivering the same sentence of exile. Again he found himself guilty of staring.

"Have you ever seen a real, honest-to-goodness amulet, Miss Williams?" he asked eagerly, reaching into his pocket. "I'd like to show you mine before I go, if I may." He slowly unfolded the dollar bill and held out the hand-painted blouse pin, watching her closely.

"What a pretty pin!" she said in a flat, disinterested voice. She looked at it perfunctorily. "I know a man who used to carry a potato to chase rheumatism away. It was planted by a one-eyed, left-handed negro, born on the thirteenth of the month. I've heard of an elk's tooth for pleurisy and a rabbit's foot for evil spirits; but a pin like that? It will lead you into danger instead of away from it."

"Not when it is pinned to a canoe cushion by a beautiful girl at the hour of three o'clock in the morning in a dense fog," declared Kendrick significantly.

"That is very silly," said the haughty Miss Williams with a bored air as she handed it back to him and turned towards her typewriter. "Good-day, Mr. Kendrick. I really must get on with my work."

It was with an unreasonable feeling of disappointment that he bowed himself out. She had not blinked an eyelash! Who was the idiot who first started looking for needles in haystacks anyway? A fool's quest! Mumma! but wasn't he *de trop* with the ladies? Well, he would buy cigars with the dollar and make a present of the pin to Mrs. Parlby, his uncle's estimable housekeeper.

But he did neither of these things. Instead, he was to continue the folly of keeping both souvenirs and the equal folly of looking at them from time to time—to see if they were safe.

CHAPTER V

THE TAN SATCHEL

Ordinarily Hugh Podmore, secretary to the President of the Canadian Lake Shores Railway, took a keen interest in his work. If anything, he applied himself more industriously during the many absences of his chief than when President Wade was there to observe and commend, a zeal which might or might not have been a tribute to his conscientiousness. But to-day Mr. Podmore, although dressed with that care which habitually imparted to his well proportioned figure something of the beau brummel,—to-day he was not quite his customary polite self. Things irritated him which ordinarily he would not have noticed, and the morning had dragged for him in quite an unusual way. He had spent much time gazing absently out of the office window at the traffic in the street below, with many futile glances at his watch.

The first shop whistle that led the noonday medley found him pulling down the lid of his roll-top desk and he was reaching for his raincoat when his stenographer entered to inform him that there was a gentleman outside who would not take "No" for an answer. In no very gracious mood he snatched the card from the girl's hand; but the name meant nothing to him and he flung aside his gloves in resentment of the interruption.

"Show'm in," he growled, unlocking the desk and shoving back the lid with a bang.

The big young man who entered in answer to the summons enquired for the President. Everybody who came into that anteroom began the same way and Podmore tilted back in his chair and appraised the other coldly, noting two things particularly—the young man's athletic build and the very marked discoloration of his left eye. Another job hunter!

"State your business, please."

"You will excuse me," said Kendrick, "but the matter is entirely personal between Mr. Wade and myself. Is he in?"

It was a little thing to arouse Podmore's ire. Ordinarily Hugh Podmore was an excellent secretary; but the caller's refusal to state his business or produce his credentials for inspection angered him. He was used to this extreme anxiety of visitors to see the Chief in person; it was a characteristic of the job-hunting crowd.

"The President's out of town," he said irritably. "Besides, he wouldn't see you until you had told me your business anyway. What do you think he keeps a secretary for?"

"To be civil to the public," said Kendrick evenly. "When do you expect him back?" and there was a directness in his look which Podmore found unexpectedly disconcerting.

"Hard to say. He's on the go continually. If your business is important—"

"It is important."

"Then, if you'll give me particulars—," suggested Podmore,

reaching for his memorandum pad.

"Be good enough to answer my question, please. When will Mr. Wade be in his office?"

"Sorry, but it's impossible to say, Mr."—he glanced at the card deliberately—"Kendrick. If you are looking for a job—"

"I want to see Mr. Wade personally and as soon as possible," repeated Kendrick, keeping his temper with difficulty. "When will he be available?"

"He's gone on a trip—to the Hot Springs," snapped Podmore. "Come back in a month or six weeks and perhaps you can see him then. Good day, sir."

For a few minutes after the big young man had bowed himself out with mock humility, Mr. Podmore stood fingering the card and frowning at the window. It was an engraved card, his fingers told him. He did not like feeling that he had made a mistake in any way; but that is precisely how he did feel. Yet he was sure he had never met this young man before, in spite of a certain familiarity of face that haunted him. Not being a regular reader of the sporting pages, he was at a loss to account for this, as he prided himself on his memory for faces.

With a shrug in dismissal of the inconsequential, Mr. Podmore went to lunch. He had comfortable quarters at the Queen's Hotel, just a block from the Union Station, and after a light lunch in the big dining-room he idled about the rambling old rotunda for an hour or more, smoking many cigarettes and attempting to read a magazine. The solicitous anxiety of his waiter during luncheon had earned that surprised individual a rebuke and cost him the usual tip; the friendly advances of a hotel guest, which ordinarily would have been met by equal geniality, finally sent Podmore up in the old-fashioned elevator to his room, where he locked the door and began pacing restlessly back and forth. Not until a sixth glance at his watch indicated the approach of 2 o'clock did his unusual fidgetiness begin to disappear; but when at last he walked briskly out of the hotel Mr. Podmore, to all intents, had regained his normal self-possession.

He went straight to the down-town offices of the Alderson Construction Company, arriving punctual to the minute of his appointment. Both Nickleby and Alderson were already there.

"Well, we're all here, Alderson. Are you waiting for somebody to open with prayer?" complained J. Cuthbert Nickleby with an impatient glance at his watch after the greetings were over. "I don't see why the devil you needed me here at all, Pod. Why all the ceremony?" The President of the Interprovincial Loan & Savings Company was a thin, sallow man with a thin, tight line of a mouth. The cynicism of his expression was chronic.

"Because you'd be the first to holler if anything went wrong," retorted Podmore, eyeing him pointedly as he tilted his hat to the back of his head and proceeded calmly to skin the glove from his left hand. "We're all in this together, J. C., and that's why I insisted on you being here—to see that everything is according to Hoyle."

"Aint getting cold feet already are you?"

An easy laugh was Mr. Podmore's only rejoinder to this insult. They both watched Alderson, who had swung open the door of the safe and was reaching into its depths. The contractor was stout and florid, and his face was flushed as he rose jerkingly from his knee and tossed a package of crisp bank notes to the table.

"Well, there 'tis, just as it come from the Inter-provincial this mornin'," he remarked, and picked up his cigar from the edge of the safe.

"Look at the way he tosses it around, would you!" chuckled Podmore. "You could buy a bunch of peanuts with that package, Frank,—a million bags at a nickle the bag." This was a hit at Alderson's fondness for munching peanuts, and Alderson's tenor laugh led the trio. Podmore picked up the package and riffled the bills carelessly. "Counted it, J. C.?"

"Fifty thousand," nodded Nickleby.

"That satchel come, Alderson? Thanks." Podmore held it up—an ordinary cheap satchel of medium size, tan in color, imitation leather and imitation brass catches. "I bought this, J. C., so that we'd have one that hadn't been tampered with and that couldn't be identified as belonging to any of us, you understand. All right, Frank, seal her up."

Alderson placed the package of bills in a large, strong blue linen envelope which he had ready to hand, and carefully gummed down the flap. Under the amused eye of Nickleby he proceeded to hold a stick of gray sealing-wax in the flame of a match and to daub this additional precaution upon the flap. The envelope was then placed in the new tan satchel, the catches snapped and the satchel locked by Podmore, who thereupon walked over to the President of the Interprovincial Loan & Savings Company and handed him the key.

"That stays in your pocket till you get to Blatch Ferguson's office, Nickleby. You hand it to Ferguson personally," and again Podmore eyed the banker keenly. "Let him do the opening himself. All you're there for is to see that he actually gets this money, and that ends the transaction so far as we're concerned." He winked, and both the gentlemen laughed as if much humor underlay the remark.

"I will now proceed to put on our little private identification mark," continued Podmore with an air of having thought of everything, and he made a triangular scratch on one end of the satchel with his pocket-knife.

"Good Lord, Pod!" exclaimed the financier with a laugh. "Is it necessary to have all this fuss over this thing?"

"Take all the chances you like when you're by your lonesome, old man; but you don't do it when I'm with you," said Mr. Hugh Podmore, smilingly unperturbed by ridicule. "It's the fellow who overlooks these very things that sometimes gets stung. It isn't at all likely, I'll admit, that the simple delivery of this money a distance of a few blocks requires all this 'fuss,' as you call it; but why take chances just to save a little trouble? Pays to play safe every time, J. C. What about that detective, Alderson?"

"Oh, that feller's on the job. Here, you can see'm standin' out there on the corner, waitin' fer our man to show up." Podmore followed Alderson to the window. "Naw, over there to the right—beside the post. Must be a good half hour since his office phoned he was leavin'. Say, he's lookin' up here. I'll give 'm the high sign now."

"Well, I guess everything's O.K., then. Call in your messenger and get a move on. I'm due at the depot soon to meet the Chief." Podmore dropped into a chair and lighted a cigarette with a look of satisfaction on his face.

Alderson leaned over and pressed a button. The young man who responded was James Stiles, bookkeeper and general office clerk. As he stood in the doorway, respectful enquiry in his whole attitude, pen in hand, linen office jacket sagging at the pockets, forearms encased in black sateen sleeve-protectors and a daub of ink on his fingers, there was little to distinguish him from hundreds of his type to be seen in modern offices. He had rather a pleasant face, Podmore thought, a little dull perhaps in its ingenuousness. He was not much more than a boy.

"Jimmy," instructed Alderson briskly, "drop whatever you're at and take this satchel over to Mr. Ferguson's office in the Brokers' Bank Building. It's got some mighty important legal papers inside an' I want you to be sure an' hand it personally to Mr. Ferguson himself. I told him I'd send 'em over right after lunch; so you don't need to say nothin'—just hand it to Mr. Ferguson, y'understand. Blatchford Ferguson, the lawyer,—you know where his office is."

"Yes, sir. Want me to ask for a receipt?"

"Uh? No, never mind a receipt. It'll be all right."

The young bookkeeper picked up the satchel, nodding respectfully to the President of the Interprovincial Loan & Savings Company as he quietly closed the door behind him. He had been formerly employed at the Interprovincial; in fact, it was to Nickleby's personal recommendation that he owed his present position with the construction company.

The departure of Stiles with the satchel, of whose precious contents he had been kept in ignorance, was a signal for the separation of the trio in Alderson's office. With a wave of the hand Podmore hurried off towards the Union Station, and presently J. Cuthbert Nickleby made his way more leisurely to his waiting automobile.

On the corner opposite the building in which the Alderson Construction Company had its down-town offices the man from the Brady Detective Agency was lighting a fresh cigar. He sauntered around the corner, then quickened his pace to get closer to the briskly walking young man with the tan satchel. He continued to follow the bookkeeper at a convenient distance.

It was the season when those who have the misfortune to be confined to indoor tasks chafe most in the leash—a beautiful May day of blue sky and sunshine and balmy air that called insistently to open places of green grass and the luxury of idleness and vagrant dreaming. Young Jimmy Stiles felt the call and he skipped along with carefree enjoyment of his brief respite. He laughed gaily at a pair of dogs who seemed inclined to question each other's veracity and sent them scampering with a whoop, swinging the satchel around his head. He pulled down his vest, felt his tie and winked boldly as he passed a pretty girl. He broke into a whistle presently, practising the latest rag-time air with an earnestness which found no ennui in repetition of tune, and it was while thus absorbed that he went by the Jessup Grill. He was well beyond the entrance before he realized that his name was being called and that somebody had darted out from the doorway to overtake him.

"Oh, there, Jimmy! Won't you say good-bye to me?"

"Why, hello, Mr. Clayton," grinned Stiles as he took the extended hand. "Goin' away?"

"Holidays can't last forever, Jimmy. I'm leaving for home this afternoon—just getting ready to go to the depot when I saw you. Come on in and join me in a glass of beer for good luck."

"Nothin' doin'! 'The lips that touch liquor shall never touch mine'," recited Stiles, rolling his eyes in exaggerated piety. "No, honest, I can't," he protested as the other pulled on his arm. "I'm on an important message for the boss an' I got to hustle right back to the office."

"Aw, come on. It won't take a minute. I'm in a hustle myself to catch the train; but I want to give you a message for—" Robert Clayton hesitated, coughed in slight embarrassment, and looked helpless. "—for somebody you know up at the church," he pleaded.

Jimmy Stiles nodded in grinning comprehension.

"Well, you know how to pick 'em, Mr. Clayton. I'll say that for you. Anne's a mighty swell girl."

"I've never met a finer one," said Mr. Clayton, looking serious.

"Oh, this town's full of 'em," cried Jimmy generously. "Say, they got a long lemonade they don't make bad in here— sliced orange and a cherry on top. I'll go you one. I guess it won't take a jiff."

"Good!" cried Clayton, leading the way without more ado into the Jessup.

He picked up his raincoat which he had left on a chair near the door, flung over his travelling bag, and carried both with him through the swing doors into the buffet. Here they found a vacant table and Clayton beckoned a waiter and set his grip and coat on the floor between the two chairs. Stiles dropped the tan satchel alongside the raincoat and grinned across at Clayton with evident pleasure. This was the right way for gentlemen to bid each other farewell, and he helped himself from the other's proffered cigarette case with the air of doing this sort of thing every day. Neither of them appeared to pay any attention to the man who entered behind them, sat down at the table next the wall and ordered a glass of beer; patrons were coming and going and the man was just an ordinary citizen entitled to quench his thirst if he so desired.

The two young fellows chatted and laughed over their refreshments for perhaps five or ten minutes. It was Clayton who finally glanced at his watch and jumped to his feet. He picked up raincoat and grip and shook hands. Stiles picked up the tan satchel and out on the street they shook hands once more. Clayton boarded a street-car, and with a final wave of good-will Jimmy Stiles continued on his way.

At a convenient distance the private detective followed. He walked into the Brokers' Bank Building just as the bookkeeper pushed the elevator bell. They went up in the same elevator to the fifth floor, where they both got out. The detective, sauntering down the corridor, observed Stiles enter the office of Blatchford Ferguson, Barrister, Notary Public, etc.

With a grunt he turned on his heel and descended to the street, where he lighted another stogey and returned the way he had come. Arriving finally at the offices of the Alderson Construction Company, he was admitted at once to Alderson's presence and reported that the tan satchel had been delivered at its destination without mishap.

As he finished speaking the telephone rang and Alderson lifted down the receiver with a nod of dismissal. The detective's hand was on the doorknob when he turned quickly, viewing with alarm the sudden bewilderment and blank consternation which had crept into the contractor's heavy face as he listened to the agitated voice of J. Cuthbert Nickleby.

"Brady's man? Yes, he's here now—Sure, I'll hold him—No, not back yet—Sure. Sure I will—Eh? Say, Mr. Nickleby, fer the love o' Mike, what's wrong?—WHA-AT!"

Alderson wildly jiggled the hook of the telephone instrument, but Nickleby had rung off. He stared across at the anxious representative of the Brady Detective Agency, his thick loose lower lip hanging in dismay. For the moment he was bereft of speech.

"What's the matter?"

"Uh? Matter?" echoed Alderson vacuously. Then he pounded the desk with his fat fist while his face grew red. "*Matter!*" he shouted. "You're a heluva detective, you are! That's what's the matter. The mon—I mean—the papers—in the satchel, you fathead!—stolen right under your nose!"

CHAPTER VI

AGAIN THE TAN SATCHEL

Swearing fervently, Alderson grabbed the telephone and called for Podmore at the Queen's Hotel. A few stuttering words of explanation and the 'phone went dead once more as Podmore banged up the receiver at his end.

Nickleby arrived first. He strode in through the outer office, leaving a trail of awed employes in his wake. Alderson, who had rushed forward to meet him, fell back a step as the banker entered the private office and banged the door behind him with a force which nearly broke the glass in the partition. He carried in his hand the tan satchel and forthwith slammed it down upon the desk and took to pacing back and forth in speechless wrath. His face was ghastly, his eyes blazing, his mouth drawn down in an ugly sneer as he turned at last upon the dumfounded detective.

"You—you blithering idiot!"

"Easy, brother. Keep your shirt on, see!" advised the Brady operative with justifiable resentment. "There aint nothin' been taken out o' that there grip while I was watchin' it, that's a cinch. Say, 'bo, what was in it, anyways?"

Alderson caught Nickleby's eye and shook his head in warning. Nickleby stepped across the room, opened the satchel and flung out upon the table a package of blank brown wrapping paper, cut to the size of bank-notes and fastened together with rubber bands. He pointed his finger at it contemptuously.

"Instead of the legal papers which were in that satchel when it left this office, there's what we found when Ferguson and I opened it. Now, explain that, will you? No, wait! 'Phone your chief to come over here himself at once; I think he'd better hear what you have to say. What's your name?"

"McCorquodale. An' I takes no lip from nobody, see!"

While the man was at the telephone Jimmy Stiles knocked on the door to report that he had delivered the satchel safely to its destination. It was an amazed youth who was yanked unceremoniously into the room by the coat-collar while the irate Nickleby blazed forth anew. He took hold of the bookkeeper's shoulders and was shaking the frightened young man in speechless fury when Podmore came in.

"Here, here, leave him alone!" he commanded sharply as he stepped between them. "What crazy nonsense is this, J. C.?"

No fuss or fury about Hugh Podmore in time of stress. It was Podmore's way to turn calm and cold and calculating in proportion to the extent to which any given crisis disturbed him. The news which had reached him over the 'phone from the incoherent Alderson had been grave enough; but he was much the coolest of the three most vitally concerned in this mysterious miscarriage of carefully laid plans. The first thing he did was to have Alderson clear the outer office of stenographers and junior clerks. He suggested that Alderson dismiss them for the afternoon, and began at once to question the bookkeeper and the detective who had followed him. The two recitals agreed in every particular.

Podmore at once despatched the detective to the Union Station in Nickleby's car to find Clayton at all costs and arrest him if he would not come otherwise.

"Tell us all you know about this man, Jimmy. Take your time," advised Podmore kindly. "No occasion to get scared stiff."

Stiles said he had not known Clayton very long—just a few days, in fact. He had met him for the first time last Sunday at All Saints' Mission, where Jimmy was an usher. On Monday night there had been a social gathering of the younger members of the church in the Sunday School and Clayton had attended that and seemed to enjoy himself. He had made friends with everybody quickly and seemed to fit in so readily that he had been accepted without question by everybody, from the pastor down. He was an American who had come north to visit relatives and was on his way back to Philadelphia. He expected to return shortly, he had told Stiles, and might decide to locate here permanently. He was in the hardware business, somewhere near Philadelphia.

"All right, Jimmy, that will do. Now, better wait outside till your friend arrives. It all seems straight enough so far as you're concerned," and Podmore closed the door on him with a smile of encouragement; for young Stiles looked as if he needed encouragement. "You've scared the wits out of him, J. C. That won't get us anywhere," he reproved when the three were alone.

"I don't trust anybody—"

"Wait," commanded Podmore with upraised hand. He

stepped over to the table quickly and closely scrutinized the tan satchel. Finally he drew attention to the triangular mark which he had scratched on one end with his pocket-knife. "It's the satchel O.K. Now, who opened it?"

"Ferguson. I gave him the key, as you suggested, and he opened it in front of me. And so help me, that stuff there was all that was in it. The money was gone. I tell you I never felt so much like a fool—" Nickleby broke off with an oath, still smarting under the jibes which the caustic Mr. Ferguson had levelled at him, and beneath which the President of the Interprovincial had writhed in humiliation. "Somebody took that money out on the way over, Podmore."

"N—ot necessarily, J. C.," said Podmore judicially. "Wait, now. Think, man. Were you there when Stiles—?"

"Of course I was."

"—when Stiles handed the satchel to Ferguson? Did you see him do it?"

"Why,—no, not exactly. I was out in the general office when the kid took it in to Ferguson. What are you driving at?"

"Talking to anybody out there?"

"Yes. I ran into McAllister, of the *Recorder*, and I was so surprised at seeing the editor of that yellow sheet there— well, he got quizzing me about one or two matters."

"How long after Stiles left you before you joined Ferguson?"

"Oh—five minutes, maybe. Why, what's all that got to do with it?" He regarded the look of triumph upon Podmore's face with some astonishment.

"It's as clear as daylight to me, J. C. In that five minutes almost anything might have happened. Many of the world's great events have happened in less than that. Hasn't it occurred to you that the package of money might be removed from the satchel and the paper substituted in Ferguson's office? The lock might have been sprung, you know."

Nickleby stared, his beady eyes narrowed in a frown of thought. Then he slapped the table with his open palm.

"By —!" he ejaculated.

"I'm inclined to fancy the whole thing is a cleverly arranged scare which those fellows have chosen to throw into us in order to protect themselves," went on Mr. Podmore, nodding with satisfaction at his own logic. "You can understand that, surely. If I am guessing correctly, they have succeeded in providing a fine denial of the fact that there ever was such a thing as our contribution to the Campaign Fund."

"I told you!" cried Alderson excitedly. "The Hon. Milt said he wouldn't have anything to do with it. He said we'd contribute at our own risk, didn't he?"

Nickleby rounded on him.

"Shut up, you jackass!" he ordered angrily.

Podmore's eyebrows arched a trifle at this admission. Already he had surmised something of the kind. The Honorable Milt was nobody's fool, he knew. For the matter of that, neither was Hughey Podmore.

"They'll be expecting us to keep our mouths shut and let things take their course," he continued, choosing to ignore the interruption. "The money's not lost, Alderson. They'll keep on swearing up and down that they haven't got it, of course; but that's just the coy way in which these things are handled. It's my opinion that the sacrifice of that million bags of peanuts up the elephant's trunk will ensure a good performance when the circus starts."

"I believe you've struck it, Pod," nodded Nickleby slowly.

"I'm sure of it," agreed Mr. Podmore, allowing himself a little laugh of satisfaction. "Hadn't Frank better write Brady a cheque and get rid of him? He's probably waiting outside, and we don't want him nosing into anything."

This seemed to meet with the approval of the others, and when the check was ready the head of the Brady Detective Agency was called in and handed a cigar, the cheque and some plausible explanations which enabled him to return to his office with no hard feelings. Detective Brady never found it an inconvenience to receive money.

The air had cleared wonderfully by the time Detective McCorquodale arrived with Robert Clayton in tow—so much so that both anxious gentlemen were somewhat surprised at the smiles which greeted them. If anything further were needed to convince Nickleby that he had been too hasty in his conclusions, this frank, clean-cut young American supplied it, and as the brief interview progressed the President of the Interprovincial approached as near to geniality as his naturally suspicious and cynical nature ever ventured. The detective had found Clayton just preparing to descend the stairs to his train; but he had come readily enough when the circumstances were explained to him.

"I do hope none of you gentlemen suspect my young friend here in connection with this inexplicable matter," were his first words as he stood with a hand on Stiles' shoulder. He spoke earnestly, his grave eyes searching their faces, one after another. "I haven't known Jimmy very long, of course; but I know honesty when I see it and I'd stake my life that he has had no hand in this—this strange disappearance which I understand has upset you all. May I ask just what the contents of this satchel were? Was it a sum of money or—?"

"No, no, it's all right, Mr. Clayton," volunteered Nickleby rather hurriedly,"—just some legal documents which can be duplicated; the puzzle is why anybody should take them. The delay in connection with some business matters which their loss will entail is the only thing that concerned us; but we find that it is not as bad as we thought, and we regret very much causing you this inconvenience."

Robert Clayton made a gesture of deprecation.

"That's the last consideration, gentlemen," he smiled. "For my own satisfaction, I would like to state candidly a little about myself. Under the circumstances it is your right to know."

What he had to say merely substantiated what Jimmy Stiles had told them already. He was returning from a visit to his uncle on a Western Ontario farm, and had remained over in the city for a few days on his way home. While out for a Sunday morning constitutional he had been attracted to All Saints' Mission by its resemblance to the little church he attended at home. There he had been welcomed so cordially by Jimmy Stiles and others that it had been a great pleasure to him.

He described in detail his meeting with Jimmy, and their harmless chat in the Jessup Grill. He produced his travelling bag and insisted on opening it for inspection despite the fact that there was no possibility of confusing its travel-worn leather with the tan satchel. It contained merely the usual travel accessories, a magazine and a box of cigars. The latter Clayton insisted upon passing around. He then produced his business card and chatted for a moment with Alderson about conditions in the building trade in Pennsylvania, asking many questions about prospects in hardware lines in Ontario.

So that when at last he took his departure, laughing away apologies, he left behind him a most favorable impression. Detective McCorquodale departed next with a real cigar between his teeth and a feeling of satisfaction in the recognition that he was no longer a "blithering idiot." Stiles was told to "knock off for the day and go fishin'," and accepted Podmore's five-dollar bill only when it was forced on him.

When the trio were alone once more Alderson produced a bottle and three glasses.

"To the Campaign Fund," he laughed, holding his glass aloft.

"And the future of the Government," added J. Cuthbert Nickleby.

"And of ourselves," said Podmore reverently.

It was thus that they parted for the second time that afternoon.

Mr. Hugh Podmore went directly to his hotel. Not until he was safe in his own room did he permit any unusual elation to show in his manner. Once he had locked the door, however, and pulled down the window-blinds, he threw himself upon the bed and indulged in a toss of unrestrained mirth. Still very much amused, he felt in his pocket for the key of the old walnut wardrobe with which his room was furnished, unlocked it and lifted out a tan satchel.

Assuredly. In all fairness to himself he had to admit that it had been about as neat a piece of work as he had ever known. For a first attempt it had been carried through with credit, cleverly planned and as cleverly executed. Everything had gone like a clock. Robert Clayton, alias "Tuxedo Bob," had performed his end of it with commendable finish, and Podmore felt that he had made no mistake in hiring him to come on from Chicago. Fifty thousand dollars! It wasn't a bad afternoon's work—not at all bad!

Setting the satchel upon the table, Mr. Podmore sank into the easy chair and lighted a cigarette with a slow smile of satisfaction. The smile lingered as he ran over the whole thing. Neat was not the word; artistic was better. Clayton had "happened" in at All Saints' Mission quite opportunely. Quite. It was proof of his ability that in three days he had established himself so firmly in the friendship of young Stiles. Poor, scared, white-faced kid!

And the duplicate satchels? An old trick, of course; but in simplicity lay success. Podmore had purchased those two identical imitation-leather satchels some days ago. In one he had placed the package of brown paper, cut to banknote size and held by rubber bands, and in a certain position on the outside of the satchel he had scratched a triangular identification mark with his pocket-knife; the other tan satchel he had delivered to the Alderson Construction Company's office. There it had received the currency in Alderson's elaborately sealed linen envelope, and there in front of the others Podmore had marked it ostentatiously for identification—the same triangular mark in the same position on the outside of the satchel.

When the bookkeeper went into the Jessup Grill Clayton had the duplicate satchel which contained the worthless brown wrapping paper—had it hidden under his raincoat. When

Stiles had dropped the other satchel close alongside the raincoat on the floor he had played right into Clayton's hand, that being the very position for which Clayton was manoeuvring; an unobtrusive kick of the foot flopped the raincoat over the satchel which contained the money, so that Clayton had picked it up quite simply, leaving the duplicate satchel for Stiles.

Clayton had made straight for the Union Station, first stopping at the hotel where Podmore had hurried from the construction company's office and was waiting to receive the money satchel. At the hotel Clayton had picked up his own personal travelling bag and had gone over to the depot to wait for the Brady detective to find him in due course.

Podmore had not opened the precious satchel, the 'phone having rung with Alderson's hurry-up message just as he had reached his room. Chucking the tan satchel inside the wardrobe, he had gone back to Alderson's office immediately to engineer the covering up and to quiet the troubled waters.

It was not every day that such a golden opportunity of acquiring fifty thousand dollars presented itself. It was rarely that it could be done without the risk of discovery. But Mr. Hugh Podmore had recognized in this very secret contribution for election purposes a sum of money which was outlawed for the time being, which for obvious reasons dare not be claimed publicly by either side in the secret transaction. Ergo, it was any man's money who could lay hands on it. Ergo, it belonged to Mr. Hughey Podmore!

The beauty of it was that the idea of Ferguson removing the contents to provide a denial of the whole contribution was so patently the clever thing to do, that it was a wonder Ferguson had not thought of it himself when there was such need of secrecy. Nickleby had accepted the suggestion at once as the solution of the mystery.

Ferguson was stupid. Even Nickleby—admirable as was his smoothness—had fallen right into the clever trap prepared for him. If Nickleby did discover the truth, Podmore could give him the laugh. Let Friend Nickleby just start something and he'd find himself in several varieties of hot soup before he knew it. For did not Little Hughey know all about the crooked deal by which the worthy J. Cuthbert had ousted old Nat Lawson from the presidency of the Interprovincial Loan & Savings Company? He did! You bet he did! Let Nickleby interfere with these pickings of Little Hughey and he would be shown a thing or two that would cost him a lot more than a measly fifty thousand!

That had been a delicate touch—making Nickleby carry the key to the satchel across to Ferguson's office. The key to satchel number two, it was! Nickleby had been on hand throughout. Oh, they had nothing on Hughey Podmore in this thing, absolutely noth—!

Podmore's cigarette teetered on his lower lip. With a sudden lunge he grabbed for the tan satchel on the table. He went to the window and threw up the shade. Slowly he turned the satchel around, examining it minutely, his amazement growing. It was undoubtedly the same satchel exactly, so far as he could see,—except for one little disparity. There was no sign of the identification mark, no scratched triangle on either end!

Thoroughly mystified, Podmore fished out the tiny key that belonged to satchel number one. It would not fit!

With an oath he seized a hairbrush, smashed both lock and brush, slipped the catches and yanked open the satchel. Inside lay a roll of old newspapers, tied at the ends with dirty white string!

That was—ALL!

Hughey Podmore wiped his forehead with his handkerchief. For once he was completely non-plussed. He sank back into the chair and lighted another cigarette with a hand that shook ridiculously. For a very long time he sat there, smoking cigarettes and staring blankly at the wall, lighting each fresh one with the butt of its predecessor, end on end.

CHAPTER VII

CROSS CURRENTS

The retirement of Nathaniel Lawson from active participation in the management of the Interprovincial Loan & Savings Company had come as a complete surprise to his many acquaintances in commercial circles. For while he was frequently spoken of as "Old Nat," it was a familiarity fostered by long and friendly associations rather than declining years. Why a man in his prime and at the apex of his usefulness should drop out of harness so suddenly when he appeared to be in the best of health, was something of a mystery. Not a few missed his genial companionship, and were frank enough to say so on those rare occasions when Nat Lawson now put in an appearance at the Club. For a while rumors were rife, but gradually these subsided as his absence became a custom.

It was to that very end that the founder of the Interprovincial Loan & Savings Company made his retirement so literal. There were times when the inquisitiveness of his friends was hard to combat, when the temptation to give expression to the hidden springs of indignation that had been born within him was almost irresistible. So, acting upon his better judgment, he gradually relegated himself to the background of affairs till his tall, distinguished-looking figure was no longer a familiar sight in public places. But if his white hair, his carefully trimmed Van Dyke beard and wide moustache no longer singled him out in gatherings of his former associates his carriage lost none of its alertness, his glance none of its customary fearlessness. Nathaniel Lawson was biding his time.

Like so many successful men who have risen to places of wealth and influence, Lawson had begun as a poor boy, struggling upward over untold difficulties by pluck and determination. In his case, however, the rewards of the struggle had been swept from his reach at the very pinnacle of achievement by what appeared to be an exceptionally bold piece of financial buccaneering. He belonged to the older generation which had grown up accustomed to seeing business carried on by individuals or on a partnership basis; joint stock companies, combines and holding companies had been a development of his later days. It had taken him a lifetime to build up his financial business from very small beginnings, until it had become the big organization now known as the Interprovincial Loan & Savings Company. And because it was his nature to be generous and kindly "Old Nat" had fallen victim to misplaced confidence.

In those early years of struggle conservative methods and plain honesty had been not the least of his assets. It was upon these sound principles that he had relied throughout. The small deposits of the working classes, more or less ignored by his early competitors, had given him his start; even now the strength of the Interprovincial lay in its popularity among workmen and farmers, while its aggregate of small savings accounts was tremendous. The people trusted the Interprovincial because they had seen it grow and knew that it was administered honestly. "Catch 'Old Nat' having anything to do with the tricks of high finance!" said they, confidently, and many were the stories which went the rounds of how the "old-fashioned" financier had allowed sentiment to "interfere" with business. And the business had grown apace.

Because of this ingrained sentimental streak in his make-up and because of this inherent honesty he had created some enemies. There were those who looked hungrily in the direction of the Interprovincial and imagined what could be accomplished in a very big way in several different directions if only the man in control of the stock were—say, a little more modern. If it were not for the close tab which that energetic young secretary kept upon things, Lawson would have run the concern into the ditch long ago, whispered the ambitious ones. The young and energetic secretary, J. C. Nickleby, may have been the first to whisper it—very confidentially, of course. For it would ill become so promising a young financier as J. Cuthbert Nickleby to be guilty of ingratitude, and there had been one raw wet night in the spring of a year long past when Nathaniel Lawson had rescued a miserable travesty of a man from the gutter—a night that Nickleby, once his benefactor had set him firmly upon his feet with a new lease of life, no doubt had schooled himself to forget for all time.

At any rate there had come an annual meeting at which Nat Lawson found himself in a quandary. It followed on the heels of a rumor that it was the desire of certain shareholders to inject some "new blood," and thereby new life, into the loan company—that it would be a good thing, in short, for the "revered old Chief" to retire to a pedestal where he could sit as inanimate as a bronze bust upon the official label, "Honorary President," while a younger man took upon his shoulders the burden of the expanded business, and so forth.

The campaign against him had been of a most insidious character and Lawson had pretended with dignity to ignore it, even while his resentment grew to the proportions of great indignation. And all the time he was worried because he could not find a certain power-of-attorney which authorized him to vote a large block of stock belonging to a personal friend who had invested heavily in Lawson's company—Bradford, the arctic explorer, who had gone into the hinterland on a Government expedition, and who was not expected to get into communication with civilization again for about two years. Bradford had left everything in connection with his investment in his friend Lawson's hands. While the status of this stock on the books of the Interprovincial was unquestioned, the power-of-attorney had been given to Lawson personally and had not been placed officially in the hands of the secretary with instructions.

Herein lay the quandary. For when at the annual meeting in question Nat Lawson had tried to vote the stock in the usual way, he was asked for the power-of-attorney by some of the new shareholders and could not produce it. Proxies which Nickleby had manipulated then were thrown on the scale and when the meeting was over, the Interprovincial had a new president by the name of J. Cuthbert Nickleby. In making the announcement, the newspapers had quite a story about "Old Nat" and his career; they printed in full the account which was handed to them regarding the presentation of a gold-headed cane, suitably engraved, and an illuminated address which marked the esteem in which the directors held the retiring president and founder.

Convinced though he was that the power-of-attorney had been stolen deliberately and that the whole thing was a cunning frame-up to get him out of the way in order that certain transactions of which he never would have approved might go through—although convinced that this was the truth of the matter, Nat Lawson had no evidence to prove a case against Nickleby or any of his associates. It would have been a dangerous procedure to give publicity to his suspicions, or to attempt legal action without definite proof of his charges, as this could result only in destroying public confidence in the institution itself without in the least altering the situation. At the worst, the reign of the Nickleby faction could be but temporary, as the situation would adjust itself with the return of the explorer who owned the stock. But it was exceedingly humiliating, and there was always the possibility that those now in control of the Interprovincial meanwhile would undermine the whole financial fabric by loose policies of administration, or even by questionable practices.

These apprehensions were shared by the only two friends whom Nat Lawson had admitted fully to his confidence— President Benjamin Wade, of the Canadian Lake Shores Railway, and McAllister, the keen-eyed editor of the *Recorder*, which of all the city newspapers was the most consistently independent in politics. Wade was an old friend of long standing, himself holder of a small block of stock in the Interprovincial Loan & Savings Company, and it was to him that Lawson had turned for advice in his extremity. Immediately Wade had called into counsel the chief of his railroad's very competent detective staff, Bob Cranston, and thereupon began a series of quiet investigations with the object of obtaining the necessary evidence to depose the Nickleby faction from control of Interprovincial affairs.

Although equally anxious to help, McAllister had no part in Wade's plans; he preferred to work along special lines of his own. He and Wade differed in their theories of the situation, and much to Nat Lawson's amusement they had argued with some heat the first night that they happened to meet at the Lawson home; so that the two were somewhat in friendly rivalry, each anxious to prove that he was right, and each determined to play a lone hand.

It may have been his interest in the case that led McAllister to call so frequently of late at the old-fashioned brick house that stood back from the street, surrounded by spacious grounds and a wealth of carefully tended shrubbery, in the older residential section of the city. No doubt it was this that made him stop for a smoke with the former president of the Interprovincial about three evenings a week on the way to his office in the brightly-lighted *Recorder* building, where hummed activity during the hours that others slept, in order that the public might have a morning newspaper to prop against the sugar-bowl while it breakfasted.

Even so, it is necessary to add that Nathaniel Lawson had a beautiful and accomplished daughter whose name was Cristobel. It is necessary to record further that being a young woman of spirit, Miss Cristy Lawson had insisted upon taking up newspaper work as a profession when the need of adding to the family resources presented itself. For most of the Lawson capital had gone into the loan company and her father's philanthropic tendencies in the heyday of his earnings had made greater inroads upon his personal fortune than he had realized at the time. Her father's objections to the plan had been overruled finally when McAllister had offered Miss Lawson a position on the *Recorder's* day staff as "Society Editor," and it was not long before her interest in the work and her natural aptitude for it rejuvenated the Society Page into one of the best features the paper boasted.

Not content with this success, Miss Lawson became ambitious to try her journalistic wings in other directions; but her desire for more important assignments than the reporting of afternoon teas brought down the paternal foot—flat! No daughter of Nathaniel Lawson was going to be allowed to roam the city at all hours. "No night work," her father had insisted. Nevertheless, the young woman continued to hope that this edict would be removed eventually, and she never lost an opportunity of coaxing if she happened to be at home when McAllister was present; but there came a night finally when Nat Lawson grew impatient at her persistence and kindly but firmly put a final period to the topic.

She arrived home from a recital at the Conservatory of Music just in time to serve the refreshments and to listen breathlessly to the conclusion of the evening's animated discussion. Both Wade and McAllister were there and it was evident that they had been "at it again." From the quiet elation in the editor's eye and the corresponding amusement of her father, she judged that McAllister temporarily was having the better of the argument.

"Mac, I don't care a hoot what you've found out!" declared Ben Wade. "You can sit there and talk till this time to-morrow night, but you'll never convince me that the Honorable Milt isn't as straight as the best man who ever went into politics."

"Ah, just so—who ever went into politics," drawled McAllister with a provoking grin.

"Who ever did his duty in public life and became the victim of hidebound newspapers!" retorted Wade. "Milt Waring and I grew up in the same town together—went to the same school, played both hookey and hockey together. Why, I know him inside and out and I tell you he's as straight as a string."

"Your simile is unfortunate, Ben. The straightest string can be tied in knots."

"I see by this morning's papers that Rives has been released from the penitentiary," interposed their host. "Good conduct has got him out three years ahead of time. His sentence was fifteen, wasn't it?"

Wade nodded, but was not to be turned from his tilt with McAllister.

"What have you found out that makes you so cocky to-night?" he challenged the editor with interest.

"You'll read all about it in the *Recorder* when the time comes. You laughed at me the other night when I warned you that politics was mixed up in this Interprovincial manoeuvring. Watch me prove it. I'll send you a marked copy of the paper."

"Bluff! Listen to him, Nat!"

"I'm not in the habit of bluffing, Wade." McAllister's jaw was set as he patted the edge of the table for emphasis. "I'm responsible to the public and I tell you both right now that as sure as you're born—Ah, good-evening, Miss Lawson," he finished, rising to his feet with a smile.

McAllister busied himself, clearing a space on the table for the tray she was carrying, and from beneath his shaggy brows the railroad president's shrewd eyes carried a glint of amusement at the evident relief with which the editor welcomed the interruption. A moment more and McAllister might have committed himself to a rash statement.

"And how goes the battle, Cristy? Who won the latest bun fight?" smiled Wade by way of making conversation. "Have you persuaded your father—?"

"Indeed I have not," interrupted Cristy with an exaggerated pout. She looked directly at Ben Wade and frowned, as if the subject were one about which she would rather not be teased even by an old family friend of long and intimate standing. "It is too mean for anything! If, as Mr. McAllister has been good enough to intimate, I am capable of big successes in newspaper work, is it right to hold me back from the necessary experience? To hear Daddy talk you'd think I was a little child—"

"Cristy!" reproved Nat Lawson quietly.

"But I ask you, Mr. Wade, is it fair—?"

"Your father knows best, my child. He probably has good reasons—"

"I do not approve of you working on the night staff. I must ask you not to refer to this matter again. We will not discuss it now, please."

"Allow me to give you another cup of cocoa, Mr. McAllister?"

"Thank you, but I must be getting along," said McAllister, glancing hurriedly at his watch. "I have stayed later than I intended, thanks to the side-tracking of yon railroad president."

"I'll run you down to the office in the car for that," laughed Wade, also rising. "I'm going out of town for a couple of weeks, Nat; but the next time I see you I expect to have some news that will interest you. And I'll give it to you in advance of publication." He slapped McAllister on the shoulder and they bade their host and hostess a jovial adieu.

But once Wade's limousine was speeding down the street the magnate fell strangely silent. He passed a cigar to McAllister and lighted one for himself. For fully five minutes he did not speak a word. He listened in a preoccupied way to the editor's opinion of the new city parks by-law and to that gentleman's surprise interrupted him finally by a statement entirely irrelevant.

"Cristy Lawson is a remarkably clever young woman," he said, gazing thoughtfully at a little electric light in the roof of the car.

"For once I can agree with you entirely," nodded McAllister, flashing a quick glance at the other's upturned face.

"I don't blame her for getting sick and tired of writing your pink-tea items. Why don't you give her a chance at bigger game?"

"You heard what her father said?"

"I did. I want to make sure that you did too."

"What do you mean?"

"Whatever you like," snapped Wade. "There are some jobs that even a clever woman has no business attempting, that's all."

"Why talk in riddles, Ben? What's on your mind?"

"This wonderful graft exposure which you are planning to spring on an unsuspecting public." He rounded on McAllister and looked at him gravely. "How much of it have you told Nat?"

"I have said nothing about it to anybody," replied the editor, plainly puzzled. "Why?"

"My advice is to keep right on saying nothing about it. The less you say the less you'll have to take back."

"We'll see about that in due course," chuckled McAllister. "Do I look like a fool?"

"Appearances are often deceptive. I once knew a fellow who got so slick at gumshoeing that he sneaked up on his own shadow and made a fool of himself."

"Got married at high noon, perhaps?"

"Mac, seriously, I want you to promise me that you won't spring anything without giving me twenty-four hours' notice. It's an unusual request, I know; but I ask it in your own interests." There was no mistaking the earnestness with which he spoke, and McAllister stared at him.

"You—have some inside information to justify it?"

"Yes. I cannot tell you the details just now. I warn you that if your paper attempts the so-called exposure which you have in mind without my co-operation you'll regret it bitterly. I can help you and will be glad to; but only on condition that you warn me when you are ready. Do you promise?"

The limousine had stopped opposite the Recorder building and McAllister alighted slowly. Then he reached in through the open door and shook hands.

"All right, Ben. You're the doctor," he decided.

"Good. You can count on me, then. As a starter I can promise that the photos of the Alderson Construction Company's missing campaign-fund contribution will be delivered to you personally to-morrow night. I'll look you up when I get back in a week's time, Mac. Good-night."

McAllister remained standing at the curb till Wade's car swung out of sight around the corner. Then he struck the pavement with his cane, for it irritated him to be so completely surprised. Wade knew! How much did he know? And how in under the sun—?

"Pyed!" he grunted. "Devil take the man!"

He turned slowly and entered the building to his night's work.

CHAPTER VIII

ABOARD THE PRIVATE CAR, "OBASKA"

For many years self-repression had stood high in the estimation of Hughey Podmore as a thing worth cultivating. He had first learned the value of it in many a clandestine game of poker, which he had condescended to play of a Saturday afternoon in a corner of the deserted composing-room. In those days of his early newspaper experience the ink-daubed denizens of the "ad-alley" had paid with hard-earned wages for many a fancy vest and expensive cravat which the paper's star reporter had worn with such aplomb. And when he had adventured afield into wider pastures more in harmony with his talents, where the cards were not soiled nor the air pungent with printers' ink and benzine, he had taken with him a tendency to quiet tones of speech and quietness of movement.

Being a believer in rubber-heels and a cool head, therefore, the secretary to the President of the Canadian Lake Shores Railway went about his duties with his customary assurance. After the first excitement of his startling discovery had passed there was nothing in his manner to indicate the fires which burned within. To one who knew him well, perhaps, it might have seemed that for the two weeks which followed the mysterious disappearance of the tan satchel he was even a little quieter than usual, a little more restrained in his talk, and a little more alert in movement. Beyond this he gave no indication of the keen disappointment and mortification that possessed him.

It had been the biggest stake for which he had yet played. He had stacked the cards with particular care till, so he had thought, all element of risk had been eliminated. But for this his natural caution would have deterred him from the attempt. What he had completely overlooked was the possibility that some one else might decide this was any man's money who was clever enough to acquire it. Figure as he might—and he had spent hours in deep thought—even his keen mind had been unable to solve the situation to his satisfaction. Somebody had stepped in and walked off with this money in front of his nose in spite of the most elaborate precautions. Who had done this, and how? It had been done so cleverly that not a single clue was left for Podmore to work on—once he had proved beyond question that Clayton had not double-crossed him. Clayton had taken the first train for Chicago; but not before Podmore had third-degreed him into abject fear. No, Clayton had had no hand in it; that was certain, and with that once established, the identity of the arch-thief remained a mystery which baffled investigation—especially when the situation called for the utmost circumspection.

It was a problem which Podmore was forced to solve without consulting anyone. He could not go boldly to his supposed partners with his discovery; for thereby he would reveal to Nickleby and Alderson his own attempt at double dealing. That he had to be very careful what he did, Mr. Hughey Podmore realized,—very careful indeed. For this mix-up held many possibilities for personal misfortune. In fact, the situation suddenly had become fraught with positive danger. There were moments, therefore, when the cautious Mr. Podmore felt qualms which though not born of a troubled conscience, were nonetheless disagreeable. Conscience in the case of Hughey Podmore, if it had ever existed, had been a stunted affair which because of malnutrition long since had given up the ghost. Its place had been pre-empted by Argus-eyed regard for all matters affecting the preservation of Mr. Podmore's precious epidermis—the safety of his own skin. And Hughey Podmore was well aware that a large contribution to campaign funds by a construction company would be a matter of immediate suspicion among opponents of the Government if it became known. Such things had got people into trouble before this. It had been one of the things which had landed the famous Honorable Harrington Rives in jail—and others who were involved.

Hughey Podmore knew all about that strenuous period of political chaos. Twelve years ago he had been an eager-eyed young reporter with a large appreciation of newspaper sensations. His skill at ferreting into hidden recesses by unscrupulous methods had made him a valuable man for a paper which was willing to ignore certain time-honored traditions of the press. Under editorial stimulus Hughey had blossomed forth among the flowers of the journalistic profession as a yellow chrysanthemum. "Mum" became the word wherever Hughey showed himself! His reputation finally had ostracised him into other fields of endeavor.

Those had been the days! If only he and Rives had been working together! If he had been managing Rives' campaigns there would have been no crude mistakes to land the "people's idol" behind the bars, Waring or no Waring. He would have seen that every dainty dish was properly cooked before it was set before the King, its inner rawness safely covered, done up brown. By all means let there be lemon filling, but smothered in a beaten white purity that would pass the public censor! Under his management there would have been no tangible evidence to show that favored contractors, bidding upon public works, had been secretly advised that their tenders were too low, and instructed as to the amounts to which it was safe for them to raise their new tenders; there would have been no evidence of election contributions from these favored contractors for the amounts thus squeezed out of the public treasury.

With such an example of folly to warn him, it was no wonder that the Honorable Milton Waring had told Nickleby and Alderson he would have nothing to do with their proposed campaign fund contribution. Nickleby must have a pretty strong connection even to dare such an approach; evidently he had felt pretty sure of himself to go ahead with the plan on his own initiative.

Nickleby believed that Ferguson had the money now. What would he say if he knew the facts—that the money was really in the hands of some person unknown, some person perhaps who was interested in gathering evidence that would upset the present Government? There was only one thing for Mr. Podmore to do, now that his own pet scheme had failed, and that was to keep quiet as to his own ambitions and stick to the three-handed game which he was supposed to be playing with Nickleby and his henchman, Alderson; for Nickleby was worth tying to.

Thus ran the reflections of Hughey Podmore as he lounged comfortably in a leather chair aboard the private car, "Obaska," and idly watched the endless flow of the Algoma wilderness pass the windows monotonously. The car had taken an inspection party west to the head of the lakes, but a wire from the Vice-President was sending the President back to headquarters unexpectedly. Besides President Wade, Podmore and Taylor, the steward, the only person on board was Bob Cranston. Cranston was chief of the railroad's Special Service Department. Taylor was busy in his kitchen, preparing dinner. Cranston and the President had the brass-railed observation platform at the rear of the car to themselves and were deep in earnest conversation; they had shut the door at their backs and the sound of their voices was lost in the roar of the wheels.

Hughey Podmore smiled cynically as he watched them. There was nothing in President Wade's fine strong profile to indicate the trend of talk. Both, in fact, were men who seldom allowed what they were thinking to reflect in their facial expressions too readily. Nevertheless, the perspicacious Mr. Podmore could surmise the subject of conversation, or at any rate give a guess which was close enough to satisfy his own curiosity.

He amused himself by running over the list of possible topics. Wade was a big man in financial circles, a man of rugged and plain-spoken dealings who commanded the confidence of every associate and was respected even by his enemies. There were many matters of moment which he might have discussed with bankers or lawyers or statesmen, but which he would hardly attempt with a bull-necked bonehead like Cranston. Government railway bond issues, franchises and stock-quotations were beyond that cheap stiff's depth. Probably Cranston was holding forth in regard to some petty theft which his crew of spotters had discovered, some ticket-scalping conductor—

Or there was old Nat Lawson's case in which Wade was interested; it was a topic that was often uppermost in the railway President's mind, as Podmore knew, and Hughey smiled inscrutably at the smoke curling from his cigarette. Old Nat, the founder and former president of the Interprovincial Loan & Savings Company—the honest old fool whom Nickleby had succeeded in overcoming by a trick, and whose shoes J. Cuthbert was now wearing! It would take more than the friendship of a Benjamin Wade, powerful though that was, to salvage Old Nat. That nanny-whiskered old galoot was sunk in too many fathoms of water ever to wade ashore. (He smiled at his poor pun.) The missing power-of-attorney that had scuttled the Lawson supporters would continue missing for all time to come. Mr. J. Cuthbert Nickleby, the then genial secretary, had seen to that once for all; in fact, it had been a charred fragment of the document which Mr. Hugh Podmore had used as a card of introduction when he had had his first long and very interesting session with Friend Nickleby.

Some class to Nickleby all right. Here were methods which Mr. Podmore could understand and admire. It was because the minds of Messrs. Podmore and Nickleby ran in the same grooves that he had been able to unearth enough of Nickleby's very private plans to persuade that "rising young financier" that it was better to set another plate at the head table than to have the dishes smashed and Lucullus waylaid before he could reach the banquetting-hall.

So Mr. Podmore had hung up his hat, accepted a cigar and joined the inner ring, soon proving himself a congenial spirit and an able counsellor. And inasmuch as President Wade, of the Canadian Lake Shores Railroad, was seeking about that time for a private secretary with a newspaper training; inasmuch as it was known to J. Cuthbert Nickleby that the said President Wade hoped to restore Old Nat Lawson to his former place in the business world by acquiring control of the Interprovincial Loan & Savings Company—inasmuch did it seem desirable in the interests of Messrs. Nickleby and Podmore that Mr. Podmore should apply for the vacant secretaryship. Podmore had got the position, thereby enabling Nickleby to keep a finger upon the pulse of his opposition.

Wade was shrewd, clever, a big man; he knew many things, did Benjamin Wade, railway magnate. But, reflected

Hughey, there were many things also which he did not know, and there was a disagreeable twist in the corner of Podmore's mouth as he lounged and smoked. His revered chief did not know, for instance, that his very competent secretary had spent the better part of an afternoon alone in the private car "Obaska," listening to the click of the tumblers in the little secret wall safe which the President had had built in behind a sliding panel—listening so intelligently that the said very competent secretary had come away with the combination.

Podmore's further enjoyment of retrospection was cut short by a sudden gesture which rivetted his attention upon the two men on the rear platform. Cranston had turned suddenly and was peering in at him; almost automatically Podmore's eyes dropped quickly to the open magazine on his knee. There was a certain hint of caution on the railroad detective's face that did not escape the astute secretary. The latter's vigilance was rewarded presently by seeing Cranston reach into an inside pocket, pull out a bulky blue envelope and quickly pass it across to the President. The latter as quickly stowed it out of sight in an inner pocket of his tweed coat and himself cast a hasty glance over his shoulder to see if he had been observed. But again Mr. Podmore's gaze dropped in time and when he raised his eyes casually from his magazine it was to note an expression of satisfaction upon the faces of both gentlemen. They got up and came inside, laughing rather loudly.

"That there steak and onions Taylor's cookin' is sure goin' to hit the spot," cried Cranston, sniffing with relish. "Eh, Hughey?" He dropped into the chair alongside the secretary with a familiar slap on the latter's knee, and thrust his legs out in the sprawling abandon of a comfortable stretch.

Unfortunately he did this just as President Wade, having turned to toss away the end of his cigar, took a step forward with a hand thrust into an inside pocket of his coat, evidently intending to put away in the safe the envelope which Cranston had given him. The result of Cranston's sudden movement and Wade's awkward position was that the President tripped, lost his balance and would have measured full length on the car floor if Cranston had not caught him. In his effort to save himself the blue envelope was jerked out of his pocket and fell directly at Podmore's feet.

"Oh, I beg your pardon, sir!" apologized Cranston hurriedly.

"That's all right, Bob," laughed Wade good naturedly. "Thanks, Hughey," as his secretary handed him the envelope. "Why, what's the matter?"

Podmore's face had gone suddenly white and he was trembling visibly.

"Aint you feelin' well, Hughey?" enquired Cranston with concern. He rang quickly for highballs.

"It's all right,—thanks," stammered Podmore hastily. "I—I guess it's just a little faintness due to the fact that I ate practically no lunch—I'm all right now."

Nevertheless when Taylor arrived with the decanter Podmore poured himself an extra stiff drink. He had need of it. For a second time he had lost his poise, and it was only with the greatest difficulty that he prevented any further manifestation of the fact during the meal and the evening which followed. For unless he was very much mistaken—and he felt sure that he was not—that envelope he had picked up and handed to the President was the identical blue linen envelope that had been stolen with the tan satchel so mysteriously two weeks ago! The size of it, the feel of it, the daubs of gray sealing-wax—Oh, there was no mistaking it!

Hopkins Moorhouse

How in thunderation had it come into Cranston's hands?—
Cranston, of all men! Had Cranston pulled off the stunt? Had
Podmore been doing him an injustice? He studied the chief
of the Special Service Department with a new and wide-
awake interest. If Cranston had purloined this packet it was
under orders—Wade's, of course. Then that suspicion which
had kept recurring every time he had tried to think out the
mystery of the disappearance was correct. It was a political
move! The opponents of the Government were lining up for
the approaching election with open charges of mal-feasance,
graft,—the same old game! Wade, he knew, had had friction
with the present administration over certain legislation; that
was sufficient motive for him taking a hand, although it was
hardly likely that a man of Wade's standing would allow
himself to become involved in such back-alley tactics—
unless—Nickleby—the Interprovincial—!

Podmore's thoughts were not running as clearly as usual.
They kept pocketing themselves provokingly in blind alleys
that led nowhere, or scattering in mazes that led everywhere.
There was such a wide field of speculation open, once he
began to consider things from the political angle, that it was
difficult to reach any very definite conclusion. He was not
now so concerned as to the why or the how of what had
happened; the cold analysis of motives and methods was
dwarfed by the one big fact that here on board the private car
and within easy reach was that blessed envelope, containing
fifty thousand dollars of any man's money. For it did not
look as if it had been tampered with; the seals were still
unbroken. Right here, within a few yards of where he sat,
was that little old bunch of greenbacks that he had planned
so earnestly to take unto his bosom and that had cost him so
many heartburnings this past two weeks. Talk about luck!
Talk about Opportunity knocking once on somebody's door!
Why, the Old Dame was chopping down his door with an
axe!

With his mind in such a chaos of confused emotions Hughey found it difficult to keep up his end of the conversation and he was not sorry when the others showed a tendency to turn in early. Once the lights were dimmed he could hardly wait the reasonable length of time which must elapse before the other three occupants were asleep, so eager was he to make his investigations. But at last the snores of Cranston and the steward and the steady breathing of President Wade satisfied him that the way was clear.

Quietly he slipped from his berth. He had not undressed, except to remove his boots and coat, and in two minutes he had the envelope in his hands. He slipped noiselessly down the aisle to the steward's kitchen, switched on a light and examined the prize leisurely. He felt it carefully, hefted it in one hand, then with the aid of a thin-bladed paring-knife he succeeded in loosening a corner of the flap sufficiently to allow of a peek at the contents without disturbing the seals. His involuntary exclamation of satisfaction when he verified the contents as a package of greenbacks was drowned fortunately in the hum of the train. It was the missing campaign fund contribution beyond a doubt.

Back down the dimly lighted aisle with its swaying green curtains, past the sleepers he slipped noiselessly to the writing desk where he carefully regummed the corner of the flap, leaving no trace of his inspection. Then he sank into a leather chair and lit a cigarette with a cheerful grin on his face.

The Fates certainly were kindness itself. He had it—50,000 bucks! He actually had it in his pocket! It was enough to give Mr. Podmore a fine start on his own account somewhere far away. Nickleby and Alderson? They could go and take a jump in the lake! He had his. It was a good time to drop out of this game anyway. The political situation did not look any too good. Well, he would befriend the Honorable Milt and

Ferguson and Nickleby and Alderson by removing this little piece of election evidence from the reach of their opponents. That was a service which was cheap at the price.

Yes, it was time to say a final farewell while the farewelling was good. He hunted up a time-table. They must be somewhere in the vicinity of Indian Creek by now. Where would the west-bound limited be at that hour? He glanced at his watch, then flattened his nose against the window, until his eyes became accustomed to the starlight and he could watch the dim panorama of spruce trees and lonely little lakes sliding by in ceaseless procession. Presently he recognized a flag-station. His guess at Indian Creek as their whereabouts had not been far astray.

He made his plans quickly. He would drop off, walk to the nearest station and catch No. 1, westbound, at midnight. That would take him into the Missinaibi country by daylight, and he could afford to run the risk of discovery until then. He would leave the train there somewhere and would find no difficulty in obtaining an outfit and an Indian guide. They would hit southwest for Lake Superior, and once there he could find his way across to the Michigan side by night and so away.

Podmore laced his boots rapidly and went through his grip for one or two articles he thought he might need. He stole back to the kitchen and put some crackers and cheese in his pockets; it was all he could find that was not under lock and key. Then with the precious envelope buttoned tightly inside his coat he picked his way cautiously to the rear of the swaying car, closed the door carefully behind him and climbed over the brass rail.

For a moment he hung there, hesitating. Then he let go his hold and disappeared.

CHAPTER IX

CONSPIRING EVENTS

The President's private car pulled into Wardlow at the tail of No. 2, the east-bound express, at 3.10 a.m., and was there side-tracked upon instructions from Detective Robert Cranston. As soon as No. 2 had got away behind a fresh engine on the long jump to the next divisional point, Cranston, fully dressed, descended from the car and went across to the despatcher's office. Half an hour later he returned to the car, undressed and crawled back into his berth with a grunt of satisfaction.

The President greeted him at breakfast with a smile and Cranston responded with the grin of a man who has made predictions which have come true.

"Well, Bob, your fish bit, I see."

"Sure did, sir. He took bait, hook an' sinker at 23.20 an' I'll have him reeled in by to-morrow morning."

"Not so sure about that, Bob," said Wade skeptically. "Fish sometimes get clean away, remember. What have you done?"

"Wired his description to every section foreman on the division with instructions to notify me here and hold him prisoner till we come. Fifty dollars reward. We crossed No. 1 half an hour after Hughey jumped. Johnston has special instructions to watch out for him, and there isn't a sharper conductor in the service. He'd figure to grab the west-bound, if everything went well. If he didn't succeed, we'll nab him sure somewhere up the line during the day."

"Unless he's taken to the woods. Podmore's not fool enough to stick to the track, Bob," objected Wade.

"Excuse me, sir, but that's exactly what he's got to do in these here parts. A train's the on'y hope he's got of gettin' quick to where he can get an outfit. On'y a damn fool 'd try to make the lake immediate. I aint sayin' as he mightn't lay low for a while, but he can't stick that out long."

"Well, I'll be gone all day with Foster up the Lone Hollow spur. Back by dark. That's all the time I can give you, Bob. If you haven't a lead before No. 2 gets here, I'm afraid I can't wait." He got up from the table.

"That's all right, Mr. Wade. But I'll have a message to show you when you get back this evening," said Cranston confidently.

Nevertheless the only message which he was able to show the President on his return was a wire from Johnston that there was no trace of Podmore among his passengers, and that everybody who had boarded last night's westbound train on the Wardlow division was accounted for. It was with considerable secret disappointment that the Chief of the Special Service Department of the C.L.S. made arrangements for the President's car to continue eastward with No. 2, while he remained behind at Wardlow; for thereby Cranston was losing a splendid opportunity to demonstrate his ability at cross-questioning in the presence of the magnate. He was only human.

Cranston, however, had been taught by experience that time is never up till the last moment. Although his belongings were packed, he left his suitcase aboard the car and long after he had said good-bye to Wade, long after the President was in his berth for the night, the detective sat doggedly on in the despatcher's office, smoking his pipe. His patience was rewarded about an hour before No. 2 was due.

The message was from Thorlakson and came over the wire from the night operator at Indian Creek. The Icelander was holding Podmore at Thorlakson Siding as instructed. Cranston already had made arrangements for a special engine to run them back up the line, and having issued definite instructions he went back to the private car and unpacked his pyjamas.

One of those methodical individuals who are born every now and then with the gift of interpreting railway schedules would have had no great difficulty in locating "Thorlakson" in the main-line timetable of the Canadian Lake Shores Railway. It takes the form of a little dagger-mark which, pursued into the fine print of the "Explanatory," yields the information that "Thorlakson" is a flag-station.

Magnus Thorlakson himself, Icelander, must be credited with being one of the oldest and most conscientious section foremen on the division. He, his men, his wife, his children and everything that was his abode in a log shanty on a rise of ground close to the track. The rest of the place consisted of a long siding, a short wooden platform, a tall new standard enclosed water-tank and a little whitewashed shed where the handcar and tools were stored. A creek here slipped out of the woods to find fault with a stone culvert ere it flowed beneath the track and resought silence among the encircling spruce trees.

It was a lonesome, insignificant place with nothing to indicate its selection as a bobbin for threads of destiny. The sun was just coming into the sky above the low-lying hills to the east when the President's special steamed into the siding. From the group, clustered about the tool-shed and awaiting its arrival, a broad-shouldered young man in the flannel shirt and legging boots of a railway engineer separated himself and hurried forward. He waved his hand as he recognized Wade's sturdy figure and laughed to hear the magnate's hearty greeting of surprise, his profane enquiry as to what in Gehenna Philip Kendrick was doing away up here in the woods.

The mere sound of that big vibrant bass voice, the mere vitality of the magnate's presence was stimulating. Here was a two-fisted, hard-headed, straight-spoken man's man who had fought his way to the top by refusing pointblank to stay at the bottom. As Phil stood renewing acquaintance he realized more fully why his aunt had always had such supreme confidence in this old friend of her girlhood.

"I've been working for the C.L.S. for nearly two weeks now," he explained. "I'm chainman with the Rutland party, out from North Bay on a topographical survey. We're taking a new mileage and mapping the right-of-way. Our van's on the second siding above here."

This unexpected "vacation" had come about quite simply. On arrival in North Bay to go fishing with Billy Thorpe he had found that wide-awake young architect so immersed in an important contract that temporary postponement of their plans was imperative. As if provided specially to meet the situation along had come Rutland's urgent wire to head-quarters for a new chainman, one of his men having taken sick suddenly. Phil had jumped at the opportunity for a taste of practical survey work, and with Thorpe's assistance the matter had been arranged readily and he had left the same night to join the Rutland party out the line.

The battered old freight caboose in which the young engineers lived was moved ahead from siding to siding by passing freight trains as Rutland advised the Chief Despatcher of the work's progress. Scarcely a day had passed that had not strung a few interesting beads of incident to brighten the necklace of its routine monotonies—the squealing, kicking baby rabbit which Anderson, the head chainman, had captured; the wild duck which they had cornered in a thicket and which Bayley, the marker, had insisted upon decorating with his white paint before he would let it go; the occasional mess of speckled trout for which they angled; the fresh baked pies and cakes they were sometimes able to buy from a section-man's wife; the bear tracks and the bodies of wild animals lured to death by the glare of the powerful headlights on the fast trains at night; the excitement at the great ballast pit where the gangs at work were running an unpopular cook out of camp; the very old Indian who had stared at the dragging chain and muttered "Heap big snake," and the very young Englishman who had gone crazy from fly-bites and whom the sawmill gang had strapped to a rough litter in preparation for rushing him to the North Bay hospital by the first train they could flag. In spite of the mosquitoes, black flies and midges, which at this season of the year were a decided affliction in the country through which they were working, Kendrick had enjoyed the new experience. Twenty miles average daily working distance, frequently with an extra ten-mile walk back to the car, already had rounded the erstwhile captain of the Varsity rugby champions into tackling condition.

In spite of the fact that he had been up all night, therefore, his eyes were bright with the mirror glisten which is the gift of long hours in the open air. The black eye which had attracted unwelcome attention at first no longer contributed to the amusement of the inquisitive, the obtrusion of its remaining jaundice being overcome by the new coat of tan that encroached upon it.

His presence at Thorlakson Phil accounted for very briefly, saying merely that he had come back there to look for a lost pocketbook, containing his railway pass. But it had not been the pass or the loose change that had troubled him so greatly; it had been—well, darn it, he didn't want to lose them like that anyway!—a dollar bill, wrapped carefully around a lady's shirtwaist pin! It was his own business entirely. Luckily Thorlakson had picked it up and was able to restore the pocketbook with its contents intact.

As it had turned out Kendrick's evening hike back down the track to Thorlakson had been a lucky thing for Podmore too. Within a mile of the siding Phil had come upon him, sitting beside the track in despair of reaching human aid before he collapsed completely. He had been badly hurt in his fall from the train, and aside from these injuries his hands were swollen and covered with dirt and blood, his torn clothes encrusted with dried mud, collar and tie gone and his shirt ripped open in front, revealing neck and chest smeared with blood where the blackflies had bitten him severely.

"He had spent part of the night and the whole day in the woods and was half out of his head, poor devil!" said Phil. "I managed to get him down here and with the help of Mrs. Thorlakson's homemade liniment I fixed him up as well as I could. He insisted on me staying with him all night—till you arrived, in fact."

"Expected us, eh?" grunted Wade.

"Oh, sure. News of the—er—accident travelled up and down the line pretty swiftly. A track-walker passed the word to us early yesterday morning just as we were starting out from the caboose for the day's work. So I had Thorlakson get a message off to you; he stuck it in a split stick and the engineer of a passing freight caught it O.K. and took it up the line to the operator at Indian Creek."

As Kendrick finished speaking they both turned to watch Cranston approaching slowly, supporting Podmore. The secretary's condition had improved greatly under Phil's ministrations and the food which Mrs. Thorlakson had prepared for him. But it was apparent that he was still suffering from shock and beneath the bandage about his head the black and blue evidence of the contusion was visible. His sprained arm was bandaged also and he limped badly and leaned heavily upon the detective.

"Hello there, Hughey," greeted Wade. "Wrecked from engine to caboose, eh? What a whack on the head! Might've killed you. How'd you come to fall off?"

Podmore smiled weakly. He gazed for a moment at Kendrick as if trying to collect his thoughts. Then he explained that he had been troubled with insomnia and got up to smoke a cigarette. He had been fool enough to perch up on the brass rail at the rear of the private car, thinking the fresh air might make him sleepy. The train had been hitting up a fast pace on a down grade and as they swung a curve he had lost his balance and pitched clean down a long fill among the rocks of a creek bottom. The fall had knocked him senseless. When finally he had recovered consciousness he had been too ill to move for a long time. Then the hot sun had driven him to crawl painfully into the woods where he had lain helpless most of the day, with just enough strength to get water from the creek. When he began to feel a little better toward nightfall he had gone back to the track and started for help. Just as he was ready to give up Kendrick had found him.

Cranston and the President exchanged glances, but Wade merely nodded when Podmore requested to be allowed to crawl into his berth because he was feeling "swimmy in the head." Cranston and the steward helped him aboard and proceeded to put him to bed.

"From that little shake of the head that Cranston just passed you, Mr. Wade, I gather that he failed to find any trace of the envelope that's missing," said Kendrick quietly. He smiled at the abruptness with which the President of the C.L.S. took hold of his arm and walked him away from the car.

"Let's go over there and see Thorlakson a minute," he said loudly. "Now, shoot," he added in a lower voice. "What do you know about this thing, Phil?"

"He's been trying to fill me up with the smoothest line of bunk I ever listened to. According to him you're the sworn political enemy of Uncle Milt and have had a finger in the theft—theft, mind you!—of important secret state documents which would have been the cause of a financial panic if they had remained in your possession much longer, to say nothing of undermining public confidence in the present administration."

"Great Busted Reputations! Did he tell you that?"

"While I was bandaging him. He said he was the reporter who located the evidence that had convicted Rives and elected my uncle, and that he was acting now as an agent of the government to recover the confidential reports that had been stolen from the chairman of the Waterways Commission."

"Trying to unload the envelope on you, eh?"

"Yes. He asked me to post it for him—addressed it himself to his address in Toronto."

"What did you do?"

"Posted it, of course—in a hollow stump over there near the tank with a slab of fungus on top for a lid!"

Ben Wade laughed aloud.

"Know what's in the thing?" he demanded abruptly.

"These stolen Government documents?"

"Fifty thousand dollars, you mean!"

"The son-of-a-gun!" muttered Kendrick, looking startled.

"But he doesn't happen to know that the bills are bogus—stage money, sandwiched between a couple of genuine bills of small denomination," chuckled Wade. He stopped short and stood in front of Kendrick with one hand on the younger man's shoulder. "Phil," he said seriously, "you've stumbled in on a little game that is being played out with stacked cards. We'll talk about it after breakfast. We'll be running up as far as Indian Creek to use the Y in the old ballast pit. You're coming along. We can stop at Rutland's caboose long enough for you to pick up your nightie and your safety razor."

"I don't think I understand, Mr. Wade," said Phil, puzzled.

"Not supposed to," retorted Wade. "Fact is, you're fired! You can't work for Rutland another minute—"

"Why, what—?"

"Because you're hired! I've got to have a secretary, haven't I? There's interesting work ahead, boy, and I need you. Don't ask questions. Breakfast first. I can't talk without a cigar and I never smoke before breakfast."

"Shall I run over to the stump and get the envelope?" asked Kendrick when he had recovered from his first surprise.

"Not by a jugful! Podmore thinks you're playing his game, doesn't he? Always draw to the aces, Phil. Leave the envelope where it is. Hello, Thorlakson. Hello, boys. Good work last night. I want to thank you all. Mr. Kendrick here has just been telling me how well you did your duty. He wants you to have that fifty dollar reward—all of it."

As he spoke he took from his pocket a roll of greenbacks and peeled off five ten-dollar bills which he handed to the foreman with a twinkle of the eye. It was what they had been waiting for with a vast interest. And while Svenson, the big Swede, and the two Norwegians snatched off their caps and grinned, Thorlakson endeavored to convey their entire satisfaction.

"Yaow, Meester Vade, sir, it is wery suffeecient," he assured in his best English as he shook hands with profound respect. When he turned to Kendrick there was added his evident admiration of the young man's generosity.

Smoke was curling up from the kitchen end of the private car and the welcome aroma of coffee announced that Taylor had breakfast ready. They climbed aboard forthwith, but the special remained sidetracked to pass a fast freight. It thundered by before they finished the meal and by the time Kendrick found himself on the observation platform at the rear of the car the special was on its way.

Wade carefully shut the door behind them. Podmore had fallen into a sound slumber while Cranston was busy at the writing-desk, and it was with a lively interest that Phil settled himself to listen to whatever confidences Ben Wade might see fit to impart. For some time, however, the President of the C.L.S. smoked in silence, his shaggy eyebrows puckered in a frown and his gaze fastened thoughtfully upon the serrated skyline of the spruce tops that ran rearward unceasingly.

"We've come across two or three places like that on this division the past two weeks," said Phil to break the silence. He nodded towards the disused station building that was receding down the track, its boarded windows and broken platform eloquent of desolation. "I've wondered why a perfectly good station like that should be built in the first place if it was to be abandoned later on without even a day telegraph operator?"

"Eh? Oh, there used to be some lumbering around here when we first opened up. Also the road's required to put up a station every so-many miles without regard to the surrounding country—just a fool charter obligation, that's all; sometimes we use an old box-car—" Wade carefully picked away the band of his cigar. "Phil, I'm going to ask you to undertake a somewhat unusual commission for me with no very definite idea of what it may lead you into. There may be even some danger attached to it. It is my duty to mention this possibility, although I know you'll consider that not at all when I tell you that the results may have some bearing upon the welfare of—your uncle; indirectly, perhaps your aunt.

"Let me give you a few facts. If you've cut your eye teeth you know that just as man does not live by bread alone so elections in this fair land are not won nowadays by mass meetings and fine speeches, but by hard cold cash and organization. Things have come to such a pass that it is largely a matter of machinery. The side with the biggest machine and the most oil—and gas—is pretty sure of passing the grandstand in the lead. The oil is most important, and long before the race it is gathered into a large tank called the 'Party Campaign Fund,' by henchmen who call upon various friendly corporate institutions. You follow me?"

"Right at your heels," smiled Kendrick.

"Well then, one of these substantial little contributions not long since while on its devious way to the Place of Burnt Offerings was ambushed by somebody with a hankering for the fleshpots of Egypt—fifty thousand dollars cold, stolen as slick as a whistle. I happen to be one of the very few, outside of the principals in the transaction, who know anything about it; for campaign fund contributions are among those things which men of discretion do not discuss from the housetops. I'm not going to say just now how this information reached me; but it is necessary for you to know that the Inter-provincial Loan & Savings Company is vitally interested in the recovery of this money, or at least in the identity of the thief. And when we speak of the Interprovincial in these halcyon days we speak of J. Cuthbert Nickleby, its astute president. A thing like this could never have happened if Nat Lawson had been in the saddle.

"Mention of Nickleby brings me to Podmore, who is nothing more than a tool of Nickleby's. I knew when I hired Podmore as my secretary that I was hiring a spy. I knew his record. You see, they were aware of the fact that I was interesting myself on behalf of my friend, Lawson. Podmore hadn't been with me two days before the beggar had the combination of the safe aboard this car. He's a smooth one. But I figured to learn as much from him as he got from me. Before we get to Toronto I'll give you the inside history of that Lawson situation; for it's mixed up with the rest of it.

"But let me get back to this stolen money. It was done up in an envelope just like this one which Podmore stole from the car the other night; fact is, they're duplicates. It was a little experiment which Cranston and I decided to try out to get Podmore where we wanted him. We're going to have an interesting session with him after a bit on the off chance of securing some information. I haven't a great deal of confidence in third-degree methods; but I'm letting Cranston have a fling at it on the chance that Podmore will drop a stitch. He's yellow enough for anything.

"Now, here's where you come in, Phil. Podmore thinks you intend to help him out and that is exactly what I want you to pretend to do. We'll stage a little drama and we'll have you on the carpet along with him. You'll deny all knowledge of the envelope. I'll fire you. You'll get mad and come back at me with red-hot talk for doubting your word and so on. We're going to let Podmore go when we get to the city. You'll go with him. The chance to sic you onto him is too good to miss. So we'll turn you loose together; it will be up to you then to mix in where you see fit. Is that all clear?

"All right. What I want you to do is to keep an eye on him. Find out what his next move is. He told you he was the reporter who had located the evidence that convicted Rives. Did he tell you how he got hold of it?—how he double-crossed Rives by low-down trickery? He doesn't know how to be loyal to anybody. I'll be surprised if he doesn't repeat on Nickleby.

"Then there are some things I want to find out about Nickleby and his associates. I want you to move carefully, Phil. I had one of Cranston's best men on the job until recently; but his usefulness was ended by unexpected developments. I'm working to put Nat Lawson back at the head of the loan company; Nickleby is an interloper and he's playing ducks and drakes with the concern. Tell you about it later. Are you agreeable to act as my secretary in these matters and to carry out instructions—blindfolded, so to speak?"

Kendrick had listened intently to this recital. Now he deliberately lighted his pipe before replying, and when he did it was to ask a blunt question.

"Does Uncle Milt figure in this?" and he noted the shadow that crossed the magnate's face.

"I wish I really knew that, Phil," said Wade seriously. "Time will tell. I'm banking on your uncle to stay square to the finish; but there's nothing to be gained by shutting one's eyes to the fact that many a good man has found the political game as it's being played these days too many for him. There are those who are inclined to doubt all politicians, your uncle included. I don't set myself up as any high-minded reformer; if you're sitting in on a game at all, you've got to play it according to the rules that are handed you—or quit."

Phil smoked in silence. He was thinking of that strange interview with his uncle the night of the fog; but he gave no voice to his thoughts.

"Your aunt has some of her private funds invested in the Interprovincial Loan and that's one of the reasons I want you with me, Phil." Wade turned and laid a hand on Kendrick's knee while he looked the young man quietly in the eye.

"There are stronger considerations than the money side of it, though. All I can say is that the happiness of your aunt is as dear to me as it is to you, or as it would be to anyone who had learned to respect and admire her as we have. That happiness has got to be guarded, Phil, even at the sacrifice of—everything else."

His gaze wandered away again to where the twin rails converged, and for a moment the rhythmic beat of the wheels over the joints held sway. Rather surprised, Phil stole a glance at the virile face that was turned so steadfastly away and recalled an item of gossip he had once overheard somewhere—that Mrs. Waring was the real reason Benjamin Wade was still a bachelor. He wondered if there could be any truth in that idle rumor.

"I'm sorry that I can't be more explicit. Did you ever try to piece out a puzzle, Phil? That's what I'm up against now. I'll tell you all about it—as soon as I know myself. There are men in this world who stop at nothing—"

Phil turned abruptly, a startled look in his eyes; but the other did not finish the sentence.

"Harrington Rives is out of jail—" he began.

"A case in point, if you like," nodded Wade. "But don't let's talk to no purpose. We'll be passing Rutland's car in a minute. Do we stop for your things?"

"You hired me back there at Thorlakson's," Kendrick reminded.

In this simple fashion were events conspiring.

CHAPTER X

THE STENOGRAPHER STILL LISTENING

The visitors who came and went occasionally up the back stairs at Blatchford Ferguson's office were a motley lot. Silk hats and expensive overcoats sometimes hung on the hooks in the corner. Again, ill-kempt figures slunk up that back way and signal-tapped an entrance; for in his police-reporter days Blatch Ferguson had been interested in the study of underworld types and he made no secret of his intention of one day writing an authoritative work upon the psychology of crime.

The big leather chair, so placed that it faced the light and left the lawyer in partial shadow behind his desk, had held many a strange and anxious caller in its day. Great men, men of national importance, had sat in that deep old leather chair; but with fine passivity it yielded the same comforts to men who only thought they were important.

Just now it was occupied by Mr. Hugh Podmore—within an hour of that worthy's arrival in the city. At three p.m. his new-found friend, Philip Kendrick, had agreed to call upon Ferguson to corroborate the story which Mr. Podmore had just finished telling and to which his auditor had listened with great intentness, that being the only indication of surprise which the practiced Mr. Ferguson permitted himself to exhibit.

"You always were pretty cock-sure of yourself, Poddy, even back in the days when we both worked on the old *Tribune*," commented Ferguson with a smirk of amusement. "But this proposition of yours is the deckle-edged limit and no mistake. If you were anybody else I'd have a lot of fun— kicking you downstairs!"

"Old stuff, Fergey!" grinned Podmore, unperturbed. "You don't need to pull that for my benefit. Talk brass tacks. Kendrick will be here in ten minutes with all the proof you want that I'm handing it to you straight and that that campaign-fund wad of Nickleby's is where I can lay hands on it. Do I pass it to you or must I hand it over to Charlie Cady? Guess the Opposition'll know what to do with it. I'm asking you this: What's it worth to the Government to win the next election? That's the little old answer I want."

"Would a couple of million satisfy you? How'll you have it?—in fives and tens?" and Mr. Ferguson gravely stroked his fleshy red nose.

"Be serious, Fergey," protested Podmore. "You can see for yourself that I came near getting killed, lining this thing up."

"I could not be more serious if you really had got killed, Poddy," and again he stroked the emblem of his *entrez* to the social functions of John Barleycorn. "I'm afraid your mind is warping in the sunshine of your own cleverness, Poddy. This fool notion of yours—coming to me about this money Nickleby's lost—if anybody had told me that once that long green was in your possession you'd come away back here—"

"What do you take me for, Ferguson?—a thief?" glared

Podmore angrily.

"Opportunist is not so harsh a word," soothed the lawyer, thoroughly enjoying the baiting. He frowned with an abrupt change of manner. "You want brass tacks, do you? Here they are, then. That money is none of my business, none of the Government's business. Understand that clearly. You say it was a campaign-fund contribution. How do I know it was? It never reached us. It's Nickleby's money and its loss is his funeral. Go and report to him and try to understand the meaning of the word 'loyalty.' Our party doesn't care a tinker's dam who has had, now has, or will have that envelope. And if you want to get thrown out by the scruff of the neck just try going to headquarters with your crazy proposition."

"You—surely you don't mean that, Fergey, old man?" said Podmore, searching the other's face with misgiving.

"Every word of it. And here's something else, Podmore, that I won't charge you for. If you're wise you'll take a straight tip and get out of this office as fast as you know how—out of town—clean out of the country! You don't seem to keep as well posted on the latest news as you used to. Have you read that?"

Ferguson had opened a drawer as he spoke and tossed out a newspaper, so folded that an item encircled by red ink was uppermost. Podmore slowly picked up the paper. As his glance travelled quickly through the marked item his face paled—what part of it was not black and blue.

"Oh, Rives, eh? I—No, I didn't know he was out of the pen." He tried hard to keep his voice steady, but did not succeed very well.

"He's been out over two weeks now," nodded Ferguson,

making no effort to conceal his contempt. "And he hasn't forgotten that a fresh newspaper reporter by the name of Podmore played him a dirty trick twelve years ago. He's sworn to get you for that."

"How—how do you know this?" asked Podmore hoarsely.

"'Itchy' McGuire called to see me day before yesterday. He's met Rives. If I were you I'd hunt me up a nice little island somewhere in the Tropics where you can live with the rest of the monkeys; they might elect you to Parliament or crown you king or something. Rives is one bad actor and he's sore—good and sore."

Podmore's attempted laugh had no mirth in it. He reached for his hat, and as he said a hasty good-bye he did not look at all well. For several minutes after he had closed the rear door Blatchford Ferguson leaned back in his chair, chuckling.

Now, while this remarkable interview was taking place in the inner sanctum Phil Kendrick was again shaking hands with Conway in the outer office. A moment later he went on through to the secretary's office, speculating on just what he should say to the self-contained Miss Williams. But, as before, he found her office deserted. To his amazement when he glanced through the inner doorway he saw her for the second time on one knee in front of the keyhole of Ferguson's private office.

She came towards him swiftly, closing the doors behind her as she had done on the occasion of his first visit. She was very angry; that much was apparent.

"I'll admit, Miss Williams, that it is often extremely difficult to break off a bad habit—"

"Mr. Ferguson is busy," she snapped.

"I would judge as much," said Kendrick dryly. "He is expecting me. If you will just hand him my card please,— Thank you."

He was surprised at the look of disdain with which she took his card. Surely this girl whom he had caught twice in the act of eavesdropping upon her employer ought to be grateful for his silence, his toleration of such an utter misdemeanor! Instead, her whole attitude was one of dislike. She made no attempt to conceal it. It might do her good to get a sharp rebuke from Ferguson, and he was of two minds whether or not to speak to the lawyer about her. Then he remembered that she was only substituting and that dismissal would not mean much to her. There was the chance that it was just her woman's curiosity to know what was going on. Women were often like that, he had heard.

"Mr. Ferguson will see you now. Tell him anything you like." She eyed him coolly.

Phil gave her a cheerful smile as he passed on into the private office. Podmore had just gone.

"I had no trouble in getting a line on him for you, Phil. He came in right after you 'phoned and has been here ever since. Now, what the devil's the meaning of all this? What are you up to?"

"Tell me just what he said to you, Blatch," said Kendrick, refusing a cigar and filling his pipe.

"He said he gave you the envelope to mail and that you hid it for him in a hollow stump near the water-tank at Thorlakson Siding when Wade came after it. He said that Wade and

Cranston gave both of you the third degree and that you lit into Wade and gave him one awful calling down for not accepting your word that you hadn't seen any envelope and knew nothing about it. He said it made Wade so mad that he not only fired Podmore but told you also that you couldn't work for the C.L.S. another minute, so it was no use you rejoining this survey party you were with. It's a swell kettle of fish you've got into, Phil. What's your uncle going to say to all this?"

"Nothing. Unless you tell him he won't know I've bumped into this mix. He's got enough worries of his own without bothering about me."

"But Phil,—"

"Listen, Blatch. I know what was in that envelope and where it came from. I want to know where Uncle Milt stands in connection with this campaign-fund money, and I want to know what Podmore is trying to do. What did he want?"

"Podmore isn't as clever as he thinks he is," Ferguson laughed. "He actually came here to see if he could work out a little graft proposition by threatening to expose a deal which he imagines has taken place between the Alderson Construction Company and your uncle. His mind works that way. He thinks everybody is as crooked as himself and that all governments are like the late Rives administration. Well, he knows different now."

"Then no such deal is involved?"

"Good heavens, Phil! Surely you didn't think that? Neither your uncle nor the Party cares a hang about this money of Nickleby's or Alderson's, or whoever owns it. We're not interested in what becomes of it. There's been no deal of any kind."

"That's all I want to know, Blatch," said Kendrick, rising. "It's just one of those things a fellow bumps into now and then, and if Uncle Milt needed my help at all I wanted to know it, that's all. I know he's absolutely on the square, of course."

"Absolutely," assured Ferguson earnestly. "Your uncle is one of the hardest working, most conscientious and high principled public men of the day, Phil, and perhaps I have had greater opportunity of knowing that than most. No man can hold high public office, seemingly, without paying the penalty of prominence—petty jealousy, envy, deliberate misrepresentation, even underhand attacks upon his character. A certain class of political aspirant seems to look on that sort of thing as part of the game, and you don't want to believe all you see in some newspapers around election time. That's the way it's been. But false accusation never yet downed an honest man, Phil. Remember that."

As Kendrick noted the expression on the lawyer's face he thought to himself that in spite of the marks of dissipation which marred it, there was a finer side to Blatch Ferguson's character which few would suspect.

"Please say nothing about my connection with Podmore, Blatch. It was an unavoidable unpleasantness which is now over. Some day soon when I have more time I'll drop in and give you all the details."

Miss Margaret Williams was nowhere about, he noted, as he took his departure.

Kendrick caught the next ferry across the bay to the Island and walked in on his uncle's housekeeper. He found that once more he had the big summer residence to himself, that his uncle had taken a flying trip to New York. That meant that his aunt would be alone in the summer cottage at Sparrow Lake, except for the servants, and he decided suddenly to run up and see her that very evening. After glancing through a slight accumulation of mail he changed to outing flannels and hied to the boathouse for an hour's run in the launch—out through the Eastern Gap into the open lake, where he could cut away across miles of blue water that danced invitingly in the golden sunshine on and on to the horizon's clear rim. All alone out there with the wash of the water, the steady undertone of the engine throbbing in his ears and the cool breeze blowing through his hair, he could sort out his thoughts.

They were inclined to tangle. He had yet to plan how he would proceed to obtain the information which Ben Wade wanted in regard to J. C. Nickleby. The railroad executive had traced certain consignments of cheap whisky which had been run through to construction camps in the northern part of the province and had his own suspicions as to the source from which the bootleggers were obtaining funds. If the luck which had attended Phil's first efforts to learn what Podmore was planning held good, it ought not to be difficult; but there would be no Blatch Ferguson to help him out in a task which would call for the utmost circumspection.

Podmore could be dismissed as of the brood of Esau, willing to sell to the highest bidder anybody's birthright upon which he could lay hands. Ferguson's confident assurance that the stolen campaign fund contribution,—if that was what it had been intended to be,—implicated the Government in no way, could be accepted without question. Had it been otherwise, Ferguson would have been galvanized to action of some sort. At any rate, the sudden disappearance of the money before it reached its destination eliminated it so far as the Government was concerned.

This much was clear to Kendrick. Beyond wondering greatly how such a substantial sum as fifty thousand dollars could drop from sight mysteriously without creating general excitement, he dismissed the matter as outside his immediate concern. If the actual money had been in Wade's possession, as Podmore had been led to believe, Phil would have been more perplexed about it; even Wade's evident inside knowledge of the transaction was sufficiently mystifying. That probably was part of the "puzzle" which would be divulged in due course. Kendrick knew that in the modern business world with its constant clashes between powerful financial interests there were many undercurrents which a young man fresh from college could not hope to gauge. He was content, therefore, to accept Wade's superior judgment without question, to follow instructions faithfully, secure in the knowledge that Benjamin Wade was a man of the highest integrity.

The railroad president had gone on to Montreal and beyond delivery of a letter to Nathaniel Lawson and the obtaining of an answer to it, his final instructions to his new secretary had been simple.

"If you can get Nat Lawson to tell you his story, Phil, you'll spend one interesting evening," he had suggested. "Good business for you to know all about the Interprovincial. Use your own judgment and good luck to you."

There was no hurry about calling on Lawson; it could wait till he got back from this rush visit to Sparrow Lake. But what about this girl in Ferguson's office? What a pippin! Phil was unable to decide whether she had been listening at the keyhole because she had gone there for that very purpose or whether he had surprised her merely taking advantage of accidental opportunity to satisfy her curiosity. She interested him greatly—probably because she was so pretty and had rebuffed him so unmistakably.

He amused himself by absurd speculations about her. If she did have a definite object in spying on Ferguson, the solitaire diamond on her engagement finger might be a bluff; her cheap manner, so out of keeping with refinement of feature and dress,—that might be faked likewise. If she were one of these female detectives you read about, who had hired her? Was she in the pay of Nickleby? If she were, it was Kendrick's duty to keep an eye on her, wasn't it? And she was a tonic for any eye!

Phil laughed at himself as he put the wheel over and swung back towards home. He was becoming an utter fool! Darn girls, anyway! This was the second one on whom he had wasted thought—one probably a thief and the other a gum-chewing stenographer who was going to marry somebody in Buffalo! And that, too, after each had told him quite plainly that if he would just remove himself entirely from their ken they could go on living happily! Just because he had happened to meet these two girls under exceptional circumstances was no justification for placing them on pedestals. King Solomon had the right idea. Poof! the seven seas were full of fish!

With which swaggering philosophy did this strong-minded young man sweep all womenkind from his thoughts—all but Aunt Dolly, who had no equal anywhere in the world. He had left himself just enough time to get to the station without undue haste. Sparrow Lake was a popular summer resort for those who wished to forget the noise of the city and enjoy the quiet surroundings of forest and lake, where good fishing was to be had in combination with fresh cream daily and vegetables in season. The cottage the Warings had rented for the season was on one of the islands, and two hours later Phil was rowing eagerly over from the station landing. He let out a whoop like a wild Indian to announce his arrival and his aunt came running down to meet him, her gentle face alight with pleasure and surprise. He swept her up off her feet and kissed her till her cheeks were wild-rose pink, very becoming with her fluffy aureole of snow-white hair.

Arm in arm they went towards the cottage, talking and laughing. The two were very near to each other and he had a lot of interesting things to tell her. He knew she would be delighted to learn of his new position as Ben Wade's private secretary and she was; but he was careful to keep from her any details of recent happenings that would be liable to cause her anxiety. The conversation arranged its own itinerary over such a wide range of topics that it was late that evening before they had "talked themselves to a standstill," as he put it.

Phil did not feel sleepy. Instead of retiring at once he lingered on the screened balcony just off his room and lighted a final pipe of tobacco. Back came the two mysterious young women to trouble his thoughts and he did not dismiss them. The night was in harmony with mystery; also there was a rising moon, hung low, golden like a lamp, its dull glow lighting only the outer water spaces.

In that lake and forest country Nature seemed to brood in a deep hush which but gathered accentuation from the raucous bass of the bullfrogs and occasional weird night sounds of birds and animals in the depths of the woods. The deep quiet was oppressive after the city's multitude of noises. Earlier in the evening while he talked with his aunt he had remarked upon the great distinctness with which the *putt-putt* of a motorboat somewhere on the lake had carried. Now when a whip-poor-will flew to a nearby tree its rapid-fire call flung wide insistently: *Whip*'rweel, *whip*'rweel, *whip*'rweel, *whip*'rweel, *whip*'rweel, *whip*'rweel. . . .

"Go to it, old boy;" murmured Phil with some amusement, his thoughts recalled at last to his surroundings.

As if insulted, the bird ceased abruptly and flew away. A dead stick snapped at the edge of the clearing. It sounded like the report of a small pistol and as Kendrick smiled at the start the sound gave him he was sub-consciously aware that the bellowings of the frogs had stopped. His glance in the direction of the sound was purely automatic, but his attention was rivetted instantly by a movement among the trees at a point where they thinned out against a silvering background of the lake.

There was no mistake about it. The slinking figure of a man was visible against the water.

CHAPTER XI

GROWING ANXIETY

For some moments Kendrick watched him as he moved cautiously from one vantage point to another, not a little surprised to discover that the intruder was spying upon the cottage. Some belated camper, probably.

But there was no harm in making sure. Phil crept noiselessly off the balcony and slipped quietly downstairs and out the back way. It was his idea to come upon the man from behind and demand what he wanted; but a careless step revealed his approach and sent the fellow running at top speed through the bush to the edge of the lake, where he jumped into a small launch which he must have paddled inshore very quietly. No such caution marked his actions now, however. He started his engine and went *putt-putting* madly out across the lake.

Thoroughly aroused, Kendrick ran to the little landing where the launch rented for the season was moored. He leaped for the engine, a moment later had swung clear and was off in full chase.

As he nursed the engine to top speed it soon became apparent that his was much the superior boat. Added to this he had the advantage of a complete knowledge of the inlets and topography of Sparrow Lake. He knew for instance, that the long neck of heavily wooded peninsula which jutted out for some distance in the immediate vicinity was bisected by a narrow channel of deep black water where a motor boat could negotiate a passage without difficulty.

Kendrick headed straight for the half concealed entrance to this channel. The stranger had gone tearing off to round the point. The result of the channel manoeuvre was that Phil came out into open water directly in the path of the fleeing launch just as it had rounded the point.

At once the intruder shut off his engine, put a foot on the gunwale and took a header into the lake, swimming vigorously for the shore close by. This was confession of an intense anxiety to escape and for the moment it did look as if his chances of getting away were excellent; the unexpectedness of the action made it necessary for Phil to make a wide parabola to bring his boat equally close inshore and to check its speed. Without a moment's hesitation, however, Kendrick also shut off his engine and dove overboard as he swept by. A strong swimmer, he was soon climbing ashore.

By this time the man he was after had started away, *swish-wish* through the underbrush; but he was only a few rods in the lead, and one of thickset build was no match for Kendrick in a footrace. As Phil overhauled him he turned suddenly and fiercely grappled with his pursuer.

This again was something at which Kendrick was proficient and he threw the man easily enough with a half-nelson. They were wrestling it out in an open space in the bushes where the light was not quite so dim, and at last Phil had the hold for which he had been playing.

"I can break your arm—quite easily," he panted in sharp warning. "Are you ready to behave if I let you up?"

Upon receiving a strangled grunt of affirmation he released his antagonist.

"Gee! 'bo, aint there nothin' y' aint good at? That's second time—y've got my nanny fer fair!"

At sound of a familiar voice Phil opened his waterproof match-safe and struck a light. He found himself gazing with some amazement into the grinning homely face of "Iron Man" McCorquodale, the ex-pugilist with whom he had exchanged sparring compliments the night of the fog.

"McCorquodale! How'd you get here?"

"On the too-too," responded the Iron Man, rapidly recovering both breath and good humor.

"Don't get fresh, McCorquodale. What were you doing just now, sneaking around our cottage over there?"

"Dry up, kid, on that 'sneak' stuff. I ain't answerin' a damn thing, see,—not till we gets over to where I'm campin'. An' if that aint suitin' you, y'knows what y'can do, don't youse?"

"You seemed keen enough to get away."

"I had m'reasons," grunted McCorquodale. "I ast you to dry up, didn't I?"

"I'd sooner dry off," smiled Phil, pulling at his wet trousers. "Where's this camp of yours?"

"Over that way," said McCorquodale, pointing. "We'd better

get them boats first, 'fore they drifts too far away."

They found them floating close together, down near the point, and McCorquodale undertook to swim out and bring them in. It was a tribute to him that he was permitted without demur to have such a golden opportunity of escaping and a tribute to Kendrick's judgment that he took no advantage of it.

He had pitched his small tent back from the lake about a quarter of a mile in a gully, where it was hidden completely by thick undergrowth. A spring bubbled not far away and the music of the tiny creek that trickled from it through a bed of water-cress provided a pleasing lullaby. His visitor nodded approval of the snug arrangements. Apparently McCorquodale was an old hand at this sort of thing.

"Seem to have prepared for quite a stay," remarked Phil, turning from inspection of the "kitchen," which had been built into the embankment and which, with its sheet-iron stove-top and all, afforded culinary facilities of a practical kind. "I suppose you have your refrigerator sunk beside the spring, eh?"

"Got a tin box there—yep," confirmed McCorquodale as he fed the fire he had started in front of the tent. "I've been here goin' on two weeks an' I figger to make m'self comfortable when I goes fishin'."

"Fish much at night?" inquired Kendrick suspiciously.

"Yep. Night's best time to catch my kind o' fish," grinned his host. "You come on over here to the fire an' get dried an' if y'll promise to keep it to y'rself, I'll put you wise."

So while Kendrick sat on the opposite side of the fire McCorquodale volunteered the information that he was a detective—in short, that he was attached to the Special Service Department of the Canadian Lake Shores Railway.

"You'll be interested in that, then," said Phil as he selected an envelope from the papers which he had spread out to dry by the fire.

"Sort o' related, you an' me,—by employment," grinned McCorquodale as he passed back the credentials. "I knowed already you was Wade's new secretary. Got a letter from the Chief himself 's mornin', so advisin'. Fine man to work for, Wade is. He never overlooks nothin' an' I guess he figgered you'n me might meet up here, seein's it's my special job just now to watch your aunt's cottage."

Since Kendrick had seen him last the "Iron Man" had grown a little moustache, a weird affair of reddish bristles which a scar on his lip compelled to lean mostly in one direction with a windswept appearance. It looked like an old toothbrush which has had desperate adventures in an overpacked travelling bag. This hirsute anomaly Mr. McCorquodale now stroked complacently, enjoying the effect of his surprising speech.

"The reason I beats it just now," he went on, "is 'cause I thought 'twas Long Jawr, the butler, as was after me. I gotta keep incog with the servants, see. If I'd 'a' knowed it was you as was chasin' me—that's different, see."

Kendrick's questions came in a fusillade. He was more than surprised; he was vaguely alarmed. Wade had said nothing about having placed one of the C.L.S. detectives at Sparrow Lake and the knowledge that such a course had been deemed advisable was disturbing. Why was it necessary to watch the Waring cottage at this peaceful summer resort? The thing was ridiculous.

The detective was ready enough to answer to the best of his ability, but it was soon evident that his own information was limited. Cranston had called him in off another job to tell him that the "Old Man" wanted him for some personal work, and therefore he was excused from officially reporting for an indefinite period. Mr. Wade merely had told him to go and take a holiday at Sparrow Lake—camp out and fish; incidentally, to keep an eye on the cottage which the Warings occupied. He was to report instantly to the president personally if he noted any suspicious characters hanging around and to trail the stranger or strangers without fail. He knew nothing of the reasons for these instructions. He wished all his assignments were "as big a cinch" as this one.

Phil knew that McCorquodale was not concocting a yarn and his face showed his anxiety. He questioned the detective so closely that that worthy was moved to protest.

"Hot tamalies! Y'r auntie aint goin' to get croaked n'r nothin' like that, kid! Not with me here, lookin' after her. What's eatin' y'anyways? Everythin's ridin' along Jake, see. An' speakin' of eatin', s'pose we has a bite. I can give you toast, tea an' a Welsh rabbit or hot dogs, dill pickles—"

Phil smiled at his host's efforts to reassure him. Certainly there was something so quizzically human about the whimsical McCorquodale that in his presence it was difficult to entertain thought of impending trouble. But as Phil toasted the bread on the end of a stick his mind was busy beneath the surface of his camaraderie. He was trying to recall everything Ben Wade had told him that morning they had ridden on the back platform of the president's private car and the exact way he had said it; but there was little which could have any possible bearing upon the need of posting a man at Sparrow Lake.

"Wade's got you workin' on that Nickleby dope, aint he?" enquired McCorquodale after the fire was going beneath the kettle to his satisfaction. "He had me moochin' around on it fer a while, but they're a pretty smooth bunch, them fellers, an' I had to quit final."

"How was that?" asked Kendrick with interest. "Did they catch you at it?"

"Catch me?" repeated McCorquodale with an injured air. "Not me, kid! Y'see, I hires out to that Brady Detective Agency that Nickleby does business with, thinkin' to get right into the middle o' things—walk right in through the front door an' pick up whatever I wanted. But the very first job they puts me on gets me in bad with Brady. They ast me to trail a kid with a tan satchel from the Alderson Construction Company's office over to a lawyer's office an' I did; then they turns around an' says somebody's gone an' swiped what was in the satchel an' blames me for not lookin' after it. But there wasn't nothin' taken out o' that there satchel for I was right behind it all the way. Somethin' damn funny 'bout that."

"What was in it?—in the satchel?"

"Oh, just some legal papers o' some kind. Say, d'you like y'r tea pretty black, Mr. Kendrick?" He got out the dishes and took another look at the kitchen fire. "Wasn't my fault I had to get off that job. I'd 'a' hooked them fellers up with this here whisky-runnin' gang up north as sure as shootin' if I'd had a chanst. They're in it somewheres. But I didn't get a look-in."

"What makes you think they're in it? Who do you mean? Nickleby?"

"Nick don't work straight from the shoulder, Mr. Kendrick; but he's got a long arm with a lot o' elbows in it." McCorquodale shook his head. thoughtfully and looked serious. "There was a guy named Weiler hangin' around—I dunno. It's just one o' them hunches a feller gets now 'n' then."

"But a financier with the standing Nickleby has—"

"Excuse me, but y're startin' off with the wrong foot," corrected McCorquodale. "Nickleby aint no financier; he's a smooth pebble, that's all. His standin's faked an' behind it he's layin' low or I misses my best guess. If he aint a crook I never seen one."

Phil was silent for a moment. Apparently McCorquodale had not been informed as to the real contents of that tan satchel he had been assigned to guard. Wade and Cranston were following that line of investigation under cover for the time being. But it was likely that the bootlegging operations had no connection whatever with the missing money and that the evidence Wade wanted was merely an additional net with which to close in on this man who had usurped control of the Interprovincial Loan & Savings Company—misuse of trust funds or something like that.

"Listen to me, Cork. I've been thinking out a plan for getting to the bottom of this law-breaking booze business that we've got a line on, but I need another man to work it out right, and you're elected."

"Attaboy!" cried McCorquodale enthusiastically.

"We can't get busy on it till Mr. Wade gets back from Montreal in a few days. I'm going to find out what lies back of the instructions you got to come here and watch our cottage, then ask him to let you join me on the investigation.

at once on a friendly footing. It was a little early yet to see the wonderful garden at its best, his host explained after they had made a tour of it; he must come and see it in another month or so, or even in a few weeks, when the pergola would be smothered in roses.

Among other things contained in Wade's letter, which Phil had just delivered, it was evident that his new chief had asked Lawson to post the bearer in regard to Loan Company affairs, particularly to tell all he knew about J. C. Nickleby; for of his own accord "Old Nat" began to talk freely of the past. It was soon apparent that he considered Nickleby an impostor whose motives were not to be computed by a self-respecting comptometer.

"Nickleby is a scamp and I might even qualify the statement, sir, by addition of the word, 'damnable.' There you have my opinion, sum total, and one of these new adding machines cannot give it to you more quickly or accurately." The smile with which he said this faded as he smoked for a moment in silence and a grim look settled in its place. He stood up abruptly. "Excuse me a moment while I get a photograph which will serve to illustrate a little story I'm going to tell you."

When he returned presently he thrust into Phil's hand the photo of a young man whose expression was boyishly ingenuous.

"Nothing dishonest in that face, is there?" demanded Nat Lawson. "That's Jimmy Stiles. He had to quit school to find work to support his mother when she was taken sick. He came to me and I gave him his first job. I found him loyal and trustworthy; but he made one little slip that I want to tell you about."

It appeared that the boy had been inveigled into a get-rich-quick investment which had gone the usual way of such things and left him in a desperate plight; so that he had been tempted to "borrow" a few dollars from the Interprovincial without permission. This money he began putting back secretly every week, bit by bit out of his salary. He had refunded about half of it when Nickleby discovered the small shortage in the young bookkeeper's accounts. Instead of reporting the matter, Nickleby, at that time secretary and office manager, told the boy he would let him off if it did not occur again and made a great show of befriending young Stiles.

But Stiles was so systematically reminded of his obligation to Nickleby that he worried constantly over what he had done—came to such a keen realization of his fault that one night he could stand it no longer and went to the Lawson home. With nerves at the breaking point he confessed his wrong to both Nathaniel Lawson and his daughter. The boy's contrition had been so sincere that they both forgave him on the spot, "Old Nat" patting him on the shoulder and assuring him that nothing more would be said about it. Stiles said nothing to Nickleby about this secret confession and for a time he recovered his spirits.

Then came the change in management. Nickleby's first move was to dismiss one employee after another until almost the only member of the old staff left was this young fellow, James Stiles, for whom Nickleby seemed to have taken a strange fancy. The reason was not long in doubt; for though the indebtedness long since had been wiped off the slate the new president began to threaten exposure unless Stiles did exactly as he was told, even when the instructions were contrary to honest business ethics.

"That's the kind of man Mr. Nickleby is," concluded

Lawson. "Cristy and I—my daughter, Cristobel, Kendrick,—have tried to give Mrs. Stiles financial assistance in the past, she being an honest deserving woman; but of late we have not been able to do so much. For his mother's sake I hope Jimmy turns out all right. But there are times when I wonder if it would not have been better for him had he gone somewhere out of reach of a man who would take advantage of a mere boy instead of trying to help him to a fresh start."

With renewed interest Phil studied the photo in his hand before returning it. The case of Jimmy Stiles did indeed throw a sidelight upon the character of Nickleby. By adroit questioning he led the founder of the Interprovincial Loan & Savings Company to continue talking of the institution which represented his life's work and in the welfare of which his whole soul was wrapped. Once started in these reminiscences of his early struggles and hopes Nathaniel Lawson proved himself an interesting talker and the hour was well advanced when Kendrick finally glanced at his watch and, refusing any suggestion of refreshments, prepared to go.

"I'll have the answer to Wade's letter ready for you first thing in the morning," said Lawson as he shook hands heartily. "I've enjoyed the evening immensely, Kendrick, and I hope I haven't bored you so much that you won't come again. You'll be welcome any time."

Phil left the house with the feeling that he had spent not only a very pleasant evening, but a profitable one. He had acquired a new appreciation of "Old Nat" Lawson and, as Wade had predicted, a better understanding of the situation which would help him in his investigations. So absorbed was he in reviewing what he had learned that he had walked several blocks before he became conscious of somebody following him. What was at first merely a suspicion became a certainty when he deliberately turned several successive corners only to find the figure still in the rear.

The discovery was interesting, though entirely ridiculous. Who could be interested in his movements? He resolved to throw the fellow off the track and have a closer look at him. It should not be difficult to do this in that district of tall hedges. He broke abruptly into a run, dodged around a corner and dropped over behind the nearest hedge.

The sound of running steps ceased. But the man evidently was attempting something to which he was unaccustomed; for on reaching the corner he stopped, bewildered by the sudden disappearance of his quarry. He stood there foolishly, staring about uncertainly and grumbling to himself.

Kendrick peered out from his hiding-place with some amusement at this discomfiture. The nearest arc light was too far away for a clear look at the man; but just as Phil was about to jump the hedge and boldly demand an explanation the other lighted a cigarette and with a shrug of the shoulders went his way, leaving Kendrick sitting back on his heels, racking his memory.

Revealed in the glow of the match the face had seemed familiar. The young fellow was a full block away, however, before he recalled the features. It was James Stiles, the young chap Nat Lawson had just been telling him about and whose photo he had been studying with much interest an hour or two ago.

Over the hedge went Kendrick just in time to see Jimmy Stiles disappear around a corner. He ran rapidly down the street, keeping to the boulevard turf, and when he reached the corner he waited until his man was sufficiently in the lead to avoid discovery, then sauntered along in the same direction just far enough behind to keep the other in sight.

For Phil's curiosity was now justifiably awake and he determined to find out where young Stiles went, perhaps overhaul him and ask him to explain himself.

With the situation thus reversed they progressed for several blocks without incident. Jimmy Stiles was stepping out with the briskness of one who knows exactly where he is going and is in a hurry to get there. He did not alter his stride for perhaps twenty minutes; but as they swung down towards Allan Gardens his pace became more leisurely, and opposite the park itself he abruptly halted, looking this way and that as if expecting to meet somebody here. In further support of this interpretation he began to stroll slowly back and forth, occasionally glancing at his watch.

Kendrick took up a position in the shadows where he could look on without danger of observation, and waited patiently. Before long a young woman approached from a sidestreet. Stiles raised his hat and the two went into the park and sat down on a bench, where they soon become lost in earnest conversation.

"'In the Spring a young man's fancy—'" murmured Phil with a nod of comprehension; but he did not complete the quotation. There was nothing lover-like in the actions of the pair on the park bench; in fact, the young woman appeared to be taking Stiles to task about something. Did the circumstances justify a closer approach with the object of overhearing the conversation?

Kendrick still was debating this delicate problem when he saw two men slinking cautiously behind the bench from the concealment of the park shrubbery. Before he could shout a warning they had closed in silently and swiftly upon the unsuspecting occupants. The girl's cry was smothered by one assailant and Stiles was struggling desperately with the other.

It happened so unexpectedly that Kendrick stood for an instant, held by his amazement. Then without a sound he sped across the street, vaulted the iron fence and charged into the middle of the excitement with ready fists. The man who had Stiles down was nearest and Phil paused long enough to send him reeling with a well-directed blow on the side of the head. He leaped the overturned bench, and made for the girl's attacker, who promptly took to his heels.

Phil chased him for several rods through the shrubbery before he swung back toward the bench. But in the brief interval both the other fellow and young Stiles himself had vanished and he found only the young woman, calmly dusting her skirt. She stood in a finger of light from the neighboring arc lamp and Kendrick stopped short, getting back his breath and staring at her in undisguised astonishment. It seemed as if she was always to find him staring at her—this cold and haughty and very pretty stenographer from the office of Blatchford Ferguson!

"Why, Miss Williams!" he exclaimed, and stepped forward quickly. "Are you hurt at all?" He righted the bench. "Perhaps you had better sit down," he urged with polite anxiety.

"It's Mr. Kendrick, aint it? No, I'm all right." Nevertheless she seated herself, patting nervously at a disarranged strand of hair. "It was so kind of you—"

"Nonsense!" interrupted Phil in deprecation. "I was passing along the street and luckily happened to glance over at the park just as those fellows attacked you. How many of them were there?—three?" he asked innocently. "I wasn't sure which of those two who were fighting I ought to hit," he laughed.

"It was a case of purse-snatchin'," she said hastily with a shrug of unconcern. "They—they were fightin' over it." He had hard work to maintain the proper expression of polite interest under the direct appraisal of those grave eyes. "The purse set me back on'y fifty-eight cents at Eaton's at a Friday sale and it had in it on'y some street-car tickets, a handkerchief, about thirty-five cents change an'—a nickle's worth of gum. So, you see, it really aint worth botherin' about." She smiled faintly as she stood up and held out her hand. "Thanks again, Mr. Kendrick. I must be toddlin' along."

But Kendrick was not to be dismissed in this arbitrary fashion. He insisted upon seeing her safely home and as it was so logically the thing to do, she accepted his escort with what grace she could. Throughout the short walk, however, her manner toward him was one of cold formality, and although Phil was by no means an uninteresting conversationalist on occasion, his best efforts failed to break down this reserve.

Several times he deliberately directed the conversation to afford her the opportunity of referring to the keyhole incidents only to have her ignore the opening altogether. It was equally apparent that she had no intention of mentioning Jimmy Stiles, and he was half inclined to regret the lead he had given her in this connection. Why had she been so eager to misrepresent the situation? Why had Stiles disappeared so suddenly? What was the meaning of the attack by these two ruffians? Was robbery really the motive, or was she lying about that, too? He had seen no sign of a purse. Why had she and young Stiles met by appointment at that late hour and in that particular place? It must be some very secret matter to require a clandestine meeting. And she had been scolding Jimmy Stiles—no mistake about that.

Thus ran the undercurrent of his thoughts as he tried to

decide whether he had better shatter that self-contained keep-your-distance attitude of hers with plain questions. He would have to right-about-face on the whole situation to do it, and he was not sure that this was wise just then. One thing was certain, Miss Margaret Williams was worth studying very carefully and he could not afford to make any mistakes in his approach.

She settled his indecision for him somewhat unexpectedly by stopping abruptly opposite a row of old brick houses with red sandstone fronts.

"Here's where I live," she said. "'Night, Mr. Kendrick, an' thanks awfully."

Phil raised his hat. Before he could say a word she had left him and running up the steps, disappeared inside the nearest vestibule.

For a moment only he hesitated, then went far enough in the walk to make sure of the house number, jotting it down on the back of an envelope. A large white card in one of the front windows announced "Board and Rooms." He went away, determined to return next day and have a chat with the landlady. Perhaps he might even go so far as to rent a room from her for a time.

But when Kendrick called next morning in pursuance of this plan he was surprised to find that no young woman such as he described lived there. The landlady proved to be an elderly widow who was quite talkative once she had satisfied herself that the polite, good-looking young man with the pleasant smile was not an agent seeking to walk away with some of her hard-earned dollars. Miss Margaret Williams? No, there was nobody living there by that name. The only stenographer she had among her boarders at present was a

Miss Turner who worked in the office of a candy factory, not a lawyer's office at all. And sometimes of a Saturday she brought home a big box of candy for Sunday, knowing that Mrs. Parker had such a sweet tooth, and she was such an obliging girl, was Miss Turner, and getting along so well at the office, she was. Only the other night she had made the remark—

Phil got away at last. He was not interested in the fortunes of Miss Turner or the gossip of Mrs. Parker's boarding-house. He was too supremely interested in the strange actions of the mysterious Miss Williams. Darn the girl anyway! She deliberately had run inside the first boarding-house they had come to, stopping calmly in the vestibule until he had gone his way, when she probably had come out again and gone home without an escort. Or perhaps she had met Stiles again. Or perhaps—

"What d'you know about it?" he muttered as he sat down on a boulevard railing and mopped his forehead in disgust.

Well, if this girl sought to avoid him she was going the wrong way about it. You bet he would make it his business now to find out exactly what was what; also what her friend, Jimmy Stiles, was up to. People here in Toronto didn't go around following other people and being set upon in the public parks—not ordinarily. The more he thought it over the more certain he became that their actions were linked up somehow with his own investigations. Why not? The girl had spied upon Podmore, who was in league with Nickleby; she had dealings with Jimmy Stiles who, according to Nathaniel Lawson, was very much under Nickleby's thumb. There was enough Nickleby mixed up in it for all sorts of possibilities. He wondered what Podmore knew about her.

There was the next move for him to make—go and see

Podmore and find out. He got to his feet at once and started for the nearest street-car line. He ought to be able to catch Podmore just finishing a late breakfast at the Queen's.

"Sorry, sir, but Mr. Podmore checked out last night," the clerk informed him when at last he reached the hotel.

"Checked out?" echoed Phil in surprise. "Last night, you say? Did he leave any message for me?"

"No, sir."

"And you don't know where he went, eh?"

"I'm sorry, sir; but he didn't say. I believe the porter took some baggage for him over to the Union Station; so he's evidently gone out of town."

Kendrick walked off slowly. It was not hard to guess whither the time-serving Mr. Podmore was bound. He was running true to form and Phil grinned as he thought of the surprise that lay awaiting in the hollow stump beside the tank at the Thorlakson siding. It would be worth something to see the expression on Podmore's face when he opened that fake envelope of Wade's with its bogus bills.

Well, he could eliminate Podmore for the present. What now? Had he better go down to Ferguson's office and boldly demand from the haughty Miss Williams answers to a few pointed questions, or had he better locate Stiles first and choke the truth out of him? He glanced at his watch. Nat Lawson would be expecting him to call for that letter to Wade and he decided to go there first. After that he would be free to follow his own investigations in his own way.

Nathaniel Lawson was at work in the garden, but went into

the house at once for the letter and insisted on Phil going inside for a cigar.

"Now you sit down in that big chair there, Kendrick. I'm the celebrated inventor of a new phosphate drink that ought to hit the spot on a morning like this. Trouble nothing, sir! I was just on the point of mixing one for myself. Make yourself at home, my boy. I won't be long."

Kendrick lounged gratefully in the comfortable leather chair. He had not realized just how hot it was outside until he found himself thus ensconced in the cool interior of what his host had called "the den." A good old scout, Nat Lawson.

Phil had decided it was best to say nothing of his previous evening's experiences, but he had asked where young Jimmy Stiles was working now and learned that the bookkeeper was with the Alderson Construction Company. It was one of Nickleby's "mushroom" concerns and apparently Nathaniel Lawson did not have much respect for any side-line enterprise in which Mr. Nickleby was interested. Phil smiled as he jotted down the address. Nobody who had heard the Lawson side of the situation could blame him for that attitude.

So Stiles worked for the Alderson Construction Company, eh?—the concern that was mixed up in that campaign fund contribution that had been stolen. Question: Had Jimmy Stiles been forced by Nickleby to—? No, that was not tenable because Nickleby would not be trying to steal from himself. Well, he'd soon get the hang of things when he went to see Stiles. It was going to be an interesting little pow-wow with that young man.

Kendrick idly watched the smoke from his cigar sail towards the long box of geraniums on the sill of the open window. He whistled to the canary that swung in a brass cage above the foliage. Then his glance wandered about the room, over the bookcases, the bric-a-brac on the mantel, the—

He sat up in his chair rather suddenly. He stood up and hastily crossed the room for a closer look at a large, attractive photo which hung above the mantel in a silver frame—the photo of a beautiful young woman in a summer dress. The face was unmistakable. He was gazing at the photo of the stenographer in Blatch Ferguson's office—the girl who had listened at the keyhole, who had met Stiles in the park last night and had been attacked by the two strangers, who had taken so much trouble to get rid of her escort by the ruse of the boarding-house! The elaborate coiffure was missing; but those beautiful classic features were the same.

He turned as Lawson entered the room, stepping slowly and carefully, with a tray and two goblets which tinkled with ice.

"I was just admiring that photo in the silver frame, Mr. Lawson. It is a remarkably fine piece of photography. The tones are wonderful. Would you consider it rude if I asked who the young lady is?"

Nat Lawson slowly deposited the tray and chuckled to himself. Unconsciously he raised his head proudly.

"That is my daughter, sir,—my daughter, Cristy. I'm sorry that just now she is not at home."

CHAPTER XIII

AND CONVERTS A GOAL

Phil Kendrick sipped his drink with what he flattered himself was a fine show of unconcern. He even smacked his lips and complimented Mr. Lawson upon the tang of that phosphate mixture he had invented; for it was indeed of fine flavor, quite a delightful beverage.

"I believe you mentioned last night that Miss Lawson had gone in for some kind of newspaper work—was on the staff of the *Recorder*, if I remember rightly," said Phil with an air of one who makes conversation for the sake of politeness. "I know the sporting editor of that paper and I have heard McAllister spoken of as one of the livest and most conscientious editors in the country. His staff swears by him. Is—er—Miss Lawson still with the *Recorder*?"

She was. And very fond of her work. She had been inclined towards literary matters almost since she was old enough to read. She wrote her first verses when she was ten, although if she knew that her dad was giving that away she would box his ears, and Nathaniel Lawson laughed to himself reminiscently.

Two things were plain to Kendrick as he listened with

interest to Old Nat's homily upon the caprices of the eternal feminine—that this high-spirited motherless girl and her father were very close to each other and, paradoxically, that he knew nothing of her present masquerade as a stenographer in Ferguson's office. For masquerade it evidently was, and Kendrick's mind raced along new channels of speculation which this realization opened up.

He was eager to get away and at the risk of discourtesy he emptied his glass rather hurriedly, refused a second one, refused an invitation to stay to lunch, and once outside the grounds fled in untoward haste.

He went up the stairs at the *Recorder* building two steps at a time and found himself at last in the little cubbyhole where Chic White sat, surrounded by walls that were papered with half-tone pictures of pugilists, baseball and football stars, and other athletic celebrities. Phil was rather amused to note his own picture in football togs among the rest. It served to open a desultory conversation which had no bearing at all upon the object of his visit. It was some minutes before he finally veered to the subject of women in athletics and from that to women in newspaper work and from that again to the women members of the *Recorder's* staff. In response to his somewhat too casual enquiry concerning Miss Lawson, Chic sat back and grinned provokingly.

"Sure Mike! She's on the staff," he admitted after indulging in that disgusting habit of his, an extra-dry spit. "She does special assignments for McAllister. Fact is, she's out of town now on one of 'em."

He eyed Kendrick shrewdly.

"Some doll, eh? But you aint got a look-in, Ken. Why say, boy, there aint a guy on this rag that wouldn't walk up a church aisle with Cris Lawson any old time she passed the high sign. She's got 'em all buffaloed. But they say she 'n' the Boss understand each other pretty well. Anyway she's sportin' a solitaire," and again White grinned and spat deliberately.

Phil got out as fast as he could. He was in a strange state of exhilaration at his discovery which not all the gossip of a hundred newspaper offices nor all the solitaire diamond rings that ever were could have dampened just then.

He hastened now to the office of Blatchford Ferguson over at the Brokers' Bank Building, buttonholed Conway and informed him that he had an important message for Miss Williams which he must deliver in person at once. Only to have Conway shake his head. Miss Williams was not there any more—had handed in her resignation last night.

"Rather sudden, wasn't it?"

"I should say so! We all knew she was here only temporarily, but she certainly left rather suddenly. Young Roy over there was awfully stuck on her; he hasn't been fit to live with all day."

"Do you know where I could catch her now? Did she leave any address?"

"Why no, she didn't," replied Conway. "I believe she expected to be married soon to a chap in Buffalo and I rather think that's where she went."

Kendrick bit his lip for a moment, considering. Then he asked for the telephone directory, thought better of it and decided to call at the office of the Alderson Construction Company unheralded. The young man who came to the counter was Jimmy Stiles himself, Kendrick surmised; but he merely asked to see Mr. James Stiles.

"That's my name," said the bookkeeper, casting a glance of quick suspicion at the caller.

"Glad to know you, Mr. Stiles," smiled Kendrick, holding out his hand, and he passed his card, dropping his voice to a more confidential tone. "I wonder if you'll do me the honor to take lunch with me in an hour's time, or if that's not convenient—?"

"Why? What do you want?" Stiles' face paled slightly, Kendrick thought. He glanced over his shoulder rather nervously, too, as if fearful of surveillance. "I—You are a stranger to me, sir. I do not see why—that is, do not know what—" Plainly he was embarrassed by the invitation.

"I want to talk to you on several important matters of considerable interest to yourself. I have some questions to ask you concerning Miss Cristy Lawson," said Kendrick directly.

"Oh, you have? How d'you know I got answers to them?" There was no question about the pallor of young Stiles now. "She aint nothin' in my young life an' I don't know 's I got the time."

"Listen here, Stiles," said Kendrick sharply. "I'd advise you to meet me as I suggest—in your own interests, let us say. I happen to know a few things which must be cleared up at once and only you can do it. Understand? You don't want me to start something and—well, spill the beans? Do you?"

"Wh—what—er—beans?" stammered Stiles, plainly frightened.

"I'm not talking about Boston baked anyway," smiled Phil. "You won't get hurt if you play fair with me." He frowned. "I guess you know what I'm referring to. Will you take lunch with me and talk it over pleasantly or do you want me to go and see—Nickleby?

"Well, we aint buyin' no more stationery just now, sir. Call again some time. Perhaps later on we may be needin' somethin'."

"Oh, very well then," nodded Kendrick easily, at once sensing the effort of a clerk to overhear the conversation—a man who had sauntered over to the counter and was making pretense of examining a directory within earshot of the two. "Our carbon paper is exceptionally fine. If I call some day about—shall we say twelve-thirty?"

"Yes, that hour will be O.K., sir," he said aloud. "Thanks. Meet me at the corner," he added in a whisper.

So Jimmy Stiles was being watched in that office, thought Phil as he went down in the elevator. What for? Who by? A couple more questions to add to his collection. Well, they'd go over to the Island residence for their lunch where they would be undisturbed. He had telephoned already to Mrs. Parlby to serve luncheon for two, and dropped into the National Club to fill in the interval till twelve-thirty.

Sharp on time Stiles put in an appearance at the appointed place, but he demurred upon learning where Kendrick was proposing to take him.

"Gee Whiz! I got to get back to the office inside an hour," he objected.

"I'll promise to get you back on time," assured Phil. "The

launch is moored down at the Canoe Club and she can do forty-five under pressure."

In spite of Kendrick's efforts at conversation on the way over, it was plain that his guest was ill at ease; but it was not until they were comfortably seated in the library that he undertook to relieve the bookkeeper's anxiety to know what was in his mind.

"I think perhaps your appetite will be improved, Jimmy, if we talk before we eat," smiled Phil. He offered his cigarette-case. "There is no reason why you and I should not be good friends."

Having first satisfied himself that there was no doubt whatever of young Stiles' loyalty to Nathaniel Lawson, he proceeded to recount briefly the events which had led up to his discovery of the real identity of Miss Margaret Williams. The extent of Kendrick's evident knowledge startled Stiles, if his nervousness was any criterion.

"Miss Lawson was masquerading in Ferguson's office for some reason. I caught her listening at the keyhole while Podmore was interviewing Ferguson day before yesterday. You might begin by explaining why she should report all this to you, Stiles, and why you tried to follow me last night after I left Mr. Lawson. I know that Miss Lawson is a valued member of the *Recorder* staff. Now, what about it?"

"She's doin' some special stunt for the paper," Stiles nodded after a little hesitation. "We've been good friends for quite a while, but there aint no reason why she should tell me all she knows, is there? She came to me yesterday an' asked me to keep an eye on your movements for a bit. She said you were workin' with Podmore an' that you an' him had swiped some envelope from Mr. Wade, the railroad president, and hidden it."

"That's what comes of listening at keyholes. Go on."

"That's all, Mr. Kendrick. She was kind of worried over you callin' on her father an' give me Hail Columbia for losin' sight of you last night after she'd gone to the trouble of pointin' you out to me. But I aint no dime novel detective!"

"Why should she be interested in my movements?"

"Search me!"

"Why did those two fellows jump on you last night? Don't say they were after your watch. Tell me the truth."

"Well, you seen how they was watchin' me at the office to-day, didn't you? I've been watched like that ever since—" Stiles stopped short in some confusion.

"Ever since the theft of the satchel containing fifty thousand dollars," prompted Kendrick. "I know all about that. It's all right. Go on."

But for a moment Stiles was stricken dumb by this cool speech.

"Who told you about that?" he demanded in a scared tone. "Say, how'd it be if you told me what's your side in this little gab-fest? Who you workin' for? Police? Nickleby? Say, you aint crazy enough to think I had anything to do with the disappearance of that bunch of coin, are you?"

"Hardly," smiled Phil. He handed over Benjamin Wade's letter of introduction, "to whom it may concern." The change which perusal of these credentials wrought in Jimmy Stiles was at once noticeable. He relaxed in his chair with a breath of relief and laughed.

"Why didn't you say in the first place you were Wade's private secretary?" he protested. "Gee whiz! Now I know where I'm at—if it's true," he added suspiciously, suddenly sitting erect again. "Miss Lawson said she heard Podmore tell Ferguson you hid that envelope for him in a stump up in the bush near some watertank or other after he'd pinched it from Mr. Wade's private car, and that you two fellows were friends an' had both got fired by Wade because you wouldn't tell where the envelope was."

"It isn't wise to believe everything one hears, Jimmy,—through key-holes," advised Kendrick. "That's all a bluff. It was Mr. Wade's idea that by pretending to be friendly toward Podmore I might get a line on something. We framed up the whole thing on Podmore."

"But the envelope really was swiped an' hid in the stump, wasn't it?"

"Yes, I left it there at Mr. Wade's suggestion."

"With all that money in it?"

"The bills were bogus—just stage money."

"What!" cried Stiles in excitement. "Gee-whilikins! Is that right, Mr. Kendrick?" His mouth opened in what seemed to be fear as well as astonishment. "But of course it's right. That's what he wanted me to get that duplicate envelope for. Gosh! why didn't we think of that last night?"

He got up and took a turn across the room and back in his agitation.

"You surely didn't expect—?" began Kendrick in considerable surprise.

"We haven't known what to expect," interrupted Stiles anxiously. "Anything—everything!—with fifty thousand dollars of election money kicking around loose. Why, Miss Lawson's been on the trail of this campaign fund contribution ever since that night when—that is to say—" For a second time Jimmy Stiles paused uncertainly.

Kendrick had a flash of inspiration. He sprang to his feet, reaching excitedly into his pocket.

"Has Miss Lawson ever owned a pin like this? Is this her's?" and he unfolded the dollar bill and held out the blouse pin for inspection.

"Sure, that's her's. She told me she lost one from her best hand-painted set in your canoe that night."

Kendrick sat down in the nearest chair and laughed as if Stiles had said something which was exceedingly witty. The outburst was so spontaneous and unaccountable that the bookkeeper stared at him. He could not know that Phil would laugh with equal abandon just then if somebody were to inform him that the real reason a hen crosses the road is to get to the other side.

"She seems to have taken you pretty well into her confidence, Jimmy. Perhaps you can tell me who her escort was that night of the fog—a Joe Somebody."

"Oh, that was me. I paddled her across the bay that night. We agreed to call each other by fake names in case anybody heard us talking. When she got into your canoe by mistake I was only about ten yards away, but I was scared to move. I knew she could take care of herself."

Again Phil laughed. But Stiles was growing impatient and

his worried look returned.

"Say, never mind all that, Mr. Kendrick, please. We've got to do something about this other thing right away quick. Nickleby's been havin' Podmore watched an' he had a seance yesterday afternoon with the fellow that's doing it. There's liable to be others setting out with the same idea she had—"

"What do you mean?" demanded Kendrick, seriously.

"Miss Lawson took the train west last night to get that darn envelope you hid in the stump in the woods—"

"Good heavens!"

"I told her she oughtn't to try it," went on Stiles earnestly. "She's liable to run into all sorts of trouble. But she wouldn't listen to me for a minute. She aint scared of anything, Miss Lawson aint, an' she thinks it's real money she's rescuing all by her lonesome."

"You don't mean to say she went all *alone*?" asked Phil in dismay.

"That's just it. She wouldn't have it any other way."

They gazed at each other with sober faces.

CHAPTER XIV

WHAT HAPPENED ON THE WINNIPEG EXPRESS

Thirty-six hours later Kendrick, aboard the Winnipeg Express, was rushing westward through the night. His watch told him that the hour was near midnight and in the open timetable beside him he was tracing the train's progress. Outside in the dark the great scenic sweep of northern wilderness was fleeing behind, mile on mile. He figured that they were within half an hour's run of the Thorlakson siding. The girl had many hours the start of him and no doubt he would find her safe and sound at the section shanty with Mrs. Thorlakson. The fast passenger train did not stop often in this part of the country; but he had persuaded the conductor to slow down so that he could jump for it.

He had taken a compartment in the observation car, but at the moment was lounging in a corner of the open reading room which at that late hour presented a vista of empty chairs and discarded magazines in their leather folders. The porter was nowhere about. One by one the other passengers had sought their berths, leaving Phil in solitary possession. He sat staring out the wide window at the racing double of the lighted coach, deep in thought.

Ordinarily the thing to have done was to head her off from

this wild-goose chase by reporting the matter to her father or by having her editor wire her on board train to return at once. But Stiles had pleaded earnestly that the girl's activities be kept a secret because there was much at stake which did not appear upon the surface. Miss Lawson was anxious particularly that her father did not learn of her present assignment until the task was completed as he would have worried unnecessarily, perhaps have interfered.

What that task was Kendrick had been unable to learn. Either the bookkeeper could not or would not tell him and Phil had been in too great a hurry to get into action to waste time in futile talk. The motive which actuated her must be a strong one to drive her into the hazards of foggy nights, office espionage and actual danger. He could well credit Stiles' assurance that Miss Lawson was not afraid of anything; her calmness after the trying experience in the park was evidence of that.

But the fact of her foolhardy trip into the Algoma wilderness was the main issue to meet just now, and with so much secrecy seemingly desirable Phil had decided that the best thing to do was to go after her himself, follow her, overtake her, protect her if need be. Her paper might or might not know where she had gone and why; but he would say nothing to anybody. If Miss Lawson had some secret, cherished plans her pluck in attempting to carry them out entitled her to some consideration, and she would be grateful for his discretion.

He had need of all the finesse which he could command if he hoped to win a place in her confidence. He could not afford to throw away a single card. As the mysterious lady of the fog she had called him a "fresh Aleck," thanks to his idiotic blundering; but even before that she had chosen for some reason to exert her woman's prerogative and had informed him quite plainly that she did not desire his acquaintance. That ought to have been enough! Then as Miss Margaret Williams she naturally would visit upon him her resentment at being surprised in her eavesdropping; the very stigma of the position in which she found herself before him could be relied upon to add fuel to her dislike, if it were not already sufficiently ablaze because she was beholden to him for his silence in regard to the matter. In the role of Ferguson's stenographer she had told him a second time that she did not wish to know him. Why, she actually disliked him so much that even after his timely arrival in the park had placed her under the obligation of common civility towards him—even after that it had been impossible for her to endure his forced escort a moment longer than it could be avoided!

And finally, there was that solitaire ring on her engagement finger. It did not matter much whether she were engaged to somebody in Buffalo or to McAllister, editor-in-chief of the *Recorder*. She could marry whom she pleased. He wasn't in love with her. That sort of thing was all rot! It was just that he hated anybody to think ill of him, to dislike him as much as apparently she did. He wanted to apologize for—well, for anything she might want him to apologize for. He wanted her to tell him why she did not wish to number him among her friends. He wanted to be her friend; that was it—Platonic friendship! She was the first girl he had ever fancied he might like to go and talk to once in a while. Just for the pleasure of—well, chumming with her. It wasn't a good thing for a fellow who had no sister not to have a girl chum. She was—oh, what a peacherino of a girl she was!

He smiled wistfully as he conjured a mental picture of her. Once more he took out the dollar bill, unfolded it and studied the dainty hand-painted pin and when he restored it carefully to its place in his pocket-book he breathed deeply and his eyes shone. Which, of course, is the way of things Platonic!

What a deuce of a mix everything had been getting into this last little while back! It was as bad as one of those mystery yarns in the magazines with something happening on every page! He recalled with a smile a heated argument which the fellows had got into on one of the Varsity Areopagus Club nights, when Billy Thorpe had contended that strange adventures were really occurring daily and nightly under the multitudinous noses of the modern, work-a-day world. It was impossible to be a student of history, argued he, without recognizing upon what slender threads of hazard great issues often had dangled, or a reader of the newspapers without admitting that mighty queer things were creeping constantly into the experience of some men. It wasn't necessary to seek these in the distorted perspectives of the criminal underworld or the political intrigues of Continental Europe, for ordinary people were just as liable to have adventures. The trouble with most folks nowadays was that they had been trotting the thoroughfares of every-day commonplaces so long they had got dust in their eyes till they couldn't see the bridle-paths of the Unusual, but that didn't prove that Romance wasn't doing business at the same old stand.

And they all had laughed at Thorpe's bombastic figures of speech and told him to go and talk to a credulous elevator boy somewhere, and asked him if he had the girl aboard the lugger yet and Professor Peabody had wanted to know seriously if he had found any traces of pre-Shakespearian drama in East Lynne!

But by the shade of Sheherazade! Thorpe had been right and Phil hadn't dared to tell him what had happened in the fog. "Bridle paths of the Unusual" with a vengeance! He'd soon have all the ingredients to write one of those wild yarns himself! He couldn't ask for a more beautiful or accomplished heroine than Cristy, or a more interesting place to start the love story than in a dense fog at three a.m. Then there was this fifty thousand dollars vanishing so mysteriously and Podmore—with a little polishing he would work up into a first-class villain; as he stood he was a joke and it was impossible to imagine him even risking a punch on the nose to capture the girl. Nickleby might be better for the real dirty work—or Rives.

"Sixty Buckets of Blood or The Hobo's Revenge!" Phil smiled to himself.

In case Wade got back to Toronto before his new secretary's return from this jaunt Kendrick had enclosed a note with the letter from Nat Lawson, telling the railroad president where he had gone and why.

It was well that he had. For rapid events were to intervene and the first of these happened within the next five minutes. He was slumped down in his chair, which he had wheeled about so that he could rest his feet comfortably on the window-sill, and beneath his wandering thoughts he was only dreamily conscious of cinders clinking in the lamp funnels and the low monotone of the rushing train. The woman, therefore, had run past him and had reached the end of the car almost before he was aware that he was no longer alone.

He sat up and stared after her. She wore a tight-fitting woolen sweater with a Paddy green tam to match and clutched a silver-meshed reticule in one hand. He could not see her face, for she did not turn around but quickly opened the door and went out onto the brass-railed platform beneath which the track was flowing back into the darkness.

In her hasty movements was a certain definiteness of purpose which did not escape the puzzled Kendrick. Then he saw that she was tugging to lift the trap in the platform which would uncover the steps on one side. She had swung this into place and was hanging to the bottom step, with the evident intention of leaping from the train, before Phil found his voice.

"Hey!" he shouted, springing forward. "Don't do that!"

She gave him one startled look, and before he could reach her, let go without a word.

A few seconds elapsed while the dumfounded young man peered into the black void that had swallowed her. Then he too swung down the steps, poised his body as far forward towards the engine as possible and with a quick push backward—jumped.

For the face which had looked up at him and on which the light had shone distinctly for an instant was the frightened face of Miss Cristy Lawson!

CHAPTER XV

RAPPROCHEMENT

The train roared away into the night on its long trail to the West, the noise of it lessening to a rumble off among the never-ending waste of trees and rock ridges. Gradually the little night birds recovered from their fright and their plaintive chorus resumed among the swamp grasses and underbrush.

Kendrick had landed luckily and except for the shaking up and a few bruises he was little the worse for his tumble. Still sitting where he had plowed up the ballasting, he rubbed his arm tenderly and tried to penetrate the gloom, his eyes not yet accustomed to the starlight after the bright interior of the observation car. With his suitcase receding at the rate of thirty miles an hour this was going to be a fine pickle as a result of his haste! They were miles from Nowhere, he knew, but that did not worry him much; he was used to walking— had walked that very piece of track with the Rutland party not so long ago. However, there was the girl—

He scrambled to his feet, put his hands on either side of his mouth and shouted. The unexpected loudness of the call startled him a little; it went echoing around and in the dead solitude of the low-lying hills seemed to carry for miles. But although he listened intently there was no answer other than the echo which soon drifted far away and got lost somewhere. The silence returned like a heavy blanket; even the little birds listened in fear.

He called again. Again there was the echo; then the heavy silence.

"Funny," grumbled Phil. "She's either mighty badly hurt or she's deliberately hiding on me. Where are you, Miss Wil— Miss Lawson, I mean?" he shouted.

"—awson, I mean—mean," mocked the double echo. The bellow flung away to distant cadences which settled softly into the night mysteries.

There was dankness in the air and the smell of skunk cabbage from a short stretch of swamp and brule directly opposite. Through the velvet gloom the fire-flies trailed. Rocky ridges were scattered around in the background and high on the right was a huge rounded pile of rock with a few white-stemmed birches clinging to it for all the world like thinning gray hairs on an almost-bald head. It was too dark to see the birches clearly, but the ex-chainman for the Rutland survey party knew they were there and how they looked; he had seen hundreds of such growths. Behind the big rock formation probably there was a lake.

Kendrick snatched up some pebbles and hurled them into the underbrush in anger at those pesky little birds with their mournful monotony of note. He knew she could not be far away and started down the track slowly, scrutinizing the ground on each side. He found her at last, lying very still among the bog reeds.

Gently he lifted her out onto the dry sandy ballast, greatly alarmed at her unconsciousness, and went in search of water. He located a tiny pool just off the right-of-way and realized for the first time that he was hatless. Hastily he sat down and removing one of his boots, dipped it in the water and came hobbling back with it as fast as he could go in an attempt to reach her before it had leaked out. He was so intent upon this that he was quite close before he realized that she was sitting up. She greeted him with an exclamation.

"Good!" cried Phil with satisfaction. "That's the stuff!" He sat down on the end of a sleeper embedded in the sand, and peered at her anxiously; but the light was rather uncertain and he was glad to note that eastward the tree-tops blackened against a silvering sky. The arrival of the moon would help a lot. "How badly hurt are you, Miss Lawson? Do you know that people have got killed, jumping from trains?" he reproved.

"Then whatever possessed you to do it?" she retorted. "I am not dense enough to believe it is just coincidence that you are here. You had no business to follow me, Mr. Kendrick, and I resent it very much."

"At least credit me with a sincere desire to be of service to you, Miss Lawson," said Phil, with a half humorous touch of opprobrium in his tone.

"Are you in the habit of changing people's names to suit the dictates of your own disordered fancy?" she demanded sarcastically. "I should think you would find that very confusing."

"I do—sometimes, Miss Williams-Lawson."

"In these days of neurasthenia it is indeed refreshing to meet one of such healthy nerve as you appear to possess," she said icily. "Since you have chosen to play the bell-boy in this large country hotel in which we find ourselves, I shall assume that I am now in my room and that you have received your tip. In other words, that will be all, *garcon*. I shall be able to manage very nicely, thank you. You may go! I really mean that!"

"I hope you will not find it too drafty with the window open so wide," ventured Phil, standing up at once and bowing elaborately. "You will find water just over the fence there and the passenger trains go by twice a day with a supply of clean linen. I am sorry that I cannot turn out the fireflies for you, but it is the strict rule for them to burn all night. You may find some rather ambitious bugs in the ballast of the road-bed; they belong to the order *Hemiptera*, and have beaked or sucking mouths. For downright earnestness of purpose, however, I would recommend the mosquitoes which will have the number of your room shortly. If the growling of the bears in the woods disturbs you, all you have to do is to light a fire in the very open grate."

"Are you trying to frighten me, Mr. Kendrick?"

"Sorry I can't ask you to ring if you want anything," Phil pursued with exaggerated politeness, "but this is a pretty large hotel, as you said, and I shall be about five miles away—at the Thorlakson siding where breakfast is served at five-thirty. Good-night, madam."

"Pardon my presumption for making the suggestion, Mr. Kendrick," she said sweetly as he bowed a second time and was turning away, "but with a five-mile walk ahead of you, don't you think it would be advisable to—put on your other boot?"

The moon, which had floated free of the tree-tops, was bathing their faces and for an instant they gazed at each other with ponderous gravity. Suddenly Phil sat down again and they joined in a peal of laughter.

The echo of it was still knocking for admittance among the hills when a strange wild laugh floated unexpectedly abroad from a point off to the right. Involuntarily the girl shrank closer to him.

"For pity's sake!" she gasped. "What was that?"

"Just a loon on the lake over there—a harmless goose of a thing," and Phil grinned at her reassuringly as he laced his boot. "But he isn't as crazy as his laugh. That's just his way of singing 'I Hear You Calling Me.'"

"Then give me John McCormack." He smiled as he caught her surreptitiously opening the silver-meshed reticule and powdering her nose, but pretended that he had not seen this bit of feminine incongruity. "My, how still everything is!" she said a moment later in a subdued voice as she swept a glance around at the silver landscape and up at the stars, fixed and dim in the infinite leagues of distance. "It would be possible to go crazy here very quickly, I suppose."

"You'd soon get used to the quiet; then the racket of the city would drive you crazy. Say, speaking of wild geese, Miss Lawson, reminds me that as soon as I learned where you had gone and what for, I followed you to tell you that this is a wild-goose chase you're on. That envelope contains a package of stage money. It's just a dummy, prepared by Mr. Wade to duplicate the one stolen not long ago from the Alderson Construction Company. Object: to fool that fellow, Podmore. Before we make any more mistakes, hadn't we better try to understand each other's position? As a starter I'm going to ask you to read this letter from the Chief. Wait, I'll scratch a match for you."

Before this speech was half completed he had Miss Cristy Lawson's undivided attention. She gazed at him in amazement, and as he shielded the burning match with glow-reddened fingers her eyes raced eagerly over the introduction of Mr. Philip Kendrick as the private secretary of the President of the Canadian Lake Shores Railway with the latter's full authority to act as his representative. There was no doubting the authenticity of it.

To relieve her embarrassment Kendrick hastened to explain in detail. It was only natural that she should have supposed him to be in league with Podmore. Had he but known she was on that train he could have told her everything and have saved her the inconveniences of the present predicament; but he had supposed her to be already at her destination.

She told him how her train had been held up by a freight wreck between Toronto and North Bay; so that she had missed connections there and had been forced to wait over for twenty-four hours.

"Hadn't we better be moving, Miss Lawson?" he suggested. "We'll have to hoof it to Thorlakson's and it's a good five miles from here. We can talk as we walk along."

He took her arm to assist her to her feet, but when she attempted to stand up she sat down again so suddenly that Kendrick thought she was going to faint.

"You are hurt!" he cried in alarm and was down beside her in a trice.

"Oh, it's nothing—just a turned ankle. It can't be very bad."

Nevertheless he would not let her stand on it until he had gone back to the rill to dip in the cold water the sleeve which he tore from his shirt; with this he bandaged the ankle tightly. As he steadied her to her feet again he could see that in spite of her attempt to smile the pain was acute for a moment. She tried the injured foot gingerly and presently was able to limp without his support.

"There, you see! It's getting stronger every minute," she laughed.

"You are a brave girl," he said.

"You wouldn't say that if you knew how dreadfully frightened I am of bugs. Are there really any bears in the woods here, Mr. Kendrick?" She shuddered slightly in spite of herself.

"Bugbears!" growled Kendrick. "I apologize for that, Miss Lawson. I should have known better. You're shivering," he cried with concern.

"Are you cold?"

"I am a li—ittle chi—illy," she admitted as she put a hand to her chin to keep her teeth from chattering.

He grasped her other hand.

"It's like ice!" he reproached. "Why didn't you tell me? The nights are cold in these northern latitudes even in summer, and I'm a proper chump to have allowed you to sit still so long." He clucked his tongue in self-abasement. "You're chilled right through."

In spite of her protests he took off his coat, slipped it across her shoulders and tucked her arms into the sleeves. When he had buttoned it and turned up the collar he locked arms with her and together they hopped up the roadbed till they had to stop finally, out of breath with exertion and laughter. But the exercise was warming and he kept her at it for another few rods.

"How's that?"

"Warm—as toast," she panted. "Oh, what a picture!"

They had rounded a curve and found themselves unexpectedly opposite a lake vista that lay steeped in the moonlight. It was from here the loon had called. There was a chain of little lakes, clustered with wide openings between. The shores were thickly wooded close down to the water's edge and the land ran out in long arms that threw inky shadows in sharp contrast to the panorama of silver water spaces. Out in the centre was an islet where a great rock, rearing above the surface, had gathered moss and a few clinging cedars, one of which stood out in solitary silhouette against the bright sky. The scene was like some artistic conception in black and white,—high lights and deep shadows,—and the cold beauty of it held them silent.

"Isn't that a glorious moon? What a wonderful night it is!" she breathed.

"Wonderful!" he agreed, but as he smiled at her he was not referring to the landscape or the moon. Far be it from him to dispute the wonder of a night the exigencies of which worked such magic in their acquaintanceship. He gave her his arm to lean on and they limped off up the track, each glad of the other's presence in the solitude that encompassed them. The moon was well up above the rock ridges now, and its white light was gleaming along the steel rails that stretched lonesomely away into the miles of spruce and Laurentian outcroppings.

At her request he began at the beginning and related the happenings of the past three weeks—at least, he began with his surveying experiences along this very track. Then he told how he had encountered Podmore and met the railroad president and about Wade's plan for discovering certain facts concerning Podmore and Nickleby. He realized how impossible it was for him to make first mention of what had happened on that foggy night that he had paddled her across the bay; he was not supposed to know that she was the girl and the bare thought of introducing such a dangerous topic filled him with trepidation, so that he was careful to give it a wide berth. He referred to the pleasant evening he had spent with her father and the way in which he had found out that she was both Miss Cristy Lawson and Miss Margaret Williams and how he had backed Stiles into a corner and questioned him.

In her turn she told him how she had taken up her newspaper work in the hope of unearthing, under the guidance of her editor, evidence that would help to restore her father to his place at the head of the Interprovincial Loan & Savings Company. McAllister, editor of the *Recorder*, suspected a political deal in regard to some government bids and thought that Nickleby and—and some others were mixed up in a bold attempt at graft. If the *Recorder's* plans did not miscarry there would be a sensational exposure one of these days which would shock the whole country.

She went on to speak of President Wade, of the Canadian Lake Shores Railway, in the warmest terms. She had known him all her life as a close friend of her father and he was a frequent visitor at the Lawson home.

She stumbled on a cross-tie and would have fallen but for the strength of his supporting arm. She winced a little.

"Here, Miss Lawson, try putting your arm across my back and your hand on my left shoulder for a while. That's it."

With a thrill he slipped his arm about her waist, but she smiled up at him without protest. They made better progress after that. The steel rails streaked away in the moonlight endlessly before them, endlessly behind with uncompromising sameness.

"I suppose I deserve a good scolding for jumping off the train so far from this Thorlakson place; but the sleeping-car conductor told me the train would not stop on any account, short of a damaged track, until it reached—Indian Creek, I think he said it was. My best plan, he said, was to get off there and ride back to Thorlakson on a handcar. I was warned not to try any moving-picture stunts; but when I found out we'd have to slow up on the grade near the siding, I made up my mind to risk it. So when we slowed up back there, I thought it was the place, and sneaked to the back platform without being seen by anyone but you."

Kendrick shook his head at her, marvelling at her nerve and the foolishness of the whole thing. Not many girls would have dared it. Lucky for her he had seen her or she might have been in a pretty bad plight along these lonely reaches of track before any section hands chanced to find her. He studied her anxiously and decided that it was best to keep her talking while they trudged along.

"Will you tell me how you came to be masquerading as Miss Williams?" he asked. "Or is that something you'd rather not—?"

"Oh, no," she laughed. "That was Mr. Wade's bright suggestion. You know, he's been helping me in my work quite a lot. I have had to keep Daddy in the dark about it for fear he'd put his foot down on the whole thing; so I made a confidant of Mr. Wade."

"Then I've got a bone to pick with him," said Phil. "Why in the dickens didn't he tell me about you being at Ferguson's office when we were both on the same trail?"

"It's just like him not to, Mr. Kendrick. Probably he thought your work and my own would not cross at all and the less either of us knew about the other the safer it would be. Why, he even refused pointblank to tell me what he was going to do with that money—the envelope—that is—"

He saw that she hesitated as if she had said too much.

"You mean the fifty thousand dollars, stolen from the Alderson concern?" asked Phil quickly. "I was going to ask you about that. You mean that Mr. Wade *really* has that money? You can trust me, Miss Lawson. Surely you know that," he urged. "He said he was piecing together a puzzle of some kind and would tell me all about it soon. How did he come to have that money?"

She studied him keenly before she spoke.

"I gave it to him to take care of," she said slowly.

"You! And where did you get it?"

"From Jimmy Stiles."

"Jim—my Stiles? Great Scott! And where did he get it?"

"He—stole it."

CHAPTER XVI

THE TAN SATCHEL ONCE MORE

She told him about it. He was much cleverer than most people thought, young Jimmy Stiles, and he was over-poweringly anxious to help the Lawsons. There was no length to which his loyalty to them would not carry him. Kendrick nodded, recalling the boy's story as he had heard it from her father.

"I had no hesitation in taking Jimmy into my confidence from the first," said Cristy, "and it has been a big help to have someone watching Nickleby from the inside. He is a great, little actor, that boy, and has succeeded in fooling our friend, Nickleby, into the belief that all he has to do is to snap his fingers and the frightened Jimmy will perform his bidding without question. Daddy told you about Stiles' early indiscretion, you said. Well, Jimmy has been pretending right along that he is afraid of exposure for that, and Nickleby has felt so sure of him that there have been occasions when he has permitted Jimmy to see behind the scenes and get a peek at some methods of doing business that would not stand analysis."

"Have you tried to get a line on Nickleby's past, Miss Lawson?" asked Phil with interest. "I understand that he was less than nobody when your father befriended him, and he may have drifted up here from the States and have a police record a yard long."

"We've thought of that. There is nothing in the local police records, but I believe Mr. Wade is making some quiet investigations in the States.

"Well, anyway, to make a long story short, Stiles knew the Alderson Construction Company was planning to make a substantial contribution to the Government campaign-fund—J. C. Nickleby, that is; for he really is the Alderson Construction Company. When Jimmy reported this to me I thought I saw a good chance to get some sensational illustrations for the exposure story the *Recorder* was after if only we could get hold of the money long enough to photograph it. Jimmy was enthusiastic over the idea and told me to leave it to him. On thinking it over more carefully, though, I saw risks attached to the stunt which made it very unwise, and when I met Jimmy by his own appointment at the Union Station one night I asked him at once to make no attempt to obtain possession of the money, even for a short time.

"But I was too late. He was carrying a suitcase and calmly informed me that the money was inside. I was badly frightened. If we were caught with that money in our possession we would be arrested at once as a pair of ordinary thieves. I had jeopardized my editor's plans that we had been working out so secretly and regretted the foolishness a thousand times. Stiles wanted me to take the suitcase then and there—take it home and do the photographing, then have a messenger deliver it to Ferguson's office; or, if I preferred to give it back to him, he'd arrange to get the money to its destination somehow without anybody being able to trace it.

"But I was too frightened to decide and it was not long

before I felt that we were being watched. You cannot imagine a more disagreeable feeling! We strolled around a bit to make sure that we really were being followed and when we found that the man we suspected was still on our trail, Jimmy was as badly scared as I was.

"While we were wondering what we'd better do I suddenly spied President Wade standing near the door of the big rotunda waiting-room and I had hard work to keep from calling out. I said good-bye to Jimmy, and walked over to him with the suitcase, blessing my stars for the good fortune. His private car was standing down on the track and as soon as he saw that I was in trouble of some kind he took me down to the car and I told him the whole story. There was nobody around except ourselves at the moment and he was not only greatly interested, but agreed to help me. We lifted out the envelope of money and he placed this in his safe aboard the car. He would not tell me what he intended to do with it, except that he promised it should be photographed for me and that it would be taken care of. He told me to ask no questions, but just leave everything to him and forget all about it. The less I knew about it the better, in case I was questioned.

"He had asked me a short time before if I thought I could obtain a place as a stenographer or office clerk of some kind in Ferguson's office for a few weeks and it had been agreed that I would try and, if I succeeded, I was to sit tight and keep my eyes and ears open. I have wondered how much of what happened he was half anticipating; he was so matter-of-fact. He escorted me out to a taxi and I went home while he sent a porter down to the parcel-room to check the empty suitcase. It may be there yet for all I know.

"You see now why I was so worried to learn that an envelope had been stolen from Mr. Wade's private car by Podmore and hidden up here at Thorlakson. I naturally jumped to the conclusion that it was the actual money that had been stolen. I should have known better, because Mr. Wade had asked me to have Stiles secure for him an envelope from the construction company's office, similar to the one containing the money. To tell you the truth, I had forgotten all about this and it did not occur to me that the envelope in the stump was a decoy. I see now, though, that Mr. Wade had plans of his own all the time."

"You're right as to that, Miss Lawson. This game is bigger than we think," said Kendrick thoughtfully. "One thing we may be sure of, Ben Wade can be trusted to act wisely. What you've just told me has interested me tremendously. Will you tell me something more? How under the sun did Stiles manage to turn the trick—get possession of that fifty thousand without getting caught?"

"It was cleverly done," laughed Cristy, "but like most clever things of that kind, it was as simple as A. B. C. Jimmy laid his plans carefully and the chief danger to threaten his success was that he would not be selected as the messenger between his own office and Ferguson's. He knew that the chances were he would be watched all the way by a detective; so he planned to make his substitution before leaving the building in which the Alderson company has its office.

"He had been keeping a close watch on Podmore for some days, for he did not trust him and felt sure that he would not hesitate to play false to Nickleby and Alderson whom he had been cultivating so carefully of late. Jimmy is shrewd. His patience was rewarded one day by the sight of Podmore in a leather-goods store around the corner, purchasing two satchels which were identical in size, shape and color. Stiles had the clerk lay aside a third satchel which was the mate of the two

Podmore had just bought. When one of the satchels was delivered at the office from Podmore, Jimmy knew he had guessed right. Just how Podmore was proposing to change the satchels worried Jimmy quite a bit until he began to suspect a new arrival in town by the name of Clayton. He found out that Podmore and this Clayton were meeting in Podmore's room at different times, but ignoring each other as utter strangers in the hotel rotunda. Then when Clayton turned up quite casually at All Saints' Mission—the church Jimmy attends, you know—and began to ingratiate himself, Stiles thought he saw daylight. It turned out that he was right, too, in suspecting that Clayton was Podmore's accomplice.

"It fitted in fine with Jimmy's own plan. When he came out of the office with that tan satchel, which contained the money, his kid brother—Bertie—was sitting on the bottom step of the stairway on the same floor, watching the door. As soon as he saw Jimmy come out, the kid ran upstairs to the next floor, picked up the satchel Jimmy had bought and in which he had placed some old newspapers, and took the elevator down. Jimmy got into the same elevator and they transferred the satchels going down to the street. So, you see, when Stiles walked out onto the street he was carrying the satchel that had the old newspapers inside, while young Bertie just stayed in the elevator, went up a few floors and calmly walked down the back stairs and so on home where he chucked satchel, fifty thousand dollars and all, under Jimmy's bed."

"By George!" chuckled Kendrick.

"Jimmy was able to laugh up his sleeve all the way through. I told you he was clever. Sure enough, he found Clayton lying in wait for him at the Jessup Grill which Stiles would have to pass. He almost laughed in that professional con man's face when he was invited inside for a drink and he proved an easy victim when Clayton switched the satchels on him. Jimmy saw that Clayton had spotted the detective who was trailing along and was on his guard. With that danger over, he knew everything was safe; for Podmore could not afford to do anything else but keep quiet even after he discovered that with all his slickness somebody had beaten him out. There wasn't a shred of evidence to implicate Jimmy, you see."

"He tells me they're watching him down at the office pretty closely, though," said Kendrick when she paused for breath.

"That's to be expected, of course. Those two men who attacked us in the park were private detectives in Nickleby's pay and they probably thought Jimmy was passing something on to me and it was time to search both of us. Nickleby and the others have kept close mouths about the theft of the election money because they didn't want any investigation by the regular police. I am inclined to think they planned their election contribution for a definite purpose and could not afford any publicity about it."

"They must be a fine bunch of crooks, that outfit!" remarked Kendrick.

"The fellow who was watching Jimmy and me at the station that night was probably acting on his own initiative. It was the same detective who had made such a bungle of following Jimmy in the afternoon and I guess it nearly cost him his job. He must have been feeling pretty well worked up at the way things turned out. If it hadn't been for Mr. Wade's timely arrival there's no telling what might have happened. Can— can we—sit down for a little rest?" she gasped.

Phil glanced at her quickly, apologizing for his thoughtless-ness. He had been so absorbed in her recital that he had forgotten the strain under which she was laboring with the pain in her foot. They must have covered a lot of ground while they talked. Five miles to Thorlakson's, he had told her, but it might just as easily be eight or ten.

After a short rest they went on. They passed through rock cuttings where their voices and the sound of their feet flung back hollowly from the walls. They rounded curves, looking eagerly for some sign of habitation, only to be met by the same stretch of deserted track leading off into nebulous gloom. Or perhaps they would see a dim white speck ahead or the black outlines of a rocky spur where the track disappeared and they would comfort themselves with the thought that around that particular curve or beyond that mile-post they would see buildings. But when they had hobbled down the track and gained the goal there were always more rocky spurs and more track to hobble over.

They talked of many things. Phil told her all about McCorquodale. They discussed politics and the Rives case and newspaper work and universities and music and the latest books. As the hours crept by their laughter and talk lessened and the spaces of silence between them grew longer. The girl was limping badly and leaning more heavily upon him, and for him the adventure grew more serious in his concern for her welfare.

"Aren't we nearly there, Mr. Kendrick?" she asked quietly after a long period of silence on her part.

"We must be," he answered cheerfully and held his watch close to his nose as he scrutinized the dial in the moonlight. "It's nearly four o'clock. I fancy the moon is a little paler than it was," he added, craning his neck to look at it riding high above them, "and the sky back there behind that hill—it looks lighter, too, don't you think? Daylight can't be far off now, as it comes pretty early up here and we're bound to reach the Thorlakson shanty soon, Miss Lawson."

They trudged on again while he told her about Mrs. Thorlakson, the good-hearted Icelandic woman, and the giant Swede section-hand, Svenson, who was a friendly sort of elephant. He tried to entertain her with a humorous account of his surveying experiences, information about the country and funny stories that he had picked up here and there. Occasionally they heard small animals scurrying away in the underbrush on either side as they passed by; but she had ceased to take notice of such sounds.

"I might carry you for a while, if you'd let me," he offered at last in what he hoped was a matter-of-fact tone. But she would not hear of that.

Dawn was coming quickly. The night gloom fled off the tops of the ridges and sought brief respite in the shelter of the water bottoms. The gray sky warmed to rose tints. New bird notes came twittering from the bushes on all sides, while frisky cotton-tails scampered ahead of them on the roadbed. The air seemed to take on a freshness that it had lacked before, laden with sweet scents of wild grasses, perfume of spruce and the aromatic smell of the wood mould. A wave of light crept across the hills, stole round about and it was day.

They came slowly around a long curve and when the track straightened out again Phil gave a whoop of satisfaction.

"Hallelujah! Miss Lawson, there's a light!" He pointed to where a yellow dot shone steadily, close to the track.

But the girl did not reply. She swayed a moment, then went limp in his arms.

CHAPTER XVII

DISTURBING NEWS

Magnus Thorlakson was in the habit of routing out his men early. The Roadmaster had made no mistake when he handed the stolid Icelander the responsibility for nine miles of the Company's line in the middle of one of the loneliest divisions. In the discharge of his duties there was no more conscientious section foreman in the employ of the C.L.S. He timed his slumber by the sun and his waking hours were filled with the roll of hand-car wheels, the ring of spike-mauls and the tamping grate of spades.

On this particular morning the big Swede, Svenson, had polished off his second plate of fried potatoes and was grinning in anticipation of a third helping and another couple of fried eggs, when a startled exclamation from the good woman of the house, and the smash of the plate which dropped from her fingers to the floor sent her husband's chair scraping back from the table with some suddenness. Callers whose clothes stamped them as city people would have been sufficiently surprising at any time to the inhabitants of that humble dwelling in the wild country and particularly so at that early hour; but the sight of a broad-shouldered young man in his shirt-sleeves, carrying a young woman in his arms up the embankment to their door, was ample justification even for the breaking of precious porcelain.

Thorlakson muttered profanity as he stared out the window. The big Swede looked up with mild enquiry, at the same time reaching for another slice of bread, while the other two men stopped eating altogether and gazed expectantly at the door.

"Good morning, Mrs. Thorlakson," greeted Kendrick. "May we come in?"

The girl stood beside him, huddled in the coat, her face white and drawn in the cold light of early morning. The woman bobbed her head in some uncertainty, then spoke in her own language to her husband who thrust himself into the doorway and leaned a heavy, flanneled shoulder against the jamb.

"Hello, Thorlakson! There's a sprained foot here that requires rest and attention and we would like some breakfast."

Then the Icelander recognized him, turned to his wife with quick commands, waved them inside with eager hospitality, suspicion no longer mingling with curiosity in his keen, light-colored eyes.

"*Farthu ut*! Out!" snapped Mrs. Thorlakson, clapping her hands sharply, and a touseled head withdrew hastily from the door of the little bedroom off the kitchen. It shut with a rattle. She placed a chair for the lady close to the fire, blew out the lamp on the table and after lifting it to its place on the shelf, got a broom and began to sweep up the fragments of the broken plate.

The two Norwegians at the table stared unblinkingly. The Swede paused for an instant at his breakfast, his jaws motionless during the few seconds required for one long look. At sight of Kendrick his wide mouth had expanded to a grin of welcome which exposed the food on his tongue, but as his glance fell upon the young lady and he noted that she was smiling at him he reddened bashfully to the roots of his pale hair and, as if to make up for lost time, fell to with augmented diligence.

In spite of the painful ankle and the strangeness of her surroundings Cristy almost laughed aloud at the comical expression on the big fellow's homely face. She slipped out of Kendrick's coat and shuddered close to the fire, holding her fingers gratefully over the hot stove.

Briefly Phil explained what had happened to them, aware that the recital would not have been very convincing if he had been a complete stranger to these simple foreigners with their natural tendency to suspicion. He made no mention of the envelope that had brought him back to the scene of Podmore's capture just a few days ago. It was enough to say merely that the young lady accidentally had fallen off the step of the train and he had jumped off after her.

But Thorlakson was only anxious to show that he was grateful for the young man's recent generosity in connection with the fifty dollar reward. He nodded as he listened.

"Yaow, that vould be other side Spruce Walley. Yaow. She slow opp down thar. Wery good, Meester Kendrick. Ve glad to have you stay so long as you like. Sit down thar. Planty wittles."

But Mrs. Thorlakson willed otherwise, bustling about as she spoke.

"My voman—she say vait avile," he explained. "Planty more—nice and hot."

Phil thanked him and smiled across at his companion who was cheering up wonderfully under the benign influence of the stove.

"Yaow, that vill be tventy-five cents—each vun, tventy-five cents. Yaow, that vill be suffeecient."

Having thus dismissed further responsibility in the matter, the foreman got up from the table and spoke to his men, who followed him outdoors to the day's work. Svenson lagged behind to gulp the remainder of his coffee and as his heavy boots clumped noisily across the rough wooden floor he ventured to look again timidly at the very pretty young lady who sat beside the stove. Her friendly nod and smile sent him stumbling clumsily out over the doorstep with reddened face and a huge grin of ecstatic delight.

"Delicious!" she laughed softly.

"Snf! Snf! Well now, you're saying something, Miss Lawson," enthused Kendrick who had been watching the frying-pan with fascination. "I'm as hungry as a bear."

Such an unusual breakfast as that was! Such wonderful home-made bread! Fried potatoes straight from the stove, piping hot and done brown; sizzling pork and eggs that were fresh laid by those hens they could hear clucking outside; buns and molasses; even doughnuts and good-natured looking wedges of pie with the knife-cuts far apart—a wonderful meal of the substantial sort favored by those to whom eating at any hour is a serious business. And they ate it with hunger for condiment, chatting and laughing in their enjoyment.

Mrs. Thorlakson beamed. It was the finest compliment they could have paid her. Afterwards with many duckings of tongue and shakes of the head she bathed the swollen ankle in cold water, put some liniment on it and bound it up. She was an adept in such matters.

During these ministrations Phil strolled down to the water-tank; but, as he half expected, he found the fungus gone from the top of the hollow stump and no sign of the envelope inside. Somebody had been there before them, Podmore probably. He would question Thorlakson about that later. Not that it mattered greatly. The sagacious Hughey was due for a severe jolt when he opened the precious envelope to which he was devoting so much attention.

On returning to the house he found that Miss Lawson very sensibly had retired for much needed sleep. He climbed the hill to the woods behind the log shanty and stretched out luxuriously on a fragrant heap of spruce boughs with the idea of indulging in pleasant retrospection.

The sun was well past its zenith when he awoke and his watch told him that it was nearly three in the afternoon. He rubbed his eyes, knotted his muscles in a satisfying stretch and leaped to his feet with a laugh. He found the girl in equally good spirits, the injured foot encased in a mocassin that belonged to one of the foreman's children. It was not a bad sprain; the pain and swelling had subsided, but it would be well to rest it for two or three days, Mrs. Thorlakson had told her. If they could put up with roughing it, she would be glad for them to stay as long as they liked.

"I've promised to show her a new crochet pattern and knit a pair of pullovers for little Skuli," smiled Cristy. "The poor thing is lonesome and I've half a mind to make a little visit for a few days. Do you know, she hasn't seen a white woman to talk to for six months?"

"You couldn't do a more charitable act, Miss Lawson, and I hope you'll allow the bell-boy to linger within call. I happen to know that Wolverine River down there has some fine trout in it and I confess I'd like awfully to rustle an Indian canoe somewhere and do a little exploring. Isn't this air simply great?"

They had wandered to the edge of the embankment and seated themselves for a sunning. She searched quickly for his expression, but he had turned and was gazing far up the track, his tanned face alight with boyish enthusiasm.

Time never passed so swiftly for Phil Kendrick as it did during the next two days. In the big roomy birch-bark canoe that Svenson had built he went fishing and exploring to his heart's content—with Miss Cristy Lawson. He initiated her into the mysteries of speckled trout and helped her to land triumphantly a three-pounder. She was interested in botany and he climbed all sorts of inaccessible places to pick strange plants for her. On these expeditions they took Mrs. Thorlakson and the children along; there was room for them all in the big canoe and with the men absent all day it was possible for them to make a picnic of it. He even enjoyed the evenings with the men while they smoked their pipes in the doorway through which it was possible to see Cristy, her sleeves tucked above a charming pair of dimpled elbows, helping Mrs. Thorlakson with the dishes.

But on the afternoon of the third day as they sat out at the edge of the clearing on a pile of balsam that he had gathered for her she began to talk of leaving. They would be wondering back there on the paper what had become of her and there was work to be done.

He could not take his eye off the diamond ring on her finger as she spoke. "They" she had said; but it was probably "he" that she thought, and he chucked a stone clean down to the water-tank, surprised that he could throw that far. The injured ankle was no longer an excuse for delaying their departure. So they planned to leave next day, boarding a chance freight and riding down the line to some station where they could catch the Toronto Express.

Several trains passed every day each way. Even as they sat there they heard the familiar rumble somewhere far off among the low hills westward. They listened to the growing noise of its approach. Presently the smoke of the engine became visible and around the curve, far up the track, the train trailed into view, a freight, the cars swinging into line and hiding behind the black front of the locomotive. The engineer was bowling her down towards them full "lickety-belt" with no intention of stopping to take on water—a through freight apparently.

With a deafening roar she swept in, the engineer jogging laxly on his cushions. Kendrick stood up and hollered at him. The salutation was acknowledged with a friendly wave of the hand. The long string of brown and yellow cars followed rattle-de-bang over the switch and rocked away eastward. The roar dropped off abruptly into diminuendo, punctuated by the rattle of a loose truck at the rear of the caboose.

From the cupola a brakeman with a dirty blue bandana knotted about his brown throat, waved to them and shouted something which they could not hear. He held aloft a white stick from which he had peeled the green bark, pointed to it, then cast it back towards them and pointed to it significantly.

"There's a paper of some kind fastened to it," said Phil as he signalled that he understood.

They gazed after the end of the caboose until the fluttering green flags faded out in the swirl of dust that pursued into the distance. Then Kendrick scrambled down to find the message. It was in a sealed envelope, bound around the stick with twine. One glance at the yellow telegram inside sent him back up the embankment towards the girl as fast as he could climb.

"Of all things, Miss Lawson!" he called out. "It's a wire from the Chief. I left a note for him, telling him where we were going, and just read this, sent down from the operator at Indian Creek. What do you make of it?"

She read it aloud, frowning in perplexity:

Philip Kendrick,
Toronto, July 27.
at Thorlakson Siding,
via Indian Creek.

Is Cristy safe? Wire immediately you receive this. McAllister anxious. Send Cristy back but remain there yourself till McCorquodale arrives. Important work for you there. McCorquodale will explain. Jimmy Stiles missing since day you left. Did you take him with you?

WADE.

"I should have sent a wire before this, I guess," admitted Kendrick slowly. "But I thought we'd be back before Wade returned to town. I didn't think to send it to McAllister. He's your—editor, isn't he? I'll get Thorlakson to send one of his men—"

She interrupted him with a gesture of impatience.

"The question is, Mr. Kendrick, what's happened to

Jimmy Stiles?"

"Yes, and what's happened to make Wade send McCorquodale up here? What's this important work he's talking about?"

"If Jimmy Stiles has disappeared, it hasn't been of his own free will. I'm sure of that, Mr. Kendrick,—positive!" She looked at him with anxious eyes.

"He was all right the day we had lunch together," mused Phil. "The wire says he's been missing since the day I left the city; so he must have gone that night. You know him a lot better than I do, of course; but from what you told me the other night he got away with fifty thousand dollars once before in pretty slick fashion."

"That suspicion does you no credit, Mr. Kendrick," said Cristy in quick resentment. "Jimmy hasn't absconded. He's been abducted!"

"You have a ready imagination," smiled Phil.

"I know Nickleby," she retorted.

Kendrick shook his head.

"Abduction brings to mind closed cabs and chloroform. Do they pull off stunts like that nowadays—in Toronto? It sounds too melodramatic, Miss Lawson."

"What about that assault in the park by Nickleby's hirelings the other night? You saw that yourself. I don't say Nickleby would dare to harm Jimmy Stiles; he's no fool. But I do think that he's had a hand in Jimmy's disappearance."

"Have you any special reason for thinking that?"

"Yes," she replied after a moment's hesitation. "We—the *Recorder*—Mr. McAllister has been expecting Nickleby to attempt a clean-up of some kind, preparatory to dropping out of sight completely. His present position with the Interprovincial Loan & Savings—control of the stock and all that—will come to a sudden end as soon as Mr. Bradford, the explorer, returns to civilization. Nickleby won't wait for that, will he? It looks as if he were getting ready to pull out and had found Stiles in his way. Jimmy knows too much."

"Well, speculating about things won't get us a hundred yards from Thorlakson Siding," said Kendrick philosophically. "What's needed is a train."

"There's no telling what may be going on back there while we sit here, twiddling our thumbs." She got up and walked to and fro restlessly. "Oh, if only we'd been able to go on that freight that just passed."

"We? Instructions are that I'm to wait here for McCorquodale and send you back at once. We'll flag the first train going the right way and you ought to get off by to-night. I'd better get busy and write out a reply to the wire. Mr. McAllister is anxious about your safety and it—'"

"Oh, drat McAllister!" cried Cristy impatiently.

"I beg your pardon, Miss Lawson," said Phil, "but please say that again."

CHAPTER XVIII

MCCORQUODALE EXPLAINS

On the heels of the message from President Wade came Detective McCorquodale an hour before sundown. He did not arrive on a train from the east, as expected, but by way of the old Indian trail that wound back for half a mile to Wolverine River, the trail once used by Indian hunters to go north into the game country. Kendrick happened to be lounging on the embankment in front of the section shanty, waiting for Thorlakson and his men to come pumping down the track on the handcar, while Cristy was helping indoors with the dinner. He recognized the detective the moment he saw the familiar chunky figure emerge from the woods and come out onto the track and he went down to meet him on the run.

"Well, well, well!" was the greeting McCorquodale launched. "He tore the false beard off his chin an' there—stood—Tom! How are you, Kendrick?"

Phil eyed him anxiously as they shook hands.

"Drop out of the clouds, man? I just got the Chief's wire this afternoon. In heaven's name, McCorquodale, what's the meaning of all this?"

"Heaven aint sittin' in on this hand, 'bo," grinned the C.L.S. detective cheerfully. "It's devils I'm trailin'. Hell's broke loose an' spilled 'em all over the map."

"What do you mean? What's happened? Is my aunt—?"

"Oh, y'needn't worry' bout y'r auntie none. She's all hunky-dory. It's those booze birds we're goin' after, you'n'me, see. Chief's orders, kid. An' oh boy! it's goin' to be some party, believe me! Let's sit down here an' I'll wag m' jaw."

Phil lighted his pipe; but it went out again as he listened with breathless interest to McCorquodale's recital. Up to four days ago he had had a very quiet and uneventful time of it at Sparrow Lake with nothing happening which seemed to justify his presence there at all. Then a stranger had put in an appearance and took to watching the Waring cottage—no less a person than this man Weiler who already had aroused McCorquodale's suspicion when the detective had worked as a Brady Agency operative. The German, however, contented himself with reconnoitring the vicinity between trains and asking a few casual questions about the Waring household over at the station. He took the first train back to the city. So did the "Iron Man."

On arrival in the city the detective trailed his man to a cheap little hotel on a back street, to a rear room on the top floor, where a second man appeared to be awaiting him. By climbing out a hall window onto the fire-escape McCorquodale had reached the flat gravelled roof and wormed himself along into a position where he could hear what transpired in the room. He had not listened long before he was satisfied that Weiler had been sent on this spying expedition by the man in the back bedroom and was reporting the result of his investigations; in fact, he was drawing a rough map of Sparrow Lake and marking the location of the Waring cottage when the detective found a small hole in a skylight and looked cautiously down upon the pair. The second "gink" was a big flabby-looking "duck," and when he had descended quietly the detective had no difficulty in finding out that the man was registered at the hotel as John Harrington.

"Rives!" breathed Phil in suppressed excitement.

McCorquodale nodded. By good fortune President Wade had just returned to the city and to him the detective at once reported the full circumstances. The Chief had been greatly interested and after congratulating McCorquodale on his discretion had despatched him back to the hotel with instructions to shadow Weiler no matter where the trail led. It was then that McCorquodale had learned of an expedition that was being planned by the bootlegging gang the railroad was anxious to locate, and got concrete evidence that Weiler was the Eastern agent of the whisky runners. The leader was a notorious character named Red McIvor and this man had arranged to meet Weiler at a rendezvous near Indian Creek.

Cranston and McCorquodale had held a consultation with Wade and it was decided that Cranston would watch things at the Toronto end while McCorquodale was sent out to follow developments at Indian Creek. McCorquodale had told Mr. Wade what Kendrick had suggested to him at Sparrow Lake—that the two of them work together on this bootlegging case, and the railroad president had then mentioned Phil's letter and his whereabouts and told McCorquodale to make for Thorlakson Siding and pass on instructions.

Weiler bought a ticket for North Bay. There he had hung around for a day, apparently waiting for somebody. At last three more fellows had come in on a train. Weiler met them at the station and the whole party took the train west that night, with McCorquodale trailing along. Their destination was Indian Creek and on arrival they unloaded from the express-car a Peterborough canoe, a tent and a lot of supplies. As soon as the train pulled out they got ready for a trip into the woods. Down on the riverbank, a few hundred rods through the bush back of the station, a half-breed guide was waiting for them. He had a big birch-bark canoe and the five of them began to hustle their belongings off the platform.

McCorquodale was forced to keep in the background until they had gone and he was afraid that he would lose them. He questioned the Station Agent closely; but that official could tell him nothing about the strangers except that they said they were part of a geological expedition for the Government, heading towards Port Nelson on James' Bay. McCorquodale pretended to accept this information at face value; but if those "birds" knew anything about any "ology" except boozeology he was prepared to swallow his suspenders, buckles and all. Included in their "supplies" were several cases of liquor; McCorquodale knew a case of liquor when he saw it, no matter if it was wrapped in canvas and covered with misleading labels.

It had taken him a little while to locate a canoe that he could hire together with a camping outfit; but finally he had started on the trail once more. He had overhauled them about fifteen miles back from the railroad where Indian Creek and Wolverine River joined waters. From there he had followed them up stream for a few miles, keeping his distance, till they came to a portage where the entire party disembarked. Instead of making the portage to a point farther up, they had gone into camp at what appeared to be an old lumber camp that had not been in use for a couple of seasons. It looked as if they intended to stay there for a while.

"I know that deserted lumber camp," Phil nodded.

"Well, that's where I comes from just now an' that's where we both makes for as soon's we rustles a bite o' grub," concluded McCorquodale. "I hikes down here special to get you soon's I'm sure them guys is anchored. Say, that there Wolverine's some river, aint it? I got my canoe back here a ways."

"Cork, are you quite sure that this bunch is the gang Wade's after? Supposing they turn out to be a fishing party or something?"

"Fishin' party me neck!" scoffed McCorquodale. "With all them cases o' the real McKay?"

"Fishing is often a thirsty business for more than the fish. Anyway, you don't know for sure that it's booze—"

"Don't, eh? They starts in on it las' night an' some of 'em was lit up like a corner saloon, I tell you. Didn't I see 'em an' didn't I *hear* 'em? Great snakes! they kep' me awake with their shouts an' singin' las' night fer hours an' I'm campin' a good loud holler away from their hangout at that. I crep' down clost to find out what they was celebratin' an' I hears 'em gabbin', see. The gang aint all there yet. They're waitin' fer the Main Squeeze—this here Red McIvor I was tellin' you about. I hears 'em mention his name, see, an' besides Weiler's there an'—"

"You win," conceded Phil. "Whisky traders, eh? Heading in to peddle the stuff to the Indians and around the camps." He smoked thoughtfully.

"If they keeps on lappin' it up the way they's doin' las' night they aint goin' to do much tradin' in anythin' but headaches.

Say, what about this here bundle o' phoney hid in a hollow stump? Wade was tellin' me you's up here lookin' after it. Cranston was wonderin' if Weiler'd got a line on it an' mebbe that had somethin' to do with the gang comin' together in this neighborhood. Did you find it?"

"No, it was gone. I'm pretty certain that Podmore was after it and got here ahead of everybody. Thorlakson hasn't noticed anybody hanging around. It dosn't matter. Did Mr. Wade say anything to you about young Stiles having disappeared? Miss Lawson is greatly worried over the last part of the Chief's message." He passed it across as he spoke.

McCorquodale grinned.

"Leave it to me, 'bo. Jimmy Stiles is the young gaffer I's trailin' that afternoon with that tan satchel from the Alderson Construction Company's office. No, the Chief didn't say anythin' to me 'bout him; but I knows where he is."

"You do?"

"Sure Mike! An' I proceeds to dry them tears the Queen's sheddin' by informin' her that the kid's within a few miles of her right now."

"What? You mean he's—"

"Yep. They got him prisoner back here at the lumber camp. He was one o' the three what Weiler met at North Bay an' it didn't take me long to tumble to the way they was watchin' him close. I slips him a note las' night that friends was near an' to be on the lookout f'r us. We're goin' to rescue the kid, see. He'll be our star witness."

"Well, what next!" gasped the astonished Kendrick. He

stared at the detective. "You're not joking? If so, your levity is decidedly ill-timed."

"Yeah," agreed McCorquodale doubtfully. "Uh-hunh. On'y I don't happen to be wavin' no wand an' floatin' horizontal in the air, see. I'm handin' it to you straight up an' down. Stiles is there an' we gotta get him away from those guys. As f'r any jokin'—" He drew out his police automatic and patted it significantly. "This gun cracks ten jokes without stoppin', see, if there's any funny work goin' on."

Phil's surprise at the turn events were taking was only equalled by the excitement with which Cristy Lawson received the news when presently she was called outside and introduced to the C.L.S. detective. She listened eagerly, interjecting a rapid question now and then as if her mind were racing beyond the facts of the recital to a logical solution of the mystery not apparent to the others. She nodded her head once or twice and laughed a little. When McCorquodale had recounted everything that he had observed she was silent for a moment, head bent in thought.

"How soon are you going back to the camp?" she asked at last.

"As soon as Mrs. Thorlakson will give us something to eat," replied Phil.

"Good. I'm ready."

"But—You don't understand," objected Phil. "We can't take you along, Miss Lawson. It wouldn't be—"

"Of course you can. I certainly am going with you."

"Impossible! Your injured foot—"

"Nonsense, it's all right now. I'm going with you," she repeated. "There are reasons why I must go; so please don't argue about it."

"But that's exactly what I intend to do," declared Kendrick decidedly. He shook his head. "There isn't room in the canoe in the first place and besides there's liable to be trouble. Isn't that so, McCorquodale?"

"Mr. Kendrick, as the representative of the *Recorder* it is absolutely necessary—"

"I'm sorry, Miss Lawson; but I refuse to take the responsibility."

"I'll assume all risk, Mr. Kendrick."

"You would be in our way, to be frank. We'll be bringing Stiles back here with us and you can wait till we come."

Almost tearfully she appealed to the detective to that worthy's evident embarrassment. Cap in hand, he made a profound and formal bow in an attempt to be diplomatic.

"Pardon me, lady, but you're crazy!" he stated politely. "Crazy as a bed-bug! It can't be did!"

CHAPTER XIX

FURTHER STRANGE PROCEEDINGS

The sun was dropping behind the wooded hills and only the golden rim of it peeped above the tree-tops when they set out. Before long the purple dusk came creeping in from the east where clouds were banking in the sky.

Kendrick expected to be back by daylight or at latest by noon next day. As they paddled up stream against a strong current his thoughts were busy with the events of the past few weeks, particularly those of the last four days. He marvelled at their kaleidoscopic nature. It seemed ages ago that he had fought a fist battle with this stalky, good-natured chap whose muscular shoulders were swinging in rhythm with his own; yet it was only a month. Now here they were, miles from civilization, heading into the night-obscured depths of the wilderness on an adventure of unknown hazard.

And this girl with the wonderful eyes and wonderful hair, wonderful wit and vivacity, wonderful—diamond ring on her engagement finger!

"Steady, 'bo, steady!" warned McCorquodale. "Take y'r time. We got a lot o' this to do."

Their eyes were growing accustomed to the semi-darkness of the wooded aisle through which the deep Wolverine River raced with a symphony of water sounds. The stream was easy of navigation all the way to the rapids below Kinogama Falls and it was a case of paddling without pause. Kendrick and Cristy had gone as far as the deserted lumber camp on their first day's jaunt in Svenson's canoe; they had been all over the place, little dreaming that so shortly it was to be occupied by these doubtful characters, or that he was to return to the spot on an errand of such consequence.

Not far from the portage at the foot of the rapids there was an old logging road, if they could but find it in the dark. The last mile could be covered more quickly by this route than by following the tump trail past the rapids, and it would lead them straight to the camp. The moon would not be up until after midnight and the tote road promised a more noiseless approach for the preliminary reconnoitring that was necessary to carry out the detective's plan.

It was McCorquodale's suggestion that they creep down on the camp and, if possible, get Stiles away first. After that they would go after Weiler. If they waited until the four men were asleep or were lucky enough to catch their man far enough away from the others to permit of capturing him without too much commotion, it ought to be feasible to carry him into the woods. There, as the detective put it, they could "frighten the gizzard out of him" and learn the meaning of his trip to Sparrow Lake and what Rives was up to; also they would make him tell what he knew about Nickleby's dealings with Red McIvor. At any rate they ought to be able to learn enough to decide on a definite course of action in rounding up the bootleggers. To McCorquodale it was a gratifying prospect. Lead him to it!

The night was exceptionally still, without a breath of air

stirring the forest. In the deep hush that brooded over the wilderness small sounds held sway that ordinarily would have been submerged in the paean of the wind in the firs—the whisper of the Wolverine where it swept, deep and strong; its strident chatter to a fling of gravel at occasional bends in the stream; its sucking snarl over a sunken boulder. The movements and whistlings of owls and bats in the dark, moss-clung corridors on either side were quite distinct; so were the whines and snorts of weasels and other small animals, noisy in the underbrush. And undertoning all other sounds, unceasing, like a hidden menace, rose the drone of insect life—the *hm-m-m-m-m-m-m* of the muskeg swarms.

After perhaps an hour and a half of hard paddling they reached the little lake which marked the junction of Indian Creek with the Wolverine. Beyond this point the stream narrowed and navigation became more difficult. As the shores began to widen out at the forks Kendrick, whose eyes long since had become focused to the twilight of the stars, saw that McCorquodale had thrown up his hand and was motioning for him to cease paddling. At the same time his ear caught a new sound—a chant of voices rapidly growing louder.

Cautioning silence, McCorquodale swung the nose of the canoe abruptly towards the right bank and they slid noiselessly into the deeper shadows, where the detective caught hold of an overhanging branch and held the canoe stationary. Presently Phil was able to recognize the familiar words of an old *voyageur* chantey, a paddling song of the French-Canadian rivermen:

"*En roulant, ma boule, roulant;*
En roulant, ma bo-u-le."

With paddles swinging in unison to the rhythm came four

men in a large Indian canoe, speeding with the current down the centre of Indian creek. Peering from their concealment, Kendrick and the detective could discern the blacker outlines of the craft and its occupants as it sped forth from the gloom of the forest into the starlit area of the tiny lake. The great canoe was low in the water; for heaped in the centre of it was what was evidently a pile of freight, with two men in front and two behind. The steersman swung the prow around and on they went up the Wolverine without a pause in the sweep of the paddles or the swing of the song:

> "*Rouli roulant, ma boule, roulant,*
> *En roulant, ma boule, roulant,*
> *En roulant, ma bo-u-le.*"

"French half-breeds," guessed Kendrick when the singing modulated in distance, "and they're heading for the lumber camp. What do you make out of that?"

"Looks like this 'Red' party them guys was talkin' about last night had hit camp. I'll lay even money them fellas has been down to the station fer another shipment o' booze," asserted McCorquodale. "We gotta do some careful gumshoein', old man. Them birds is feelin' their oats."

From the junction of the two streams it was only a matter of four or five miles to the foot of the rapids, and after a while they could hear the distant roar of the water. Paddling cautiously now and keeping well within the deeper shadows close to shore, they finally reached the spot where the tote road debouched on the river and without mishap disembarked and hauled the canoe out of sight into the bushes. In following the lumber trail there was the danger that they might meet some of the men from the camp; but after a whispered colloquy they decided it was a risk which had to be run. Since the old tote road had received its last "swamping out" it had accumulated enough underbrush, saplings and fallen limbs in spots to afford emergency concealment of a sort.

They had gone but a short distance into the woods, however, before both of them stopped abruptly and listened to a strange sound which carried to them eerily in the quiet night with all the mystery of the unaccountable. It was like the beat of a distant drum, a hollow tattoo that came and went at regular intervals:

Rumma-tumma-tum-tum . . . tum-tum!
RUM-tummaty-tum-tum . . . tum-tum!

"What is that?" said Kendrick in a low voice.

"It's a new one on me," muttered McCorquodale in an awed tone.

"Sounds like an Indian drum. Listen. There it is again."

As they advanced the intermittent drumming increased in volume. Presently above the trees they could see a glow in the sky. The reflection of what seemed to be a huge bonfire grew so strong that they left the logging trail for fear of discovery and stole forward cautiously through the woods.

Rappa-tappa-tap-tap . . . tap-tap!
RAP-tappety-tap-tap . . . tap-tap!

A medley of many voices rose in a weird chant which struck across the night like the wall of some stricken victim of the *loup garou*. It fell away abruptly and the drumming noise renewed.

Turning sharply to the right to get well away from the tote

road, Kendrick and his companion crept at last to the edge of the clearing and took refuge in a hollow where a fallen tree hid them completely. From behind this shelter they peered forth upon a strange scene.

In front of the bunk house, cook shanty, stables, sealer's shanty and other low log buildings that once had been a lumber-camp, was an open space, about two acres in extent, lighted up like day by a bonfire at each end. In the centre, alongside a stump, his figure boldly revealed by the firelight, stood a man with dishevelled hair and a stubby growth of black whisker. He wore the corduroys and Strathcona boots of a shantyman; about his waist was a bright red scarf. Inverted upon the stump was an empty wooden box and in each hand he flourished an empty whisky bottle.

Seated upon the ground in a semi-circle were nine of the roughest looking men Phil ever had seen, each with a piece of broken pine box across his knees and a whisky bottle or a short stick in either hand. Some of them were undoubtedly half-breeds, swarthy of skin and very unkempt; some bore the scars of knife wounds on their faces—riff-raff of the cities mixed with the off-scourings of railway and lumber camps. The whole motley crew were in various stages of drunkenness and it was evident that the whisky-traders' song they were singing appealed to them as about the funniest and most musical thing they ever had enjoyed, for each man tried to outdo his neighbor in the vim which he put into his efforts. The leader by the stump had cursed them into realization of the grave importance of pounding the accompaniment in proper unison, and after much practice had got them into some semblance of accord.

"Now fer the last time, fellers!" he shouted, and away they went:

"Rum fer Injuns when they come!
Rum fer the beggars when they go!
That's the trick, my grizzled lads,
To catch the cash and snare the foe!"

Racka-tacka-tack-tack . . . tack-tack!
RACK-tackety-tack-tack . . . tack-tack!

"This aint goin' to be no cinch, 'bo," came McCorquodale's serious whisper in Kendrick's ear. "This mob's come in durin' the afternoon. We better get back an' pick up a gang o' our own—some o' them guineas from the railroad. Then we can clean this bunch up in proper shape."

"Wait," muttered Kendrick. "What are they doing now?"

One of the men was digging a hole while two others picked up a small log which they presently up-ended in the hole, tramping the earth about it firmly. The individual who acted as master of ceremonies gazed expectantly towards the bunk house where a heavily built man with sandy hair and whiskers had put in an appearance and was waving his hand.

"There's Red and Weiler!"

"Keep quiet!" commanded Phil.

Corduroys had mounted the stump and was addressing the boisterous crowd. Apparently he was looked upon as something of a wag, for he was interrupted frequently by laughter. His voice carried distinctly.

"Gents an' fel—ler citizens," he began, striking an oratorical attitude, "we now comes to the next num—ber on the program, the which is costin' a lot o' cold coin. Fif—ty thous—and dollars, gents, is what it costs to have the

Perfessor put on his little stunt. Fif—ty thous—and dollars! We calls it 'The Double-Cross an' the Get-Away.' The Perfessor has double-crossed our friend an' worthy leader, Red McIvor, an' refuses to say where he has buried the hidden treasure. Instead of fifty thousand good bucks, he hands over a wad o' phoney bills. Instead o' fifty thousand genooine plunks we will now perceed to have fifty thousand dollars' worth o' fun—the Perfessor's treat, gents. He will now demonstrate his get-away. He is an insect an' to the insects he goes from here. He has stung us an' it is now his turn to git stung. I have grea—at pleasure in callin' upon the Perfessor."

As he finished speaking there issued from the log shanty a struggling group. Dragging between them in no gentle fashion a kicking, screaming prisoner, came Red McIvor and the German. They kicked him forward into the arms of the waiting men at the post, to which he was bound quickly from feet to waist. The firelight played upon the prisoner's distorted features as he begged them to let him go. His pleadings were greeted with shouts of laughter.

Kendrick clutched McCorquodale's arm in sudden excitement.

"By the eternal, it's Hughey Podmore!" he gasped in disbelief. "They've caught Podmore with that bogus money on him! That's what he means."

"There's Stiles—the one they're bringin' out now," whispered McCorquodale, pointing to a second prisoner who was being hustled out to witness the performance. His hands were tied behind his back and the man who had him in charge shoved him roughly to a sitting posture and pointed towards the post.

Kendrick's face was tense at he watched. His eyes smouldered with cold fire.

CHAPTER XX

A MAN OF MONEY

McIvor, the leader of the crew, was holding out the envelope taken from the stump and saying something to the first prisoner. They could not catch the words at that distance. Podmore shook his head and renewed his pleadings. The only response to these was an oath and a cruel blow on the mouth from the enraged ruffian, who now issued a sharp command.

Two of his men sprang at the prisoner and in a trice had stripped him to the skin from the waist up. They tore his shirt to ribbons. A jerk of McIvor's hand brought a third man on the run, carrying a tin can. He began to smear the contents over the back and chest and arms of the shrieking prisoner. While the onlookers rocked with drunken laughter Red McIvor peeled bill after bill from the roll of stage money in his hand and plastered them to the prisoner's naked body with resounding slaps.

"Tar an' feathers up to date—spruce gum an' greenbacks!" mumbled the detective. "Hear that feller yell!"

Kendrick's eyes were ablaze. He whipped out his revolver, his teeth clenched.

"McCorquodale, we can't sit here and see him killed in front of our eyes. This thing's gone far enough. I'm going out there—" But the detective grabbed him and with an oath dragged him back.

"Y' gone clean nutty?" he protested furiously. "Wanta get croaked, y' poor fish? Fat chanst y' got with them bohunks armed with rifles! It's six to one!"

"They're scaring the poor devil to death, I tell you. See, they're getting ready to drive him into the bush! Man, don't you understand? The flies! He'll be eaten alive!"

McCorquodale carried his profanity pretty close to the surface at all times, but the wellspring of it that gushed from him as once more he dragged Kendrick off his feet sounded the depths of anxiety and formed a lurid preface to angry argument. Had Kendrick forgotten Stiles? They couldn't hope to save both prisoners at once. Get Stiles first and they could organize a search-party for Podmore afterward.

"The whole mob'll be chasin' off in a minute an' that's the chanst we gotta lay for. Don't go 'n' spoil everythin' just as it's comin' our way. For the love o' Pete, 'bo, stuff moss in your ears an' sit tight!"

Kendrick had himself in hand again immediately. In an open fight with that gang two men hadn't a ghost of a show. As it was, their situation was desperate enough. The best that could be done for Podmore was to let things take their course for the moment. Later—

The detective's prediction was being fulfilled rapidly. The last bill had been stuck in placc and the drunken gang had staggered to their feet, jeering and laughing at the grotesque appearance of their victim. They formed in two lines with sticks in their hands in preparation for the moment when the prisoner would be released and forced to run the gauntlet of their blows in his flight to the woods.

Podmore's eyes were rolling in the agony of his terror. A crimson slobber drooled from his swollen lips. As he was cut loose from the cords that bound him to the post and the first stick thumped his back he sprang away with a frenzied yell.

There was but one path left him—straight down between those two lines of hideous leering faces. Beyond he would be free and the woods for him held no terrors to equal the panic of the moment. With arms hugged over his head for protection he made his dash to such good purpose that he leaped by the excited rows of man-baiters with only one or two bad bruises. In their eagerness to achieve a good wallop some of his intoxicated tormentors missed him altogether and succeeded only in swinging themselves off their feet as he passed. Those who thus went sprawling tripped up the others and the scramble enabled him to get a good sprinting lead. Fear sped his feet. He seemed not merely to run; he took wing and flew—a screeching, gibbering madman.

And laughing loudly, yelling, brandishing their clubs, the whole crazy howling mob took after him.

Kendrick gnashed his teeth as he watched and waited. His throat was dry, his fingers twitching with repressed rage. When at last he spoke his voice was hoarse.

"Ready, Cork? There's only one in sight. Come on!"

"Leave'm to me!" growled McCorquodale huskily, grabbing up a stout stick. "You look after Stiles."

They dashed into the open at top speed. The man who had

remained behind to guard the second prisoner was still standing in the same spot, holding Stiles by the coat-collar and listening to the receding uproar and the wild screams of Podmore as he fled for his life. Both the man and his prisoner were gazing off towards the tote road down which the stragglers of the chase were just disappearing. McCorquodale was within ten feet of them before the fellow turned. As the detective scooted at him he let out a startled yell which was effectively chopped in the middle by the descending blow.

"Mr. Kendrick!" gasped the white-faced Stiles, his eyes bright.

"Quick, Jimmy!"

He cut the cords that pinioned the other's arms and hustled the speechless youth across the clearing.

"Hi, there! Stop!"

Red McIvor at the door of the shanty had just caught sight of them. He jumped back inside for a rifle.

"Beat it!" yelled McCorquodale. "Under cover!"

The bullets clipped twigs from the trees as the three plunged into the woods.

"This way. Quick! Follow me, you fellows," cried Phil. He jumped a log and struck to the left at a sharp angle. "I know a place where we can stand them off—if we can make it."

They floundered on, barking their shins in the darkness that encompassed them beyond the circle of the bonfires. Behind them McIvor was hallooing to his scattered followers at the top of his lungs and cursing impotently between hollers as he poked about at the edge of the clearing.

The bedlam which had broken loose when Podmore was freed had trailed out to a scatter of noise in the distance. Far away the shrieks of the half-demented man of money still rose above the shouting and cat-calls, but they were growing less frequent and fainter. Podmore was making good time apparently. There was a lot of hallooing going on from one to another, while loud voices and laughter marked the return of stragglers who had dropped out of the chase.

With so many stumbling about in the dark Phil reckoned that the unavoidable snapping of dry sticks in their scramble through the undergrowth would pass unnoticed long enough to enable them to get well away. Once or twice they crouched in silence to allow groups of men to pass them; for Kendrick was now taking a course parallel to the tote road. Every little while he paused to listen for the fresh outbreak that would take place back at the camp as soon as Red McIvor had got enough of his men together to start an organized pursuit. He grinned presently as a chorus of hallooing flung wide upon the night to apprize those farthest away that something had gone wrong and to recall them. By this time, however, the three fugitives were almost within reach of their goal and could afford to slacken pace in favor of stealth.

The temporary refuge for which Phil was heading was a rocky elevation which rose not more than a stonesthrow from the logging road. It marked the end of a spur which jutted out from the ridge than ran toward Kinogama Falls. Some by-gone age of upheaval had thrust skyward a huge pillar of granite and the centuries had gathered about its base a rubble of boulders and earth in which the forest growths had taken root and spread up the slopes. On the top of this hill was a basin-like depression which made a natural rampart for defensive purposes and Phil had remarked as much on the day that he and Cristy Lawson had climbed to it. They had stood looking around at the huge broken slabs of granite and speculating upon the oddness of the formation, while their conversation had taken on an academic flavor as they discussed the nebular and glacial theories. They had discovered at the bottom of a great cleft in the rock, a spring of sparkling water, so cold that it was impossible to drink it without frequent pauses. They had named the place "The Saucer," had eaten their lunch there. He remembered how beautiful she had looked as she talked in carefree animation and he had taken her hand to pilot her among the rocks and—That was just three days ago!

"Easy now, fellows," cautioned Phil in a whisper. "It's just a short climb, but watch your step. Give me your hand, Cork, and you take hold of Jimmy's. For the life of you don't dislodge any stones. They'd go down with a crash that could be heard a mile on a night like this."

They reached the top without this misfortune, however, and dropped behind the rocks with no little satisfaction.

"Now Jimmy, what's the meaning of all this?" demanded Phil. "Keep your voice down to a whisper. Podmore—what about him? And how in the mischief did these toughs get hold of you?"

It was only by the greatest effort that Stiles pulled himself together. The excitement of seeing friends and of the escape had keyed him to the required effort, but with the tension relaxed he was on the point of collapse. None too strong at any time, the terrible experiences of the past few days had weakened him greatly; he had had little to eat and the strain of the last twenty-four hours had exhausted him. He covered his face with his hands and shook as with an ague.

"Well, never mind, just now, Jimmy," said Phil quickly as he noted this condition with some anxiety. "There's a lot of talking to be done, but it can wait. You lie down and get some rest, old man,—"

"Can it! Can it!" whispered McCorquodale fiercely. He held up his hand and listened.

After the uproar of the past twenty minutes the sudden quiet in the vicinity of the camp was ominous. There was no longer any sound of Podmore or of the chase. But now and then a dry stick snapped and there was a swishing of bushes. The sounds seemed to come from three or four points at once.

"They're searching the woods for us," whispered Phil. "They probably figure we'd make for the river. After everything's quiet, we'll slip away from here and try for the canoe, but not—"

Bang!—Bang!-Bang!

The rifle shots shattered the quiet within a hundred yards of them, down the tote road towards the river. The three fugitives leaped to their feet and strained their ears to interpret the sudden renewal of pandemonium that had broken out all around them. Men were shouting to each other and plunging excitedly towards the sound of the guns. There was a noise of pursuit rapidly approaching along the logging road. Then came a bull-like bellow of rage and a woman's scream.

Kendrick's face went white in sudden comprehension.

"She's followed us!" he groaned. "Stay here, Stiles. Come on, Cork. It's Miss Lawson!"

Trailing profanity like an express locomotive trailing smoke, McCorquodale followed down the hill in long stumbling jumps. Loose stones showered after them and large rocks dislodged and crash-smashed through the bushes. Without an instant's pause Phil went leaping over fallen trees and tearing through the undergrowth like one possessed, swearing at the occasional obstruction over which he tripped in the dark.

He broke through into the tote road just as the girl's fleeing figure loomed dimly in the twilight.

"Here, Cristy!" he shouted. "This way. The Saucer! Make for the Saucer! Are you all right?"

"Yes," she panted. "Oh, Philip,—Svenson—call Svenson!" Neither of them gave thought to the familiar names by which they addressed each other under the stress of the moment.

"Here, Cork. Help her. Hustle back, the both of you."

There was no time to lose. Members of the gang were plunging through the woods towards the spot from several directions. Kendrick sped down the tote road, revolver in hand. Svenson was not hard to locate, for he was bellowing like a bull of Bashan in the middle of the trail, shaking his fist in the air and hurling defiance at a cringing group who were just picking themselves up from the ground where they had been flung by the enraged Swede.

"Come on, Svenson! This is Kendrick. Quick, man," called Phil. "We've got her safe. But there's a million more of them coming through the woods."

They ran for it none too soon. Rifle flashes broke in the dark like fireflies elongated. Bullets were whining past them and thudding into the tree-trunks and plowing up the ground all around them as they dove into the thicket; but it was blind guess work shooting in the dark. They got through unscathed.

At the foot of the hill they overtook McCorquodale and Cristy just as the sharp bark of the detective's automatic sent three pursuers hastily to cover. The big Swede swept the girl over his shoulder as if she had been a sack of meal and started rapidly up the ascent while Kendrick dropped behind a rock and joined McCorquodale in the fusilade with his own weapon.

The firing was bringing the whole gang about their ears and as soon as he had given Svenson time to reach the top Phil ordered the detective to beat a retreat. They tumbled in among their friends, all but winded.

Svenson sat down and wiped away the blood that was trickling down his face from a scalp wound.

"*Yum*—pin' *Yim*iny!" he puffed with emphasis. "Vell, by golly!"

"Y've said somethin', Goliath," approved McCorquodale with a grin.

CHAPTER XXI

DOUBLE TROUBLE

Inwardly raging, Kendrick crept about, making anxious inventory of their hurts.

There was little use in voicing his amazement that they had been fired upon with unmistakable intent to do bodily harm—and for such trivial cause. He had not dreamed that any gang of men would dare to carry out such an attack in Northern Ontario in these days of established law and order. These were not pioneer times and a dangerous situation like this in which they found themselves was out of place except in a moving picture. One could look for anything to happen in the photo plays which staged bloody scenes in a corner of a city park, called it "the Canadian wilds" and shot at least one man every thousand feet of film. But here in Northern Ontario, a few miles from the luxurious trans-continental passenger trains *de luxe*—! Scum and all as these fellows were, they would not dare do this unless they were crazy with liquor.

There was ample proof that they were drunk enough for anything and in the face of the real danger of the situation nothing was to be gained by recriminations. It was through no fault of McIvor or his men that their bullets had not caused serious wounds or several fatalities. Phil was thankful to find that his little party had escaped. Their clothes were badly torn, of course, and all of them bore various scratches and bruises from contact with the forest undergrowth in the dark; but beyond the gash on Svenson's head and another on Phil's shoulder where a bullet had torn through his sleeve, they had escaped for the time being.

He found Cristy Lawson and young Jimmy Stiles in a nook behind the rocks, exchanging confidences with breathless interest. She had lighted a small candle and stuck it up in a recess where its feeble rays were hidden from outside view. She had brought along a canvas haversack into which she had thrust a number of things she had thought might be useful in an emergency, including sewing materials, a bottle of Mrs. Thorlakson's special liniment and a package of sandwiches. The latter she had opened and Stiles had been munching away while she told him all that had taken place since she left Toronto—nearly all, that is. But it was Stiles who was talking when Phil joined them—talking so rapidly and excitedly that he was almost incoherent. At sight of Kendrick he stopped abruptly and when the girl turned, Kendrick noted that she was scarcely less agitated.

"Jimmy has something to say that you should know at once," she explained hurriedly, averting her gaze. She seemed very much upset.

He hastened away to post McCorquodale and Svenson to watch for further demonstrations from the enemy. There was no sign of any intention on the part of Red McIvor's men to assault the impregnable position. The whole gang seemed to have drawn off, for the present at least, and it would be impossible for any of them to creep up the hill without giving ample warning of their approach. So, cautioning both to keep their ears open and to call him at the first sign of further trouble, he slipped back to hear what Stiles had to say.

The story of the bookkeeper's strange experience was so absorbing that it was not long before both his auditors completely forgot their surroundings. The gang of toughs in the camp below were running a consignment of cheap whisky and rum into the north country for distribution among the camps and various unscrupulous traders who would supply it to lumberjacks, trappers, construction gangs and even Indians in due season. This Red McIvor was a notorious character who was known in many an out-of-the-way corner of the North for the boldness of his operations and his defiance of the law.

But is [Transcriber's note: it?] was not just chance that had brought him into this part of the country on his present expedition. It was the money hidden in the stump. McIvor was open for any sideline in dishonesty that gave promise of lucrative returns and his agent, Weiler, had been very busy in Toronto recently. Somebody had tipped J. C. Nickleby as to Podmore's underhand activities—Ferguson, the lawyer, Stiles thought; but was not sure—and Podmore had been watched closely and followed when he started West. Word had been passed to Red McIvor, who had lost no time in getting on the trail of this fifty-thousand-dollar pick-me-up, with the result that he had reached out a hairy arm, twisted his fingers in Mr. Podmore's coat-collar and calmly dispossessed him of the sealed envelope which he had recovered from the stump. The chase which had ended thus had not been prolonged, as the city man had been no match for the experienced woodsman in the latter's own environment.

When McIvor found that all he had for his efforts was a package of worthless stage money he was furious. He at once concluded that Podmore had tricked him and had hidden the real money. He trusted his eastern agent implicitly and neither Podmore's own blank surprise when the envelope was opened or his most desperate protestations could change McIvor's idea of the situation. Knowing the truth of the matter, Stiles had tried to save Podmore from the rough punishment meted out to him at McIvor's camp, but his net return for his efforts was abuse; he dare not reveal too close a connection with the envelope as his own position already was too precarious.

On the night following his luncheon with Kendrick Stiles had gone back to the office to finish some work. He was in the habit of working on the books at night occasionally. He had no sooner let himself in than he became aware of a heated discussion that was going on behind the ground-glass partition which separated Alderson's private office from the general office. One voice was Nickleby's; the other he did not recognize, but from the tenor of the remarks he felt sure that what was going on was of vital interest to his friends. Instead of turning on the light, therefore, he had crept close to the partition.

He soon knew that the man alone with Nickleby in that office was Harrington Rives, late of the penitentiary, and that Rives had known Nickleby in the past. In fact, Rives was calmly advising Nickleby to remember that the police had long memories, and that away down south in the States was a certain institution which would be glad at any time to welcome home a prodigal no matter how often he changed his name. After this remark Nickleby had cooled down very quickly, as if realizing that he was in Rives' power, and it was apparent to the eager youth in the outer office that the pair understood each other thoroughly. Judging by the clinking of glass and a certain recklessness of speech, both were drawing heavily upon Alderson's stock of liquid "office supplies."

Stiles had become so excited over his discovery that for the moment he had forgotten the danger of his own position. Accidentally he knocked his knee against the partition and the first thing he knew Nickleby and Rives came into the outer office on the run. They caught him just as he had reached the door.

When they realized that he had overheard their conversation his life had been in danger for an instant; for Nickleby was in a white-hot passion and would have choked him. But the ex-politician took the situation very coolly and dragged Nickleby loose somewhat roughly. There was no use in getting excited, he had advised calmly; there were other ways of taking care of this young man. Whereupon they had shut him inside the vault while they discussed the matter of his discreet disposal.

It was perhaps half an hour later that a closed cab had driven up the lane at the rear of the building. Two men were inside the vehicle, waiting for him. It was too dark for him to get a good look at them just then. They lost no time in tying a pocket-handkerchief around his ankles and blindfolding him with another. Rives and Nickleby remained behind at the office. Jimmy knew that his two custodians were "tough," if their talk and manner meant anything, and whenever he tried to speak to them they told him to "shut up or we'll knock your block off," following up the threat with sundry kicks and blows.

"There's your melodrama for you, Mr. Kendrick," Cristy could not resist interpolating, "closed cab and all."

They left the city and drove for most of the night along country roads. About dawn they reached their destination and when the bandage was removed Stiles found himself in an empty room that was so dusty and musty he came to the conclusion it was an empty house on some little travelled side road. As soon as it grew light enough to take an inventory of his surroundings Stiles went to the window, but could see nothing except hills, valleys and bushland. Not a single habitation was in sight. He found out later that the place was down near Stockton, somewhere back in Clam Creek Valley, many miles from the city; it was from the Stockton station that they afterwards boarded the train.

Food was brought in to him regularly three or four times by a toothless old woman who refused to talk. They watched him too closely for any attempt at escape, one of his guards remaining in the room all day.

The next night he heard voices and a general stirring about the place and before long he knew that Rives had arrived. He came into the room with the two men who had ridden in the cab and they tried to make Stiles tell what he knew about the missing campaign fund money. It had been a bad half hour that followed; but at last they decided that he really knew nothing about the matter.

Rives had sent the other two out of the room then and had adopted a less truculent manner. He told Stiles that he had no desire to do him any injury and that no harm would befall him if he did exactly as he was told. It was necessary that Jimmy disappear completely for a while, and accordingly they had arranged for him to take a little holiday trip into Northern Ontario with the two "boys" who had ridden with him the night before. If he agreed to go with them and to make no attempt to escape or create a disturbance he would be treated with every consideration. There was no reason, Rives said, why the trip would not prove a genuine holiday jaunt; there would be canoeing, fishing, camping out, plenty to eat and so on and he would be back after a while with a fine coat of tan and, if he behaved himself, money in his pocket.

With his voice dropped suddenly to a strictly confidential tone, Rives had then informed Jimmy that the missing campaign fund money had been located—at a place called Thorlakson, west on the C.L.S. railway, hidden in a certain stump beside a water-tank. Very carefully he led up to the proposal that Stiles should attempt to secure this money without the knowledge of his camp-mates. It was then that Jimmy had learned from Rives about Red McIvor and the logging-camp where the party was to gather; that the station at which they would leave the train was called Indian Creek, and that it was the next station beyond Thorlakson—just a few miles away. Rives said that both Red McIvor and a man named Podmore were after the money and he was afraid that if they secured it they would steal it whereas he, Rives, was anxious to restore it to the rightful owner. If Jimmy would help him to do this, get the money and turn it over to him, he would see that he was suitably rewarded. If Jimmy refused to fall in with the plan outlined, the alternative was a jail sentence; for it had been only with great difficulty that he had persuaded Nickleby to refrain from putting Stiles in jail on a charge of theft.

Jimmy had pretended to be duly impressed and grateful to Rives. He had agreed promptly to the proposal. The situation suddenly had become so ludicrous that he had experienced great difficulty in maintaining the proper solemnity. The opportunity of getting to Thorlakson where he could report his discoveries to Miss Lawson was the thing he most desired.

But he had failed to reckon the possibility that he would be unable to escape. It had seemed to be an easy thing to give his two companions the slip; but when they detrained at Indian Creek he had been inveigled into assisting with the unloading of the canoes, and on his first trip to the creek a short distance from the station, he had found himself forced into the Indian guide's canoe and carried beyond reach of help.

He had planned then to escape after they reached the abandoned logging camp, steal a canoe and come back to the railway line and down to Thorlakson on a handcar or a freight train. But again he had not reckoned on the number of men with whom he would have to deal at the camp. McIvor's party proper consisted only of three men beside himself; but the half-breeds and others who had been invited for a spree began to straggle in till escape became almost impossible. They caught him the first time he tried it and after that he had been guarded more closely. It was plain to him that Nickleby, knowing of this McIvor expedition, had paid McIvor's agent to carry him into the heart of the wilderness with them and to keep him away from civilization.

In the light of this recital of the facts the presence of Jimmy Stiles was no longer an unbelievable coincidence, but a logical outcome. Nickleby, having made a dicker with McIvor's man to recover the money from the stump before Podmore could get it, had attempted to kill two birds with one stone by having McIvor take Stiles with him on his expedition beyond the outposts of civilization. In doing that Nickleby had no means of knowing that he was defeating his own ends by putting Stiles within reach of friends.

The end of the narrative found Kendrick full of eager questions. The definite knowledge that Nickleby had a police record, that Rives knew this and had looked him up on the strength of it, that the two had their heads together—all this boded no good, as Phil saw it. Nathaniel Lawson and Benjamin Wade apparently had been justified in their worst suspicions of Nickleby. Kendrick asked Stiles for further details of the conversation he had overheard between Nickleby and Rives. Had he been able to catch all that was said? Was there any indication that the two were planning further mischief?

"They dropped their voices pretty low once or twice," replied Jimmy with some hesitation, "but I got the most of it." He looked across at Cristy Lawson and cleared his throat in such evident embarrassment that Phil glanced quickly at the girl.

"What is it, Miss Lawson, please? You and Jimmy are keeping something back. Why? Is there something you think I ought not to know?"

She looked up at that and he was surprised at the diffidence reflected in her manner.

"It isn't that it is anything you should not know," she said with an effort to choose her words carefully. "On the contrary, you should know it. But it is never pleasant to be the bearer of—bad news."

"'Nothing is ever so bad that it might not be worse,'" he quoted, endeavoring to cover his anxiety by a smile. "What is it, please?"

"It is about your uncle, Mr. Kendrick." She turned to face him squarely and spoke rapidly. "We have undeniable proof that the Honorable Milton Waring is in collusion with Nickleby—and, incidentally, Rives—and they are planning to misuse the funds of the Interprovincial Loan & Savings Company. They are meeting about midnight on the twenty-seventh at your uncle's house—over on the Island—to close a deal which involves control of Interprovincial stock. Nickleby has agreed to dispose of his holdings and those of his clique at grossly inflated prices and to provide the money for the purchase by a large loan with very inadequate collateral security. In plain language it is a huge steal which may mean, possibly, that the loan company will have to close its doors."

CHAPTER XXII

LOWERING CLOUDS

Phil gazed gravely at the girl's flushed, excited face; then at the pale, serious Jimmy Stiles. He could not smile at this startling statement as an out-and-out absurdity when it was so apparent that both of them were sincere in their belief that it was the truth.

"That is a pretty serious charge you are making, Miss Lawson," he said quietly. "You speak of undeniable proof that my uncle is in collusion with Nickleby. I think we may eliminate Rives as impossible in this connection. As you know, my uncle was the man who put Rives in jail, where he belonged. Just what do you mean by 'undeniable proof'?"

"It is true that Rives was jailed through your uncle's efforts, but that was twelve years ago, Mr. Kendrick. Twelve years is a long time—in office. Political brooms have an unfortunate tendency of late years to lose their splinters very rapidly once they are sure of a place inside the door and it isn't a great while before they no longer sweep clean."

"'Undeniable proof,' I believe you said," persisted Phil.

"Jimmy overheard Nickleby and Rives calmly discussing the

meeting with the Honorable Milton Waring, which is to take place on the night of the twenty-seventh, and while he was unable to obtain the full details of the scheme which is being hatched with your uncle's co-operation, he learned enough to show that their plans are pretty near maturity.

"If that were all, I would be inclined to say that Jimmy must have been wool-gathering and have misunderstood what he heard; but, unfortunately it isn't all—not by any matter of means."

She paused and looked up at him bravely.

"Mr. Kendrick, several times in the past few days our conversation has wandered to political topics and once or twice you mentioned with some resentment the personal attacks which are made upon our public men by political opponents in the heat of electioneering. You said it was enough to drive all thought of taking part in the government of the country from the minds of decent citizens. You were pretty severe on the newspapers, the party organs anyway, for some of the things they have ventured to say about your uncle from time to time. I endeavored to change the subject whenever you got going along this line for fear I would say something which would hurt your feelings. I assure you it is not easy for me to do that now. I am a newspaper woman, as you know, and loyalty to my paper demands that I speak plainly. Also the situation in which we find ourselves requires me to give you facts in advance of publication— facts which have been very closely guarded by the *Recorder*—and I am trusting to your discretion under most difficult circumstances."

"I understand, Miss Lawson. It's scarcely necessary to assure you that your confidence will be respected."

"I told you the other night that my editor had grown suspicious of the Alderson Construction Company and that we had been gathering up evidence for a graft exposure that would shock the country. I regret very much that the Honorable Milton Waring is involved in these charges, along with Blatchford Ferguson and Nickleby. Alderson himself is merely a figurehead of Nickleby's; for, as I told you before, the Alderson concern is ninety per cent. J. C. Nickleby. It was immediately after a secret meeting between these four men that the campaign fund contribution of fifty thousand dollars was made by the Alderson Construction Company. You know what happened to it. Photographs of this money are now in the *Recorder's* possession.

"But before this meeting took place at all we had run down the proof of a real-estate transaction in connection with the proposed new Deaf and Dumb Institute that was traceable finally to your uncle and Nickleby and Ferguson. The three of them secretly formed a little syndicate. Nickleby advanced the wherewithal to purchase the land, Ferguson bought it up quietly and shrewdly through different agents at half its value, and the Honorable Milt's contribution was to engineer the Government's purchase of the site. In fact, we obtained the proof that it was he who proposed the whole deal to Nickleby in the first place. The site was purchased piecemeal, at sacrifice prices, from individual lot owners for a total of $50,000. Its market value was $100,000. It was sold to the Government for $200,000. The profit of $150,000 was split three ways between your uncle, Ferguson and Nickleby. These are facts, Mr. Kendrick, which have been established beyond question by my editor, Mr. McAllister, by personal investigation."

She paused and looked away from him to escape evidence of the pain which she knew her words were giving him. His face seemed haggard in the feeble flicker of the candle. Stiles had sat silent throughout, poking some dried pine-needles into a little heap with a stick. He continued carefully to poke them together and scatter them again, poke them together and scatter them again.

"You are quite sure—of the proof?"

"I'm awfully sorry, Mr. Kendrick," and he looked up at her sympathetic tones to find tears in her eyes. "There is no mistake. The *Recorder* has the sworn affidavits to prove its charges in connection with the real-estate deal and Mr. McAllister has shown me photos of the cheques."

Phil sat as if dazed. He could not trust himself to speak. He fought against belief in his uncle's dereliction, but there seemed no loophole of escape from such evidence and he knew that Cristy Lawson could have no object in attempting to deceive him. She was telling him the truth.

This, then, was the sort of thing Ben Wade had had in mind when he said there was nothing to be gained by shutting one's eyes to the fact that many a good man had found the political game as it was played these days too many for him. He knew what McAllister had up his sleeve perhaps. Was it part of the puzzle which the railroad president was trying to piece together? What had Wade done with the stolen money that Cristy had given him? He had had it photographed, for one thing, and turned the photos over to McAllister! He had been helping Cristy in her work! At the same time he had been trying to save Aunt Dolly from—what? The suffering she would undergo under the disgrace of the very exposure which Wade was helping to bring about?

It was a muddle which was hard to penetrate. What a beautiful line of talk Blatch Ferguson had handed him the other day! According to Blatch the Honorable Milton

Waring was one of the hardest-working, most conscientious and high-principled men of the day and Blatch had had greater opportunity of knowing that than most, he had said. He could say that, knowing the facts, being one of the principals himself in the graft that was going on!—could say that and follow it up with a homily upon honesty in public life—say it with an exalted look upon his face! How completely a bit of unsuspected truth could alter an entire perspective! How easily he had been fooled when he became too inquisitive!

And his uncle? Had his uncle talked to him that foggy night only for the purpose of fooling him too? "Even one man against a pack of wolves can put up at least some kind of a fight, even though he knows that sooner or later he is doomed to go down." His uncle knew, then, that sooner or later discovery must come? He had talked about having tried to do his duty and wanted his nephew to believe it no matter what happened. But, as Cristy had pointed out, new brooms had time to become worn and inefficient in twelve years of use. His uncle had been talking in the past tense! He *had* tried to do what he thought was his duty—at first, when he swept into politics, inspired by the victory over the Rives crowd. Twelve years apparently was a long time to expect an inspiration to burn in the face of besetting temptations.

Phil looked up at last, aware that the girl was speaking, tense with eagerness.

"I wanted you to know the truth, Mr. Kendrick," she was saying, "if only that it will help you to understand how serious I consider the news which Jimmy brings—this new deal that is pending, I mean. The *Recorder* must act at once to stop it. It is better that your uncle face the charges as they now stand than to have this last and blackest mark against him. I hope you agree with me?"

"Decidedly," nodded Kendrick. "What you have told me, Miss Lawson, has—well, kind of knocked the wind out of me. I can scarcely credit it. Even yet, I am hoping against hope that it is not as bad as the evidence seems to indicate. But one thing is certain, there is no use in attempting to do anything but face the music. If my uncle is guilty, he will have to pay the price; there can be no compromise between right and wrong. On the other hand—well, false accusations never yet downed an honest man."

He was entirely unconscious that he was quoting Blatch Ferguson. Impulsively Cristy held out her hand, her eyes glowing.

"I am glad to hear you say that," she said softly. "Somehow, I felt that you would take it—that way."

"There is one thing I cannot force myself to believe," he asserted confidently, "and that is that Uncle Milt would have any dealings with this man, Rives. That seems to discredit—"

"I think perhaps you have misunderstood part of it," interrupted Stiles. "Miss Lawson didn't mean that Rives was mixed up with your uncle. He's in with Nickleby, but I don't think Mr. Waring knows that for a minute. From what Rives and Nickleby said I think they're planning to give the deal away and get Mr. Waring into trouble—after they get away themselves to a safe place, y'understand. The deal's between Nickleby and your uncle, Mr. Kendrick. It was Rives who told Nickleby they'd leave Mr. Waring 'holding the sack.' That was the way he put it. I don't know whether Rives is going to be at this meeting or not; but't aint likely."

"And when did you say this meeting was?—the twenty-seventh?"

"About midnight—that was exactly what Nickleby said."

Phil turned quickly to the girl.

"And do you know what day this is?" he demanded.

"Wednesday—the twenty-seventh," she said calmly.

"Then, to-night—Listen, Miss Lawson. Do I understand that you believe an actual transfer of cash or negotiable securities will take place in connection with this thing—*to-night*?"

"Unless the date has been changed—yes. Jimmy overheard Nickleby say he had arranged it that way. It is not likely that the date has been changed, once Jimmy was safely out of the way; Nickleby and Rives would be only too keen to get it over with before some hitch occurred."

"Then we're too late!" cried Phil in excitement.

"I do not expect you to help me, Mr. Kendrick, but I do expect that your sense of fair play will prevent you from attempting to detain me."

"Detain you? I don't understand, Miss Lawson. I am ready to help you in every way I can to prevent this thing. I would be anyway, but with these two criminals planning deliberately to get my uncle—why, there's nothing we can do at this late date—"

"There's the telegraph wire. What time is it now?"

"Not quite ten o'clock," answered Phil, glancing at his watch.

"If I could get away from here immediately, I could make it—wire the story to the *Recorder* with instructions to communicate with the police—to-night, I mean. The paper doesn't go to press until after three-thirty. But there's no time to lose."

"Hey, 'bo!" called McCorquodale sharply. "Here comes the torchlight parade. Get a wiggle on. Looks like they was goin' to set the woods on fire!"

All three sprang to their feet in consternation. For the time being they had forgotten all about the McIvor gang.

CHAPTER XXIII

THE FIGHT

Kendrick joined McCorquodale on the run. It needed but a glance over the rock to observe two members of the gang approaching the base of the hill through the woods, one carrying a flaring pine-knot torch, the other a piece of white canvas tied to a stick. They were coming for a parley.

Phil summoned his little party around him for a hasty council of war. It looked to be as good an opportunity as they were likely to have for attempting to reach the river. Unless somebody had a better suggestion to offer, let Miss Lawson, Svenson and Jimmy slip away, while McCorquodale and he talked to these fellows on the opposite side of the hill.

"We'll jolly them along as well as we can to give the rest of you as much time as possible. How does it strike you, Miss Lawson? Is the ankle bothering you at all?"

The girl was quite sure of herself. The ankle was all right and she could handle the canoe. When she got to the section shanty she would have Thorlakson get out the handcar and run her down to the nearest telegraph operator and that was all there was to it.

"In that case I can be of greater service as a rearguard," said Kendrick. "Svenson's canoe is plenty large enough for the three of you without overcrowding. It's really built for four, isn't it, Svenson?"

"You bet you life Ay ben smart fallar," grinned the big Swede. "Das ben gude yob, y'batcha. Das har canoe, she ride avay vith seven, den take nodder vun. Yaw, das' rite, alrite."

"What about you and Mr. McCorquodale?" asked Cristy.

"Don't worry about us. We'll try to follow you as soon as possible, but on no account are you to wait for us, once you reach the river. We may be—delayed somewhat. If you watch your step and get any kind of an even break on the luck, you'll get through O.K.

"Svenson, listen to me carefully, now. You are to make it your first business to protect Miss Lawson—at any cost. If you are discovered by a sentry, silence him before he makes a noise. If you can't find your own canoe, take any one you see; you'll find ours drawn up in the bushes to the left of the trail, not far from the flat rock. It'll only hold two; so you get Stiles and Miss Lawson afloat, then hump back here. You understand, now? If they haven't touched the big canoe you are to go along with the others; you are to come back only if the canoe is too small to take you also. And if you get into trouble—fight!"

"Ay goin' tew rase hell," grinned Svenson, growling with delight as he swung the big club with which he had armed himself and tapped the hunting knife in his belt. "Don't Ay toll you dat Ay ben gude smart mans? Veil, by golly, das no yoke! Yust vatch may rase hell an' soak dem on da hed!"

"Not unless you can't possibly get away without a fight,

remember," warned Phil. "If it comes to a showdown, Miss Lawson,—if you are discovered—you are to slip out of sight into the woods immediately. And that means *immediately*, please. Don't wait for anything. Stiles and Svenson will hold them back long enough for you to reach a canoe. And for God's sake, get in and away as fast as you can go. You are the one on whom most depends, remember. You *must* get away without fail, no matter what happens to the rest of us.

"Jimmy, you are to stick with Svenson if there's a fight and help him all you can. In an emergency your help might just turn the whole trick. Get hold of a club as soon as you get down the hill. If we only had some more guns! There's only the two revolvers and Cork and I'll need those to put up a front. We'll join you as fast as possible if you get into trouble. Miss Lawson is an expert canoeist and the river is not difficult; so she'll be all right. Stick with Svenson, Jimmy."

Satisfied that all of them understood their parts, he told them to wait for his signal to creep down the hill, and turned to the side that faced the camp. The two men, carrying the torch and the white flag, had almost reached the foot of the hill by this time and as they showed no indication of halting, Kendrick stopped them with a sharp command.

"That's close enough!" he called in warning. "What do you want?"

"Red sent us over to find out what'n hell you fellas means by grabbin' off one o' our men."

"He's not one of your men," denied Phil.

"You're a liar!" cried the man who was carrying the flag. "He belongs to our party an' we want him back damn quick or we'll come an' take him. What're you holdin' him prisoner fer? You let him go, Mister, an' there won't be no more fuss about it."

"All right. If he wants to go back to the camp, he can go. Wait a minute and I'll ask him."

He made a pretense of doing so.

"Away you go now! Don't step on any loose stones. Good luck, Miss Lawson," was what he whispered.

The girl ran over to him and caught his hand.

"I think it's great of you, Mr. Kendrick," she murmured. "Good-bye, and good luck to you also," and with that she was gone; but he thrilled at the farewell pressure of her fingers.

"Hi, you, up there! We can't wait here all night."

"There seems to be a slight misunderstanding, old man," placated Phil. "He says he prefers to stay here. He says you kept him prisoner over there and didn't give him enough to eat."

"Aw, he's full o' *hooch*!" cried the spokesman with a loud guffaw. "He'll be gittin' a heluva lot less grub where he is. Say, are you guys goin' to be good sports or aincha? Red told me to invite the bunch over to camp fer a snort. C'm on over an' hev a drink on us an' cut out the shenanigans."

"Now, that sounds pretty decent of you," approved Phil. "Wait till I see what the rest say."

He ducked down again to find McCorquodale crossing from the opposite side of "The Saucer," where he had been keeping eyes and ears open for a surprise attack in case the white flag was but a treacherous ruse.

"Everythin' jake so far, 'bo," whispered he with elation. "They's down to level ground 'thout a peep—slick as a whistle."

"Good," breathed Phil. He climbed again into view. "Listen, boys. My friends say to thank you for the invite, but they aren't thirsty. Did you know that we had a spring of cold water up here?"

The fellow grew angry.

"If youse don't come youse'll be damn sorry, Mister. You've plugged a couple o' our fellas pretty bad an' y'aint goin' to git away with nothin' like that."

"Why, what will you do?"

"We'll damn soon show you, Mister. We've got you surrounded right now." Phil's heart sank; he had been hoping that the sound of an accordeon and singing at the camp meant that most of them were over there. "If we can't do no better, we'll starve youse out in a couple o' days."

"You can't do that," scoffed Phil. "We've got water right here and a big package of concentrated food tablets that will keep us going for weeks. Besides, let me tell you something you don't know. The rest of our Government survey party is due to join us here to-morrow morning, and I'd advise the whole bunch of you to clear out by sunrise or you'll regret it. You're breaking the law, firing at us the way you have."

"Yah! that bluff don't go, Mister."

"We have the law on our side," retorted Kendrick, "and we'll shoot to kill in self defense if you don't leave us strictly alone. We've got—"

He never finished that sentence; for rifle shots and hallooing off towards the river apprized the two anxious defenders of "The Saucer" that the worst had happened. Kendrick crossed to the opposite side in two bounds and found McCorquodale already on top of the rocks, reaching down for his leader's hand.

"We're in for it, old man," said Phil coolly. "Make straight for the trail. We've got to beat them to it."

McCorquodale only swore as he tightened his belt and for the second time they went down the hill in long jumps that sent loose stones crashing through the brushwood. Once on the level they ran for the sounds of trouble as fast as they could make headway through impeding undergrowth. They broke through at last into the tote road and ran at top speed down a straight stretch of it that was like a long aisle between the flanking trunks of spruce and hemlock. There was a sharp turn in the trail at the end of this aisle and judging by the glow of a fire that someone had lighted and the shouts of men in combat, it was just around the turn that the issue was being fought.

"Left, Cork—into the bush!" panted Phil as he heard a shout behind them.

They cut straight through for the bonfire, against the glow of which the tree-trunks began to stand out black. As they approached, Kendrick threw out his arm to stop the detective, and they dropped to the ground and crawled the remaining distance on hands and knees.

Against the firelight towered the black bulk of the giant Swede in the centre of a wild hand-to-hand fight against five of McIvor's men. They were attacking him from all sides at once, and if any of them had been armed with rifles they had thrown these aside in favor of knives and clubs. The fighting was too close for the use of firearms. A sixth man had got it on "da hed" before they had succeeded in knocking the club out of the Swede's hands; he lay, sprawled and still, near the edge of the woods. The sheath in which the sectionman had carried his hunting-knife swung empty as if the knife had been plucked out by one of his assailants; for he was defending himself only with feet and bare hands.

But it was all Svenson needed. He was putting up the fight of his life. It was a beautiful demonstration of Scandinavian defense methods—one man unarmed against five with knives and clubs! His huge arms were working like flails. His powerful, supple body bent and heaved this way and that with powerful sweeps as he met the incessant attack. As fast as they came at him he sent them hurling off their balance.

He seemed to have a defense for every kind of attack. As Kendrick and McCorquodale first got sight of him three of the gang were rushing him simultaneously. He knicked the knife spinning from one man's hand with his heavy hob-nailed boot, grabbed the fellow by the waist and tossed him backward over his head, grabbed a second one and whirled him across his hip clean into the bushes; number three he laid out with a knee in the stomach and an uppercut that must have broken his jaw. All this like lightning. Svenson was indeed proving himself "gude smart mans," and that was, in very truth, "no yoke." Svenson was making good his promise "tew rase hell."

"Oh boy! Oh *boy*!" McCorquodale kept muttering to himself, pausing an instant in amazed admiration.

One glance assured Kendrick that the girl was nowhere in sight. Evidently Cristy was carrying out instructions to the letter.

Stiles! Where was Stiles? Jimmy had "stuck," but he had gone under early. He lay prone in the foreground, his face ghastly with a smear of blood across the cheek. The fellow who had done it was still standing there, looking down at the inanimate form.

Distant shouts and the noise of reinforcements approaching through the timber announced the gravity of the situation. In another moment the whole crowd would be upon them.

"I eats this guy up, 'bo," whispered McCorquodale, pointing to Stiles' victor with his thumb, "'n'en I helps Swedie, see. You grabs Jimmy on your back an' beats it fer the canoes. The girl's away already an' Swedie an' me'll join you in a jiff an' the whole bunch of us vamooses, see. You grabs Stiles—"

Kendrick silenced him with a look and together they leaped into the fray. Phil knocked out the man standing beside Stiles with one blow on the head from the butt of his revolver. Shouting encouragement, McCorquodale went to the hard pressed Svenson's assistance—Iron Man McCorquodale, former near middleweight champion—and the light of battle was in his eye.

A man ran out of the bush, his yellow teeth bared in a snarl of rage. He wore a bandage across his forehead and came at Kendrick, levelling his rifle. Just as he pulled the trigger he tripped on a root and pitched full length into the open, the gun exploding harmlessly into the ground. Phil had him by the throat in an instant.

"Kom on! Kom on, by Yiminy!" bellowed Svenson exultantly

as he shook his tawny head and blew the blood from his mouth. "Yust took a look at may! Ay ben give you nodder bellyful, y'batcha!" He ducked low to avoid the vicious sweep of a heavy stick, grabbed the assailant by the ankles and swung him around his head as if the man had weighed but twenty pounds. Only two were left facing him now and they fell back before this terrible antagonist, swearing impotently.

McCorquodale had met a new arrival on the scene with a fierce uppercut that felled him like an ox and was slowly pressing a second arrival back into the bush with right and left swings to the face that landed so swift and sure that the fellow literally was blinded by the blows. It was Weiler, and the detective growled as he fought.

The tide of battle gradually was turning. So many of the enemy were down and out that it was beginning to look as if Kendrick and his friends would win through to the river if they could but keep up the terrific pace for a few minutes longer. This, however, was reckoning without the sudden reversion of the odds against them by the arrival of Red McIvor and two more men from the camp. They came running into sight around the turn in the tote road and McIvor was cursing like a wild man as he bore down on the struggle.

If the others had neglected the advantage which fire-arms gave them, not so Red McIvor. Within fifty paces he stopped short, dropped to his knee and deliberately raised his rifle.

"You—fools!" he yelled. "Clear away from them!"

He was aiming at the big Swede; but as Phil finished choking the halfbreed who had attacked him and sprang to his feet, McIvor swung his rifle.

Kendrick dropped in his tracks.

McCorquodale turned quickly at sound of the shot, just in time to see his leader go down. He fired from the hip and at the bark of his automatic Red McIvor pitched over sideways.

For a moment the two men beside him stood gazing down, awe-stricken and dismayed. Then they turned and ran as hard as they could go, back up the logging trail. It was the signal for the retreat of every member of the gang who could slip out of sight into the woods; but not before Svenson had gathered together every weapon they possessed.

With an oath McCorquodale started towards Kendrick; but he stopped when he saw Phil sitting up, grinning at him cheerfully. At the first move of McIvor's rifle in his direction he had thrown himself flat, disconcerting the man's aim.

The detective's bullet, however, had found its mark. Red McIvor lay sprawled grotesquely where he fell. A moment later McCorquodale looked up from his examination.

"Y' can't kill this bird with no thirty-two," he grinned. "He'll be around after a bit, cussin' a blue streak. The bullet bumped him on the bean an' glanced off like it was solid ivory. I slips the bracelets on him, see, an' we takes him along with us. I miss my guess if he aint wanted bad in 'bout every place he's been."

It was an odd procession which filed out on the riverbank twenty minutes later. First came Svenson, carrying across his great shoulder the still unconscious form of the bootlegger. Behind him walked Jimmy Stiles, supported by Kendrick. McCorquodale brought up the rear, loaded down with confiscated rifles.

They found Svenson's big canoe unharmed. The small canoe was gone from its place in the bushes beside the flat rock. In the soft earth at the water's edge they discovered a spare paddle stuck upright and to it was tied a bit of cambric, her handkerchief.

Phil struck a match and examined it carefully, making out a dim "O.K." which she had marked on it with a lead-pencil.

He heaved a breath of relief and smiled as he wrapped it carefully about a dollar bill and tucked it away in his card-case.

CHAPTER XXIV

THE RACE BEGINS

It was just a few minutes past eleven o'clock when Cristy Lawson climbed to the railroad track out of breath and hurried towards the section shanty. She had made good time in the canoe with the swift current of the Wolverine in her favor, and she was elated at her progress. The remaining stage of the journey should not present much difficulty, once she had persuaded Thorlakson of the urgency of her mission.

The place was in darkness and she tapped loudly on the window-pane of Mrs. Thorlakson's bedroom. After a little while she heard the woman stir and call out. Cristy shouted in to her and with many strange Icelandic expressions of astonishment Mrs. Thorlakson came to the door and let her in.

The kind-hearted woman's appearance in a flaming red canton-flannel nightgown, her hair comically "done up" for the night, was grotesque. But Cristy did not laugh. Instead, she asked for Thorlakson and cried out in dismay to learn that he was not there—that he had taken the handcar and had gone off with the two Norwegians to visit Bilodeau, the foreman on the section below.

Cristy poured out her story, at least as much of it as she

thought would convey the urgency of the situation; but it was rather difficult to make the woman grasp it, Mrs. Thorlakson's English being somewhat limited, while the girl had no knowledge whatever of Icelandic. At last she gave it up.

"May I have some biscuits or something from the pantry?" she asked, and at the woman's nod she rummaged around among crocks and pans in search of portable edibles. She stuffed a handful of stale doughnuts inside her shirtwaist, together with a lump of cheese.

Mrs. Thorlakson stood at the door with the lamp held high in one hand, peering in upon these operations in dumb wonderment. When she finally realized that the girl purposed setting off along the track on foot, she became loud in her protests. Cristy made out that she was anxious about the sprained ankle; but this was so entirely better that it had given her no trouble at all so far and she merely laughed away the good woman's fears and, with a hasty good-bye, ran out of the house and disappeared in the dark. For several minutes Mrs. Thorlakson continued to stand in the doorway, the lamp above her head, her face shining in the mellow glow with a queer mixture of apprehension and mystification. These city people were beyond her comprehension.

Cristy hesitated a moment as to which direction she should take. She knew that Indian Creek was west and she knew also that she and Kendrick had walked that eastern stretch of track for miles and miles. She turned west.

At first she ran, experiencing a thrill of satisfaction that her ankle seemed to be almost as good as it ever was. Lack of breath soon slackened her pace to a walk. There was a long trudge ahead of her before she could hope to reach the station above and the wisdom of conserving her energies was evident. She had no idea how far away the station might be—possibly a couple of miles; more likely many more. She had heard the foreman say his section was about nine miles long, but she was ignorant as to how much of it lay west of the shanty. She hoped devoutly that the station was not too far away. Time was precious. Time was everything.

The night had grown cloudy and dark. She could not see more than a few feet away; but that was nothing. All she had to do was to keep on walking as fast as she could until she got to the next station up the line. After that she merely had to sit down at a table in the station-agent's room and write up the whole story for her paper. The operator and the *Recorder* would do the rest. She would send a flash wire to notify Brennon, the night editor, what to expect and she would send a special message to McAllister that would send him jumping for the Chief of Police.

The *Recorder* was a morning paper. It did not go to press until about four a.m., and they could hold it beyond that hour if necessary. That part of it was all right if they could only get the police into action in time to catch the scoundrels who were plotting at Waring's house. If all went well she might expect to reach the wire by midnight. They would have her story in type in plenty of time if there was no wire trouble. That was a chance which she would have to take. It might be, of course, that Nickleby and Rives had acted already; but hardly likely, she thought.

She could not afford to fail. She MUST not fail! There was no use in trying to rake up obstacles until she came to them. All sorts of possibilities for failure at the Toronto end occurred to her; but she shut her lips tight together and thrust these doubts aside angrily.

Just then she tripped on a cross-tie, stumbled and fell. Her heart leaped in fright at thought of the ankle and she tested it anxiously; but it seemed all right. She would have to pay more attention to her feet. Here now she had gone and skinned the palm of her hand for nothing and lost two doughnuts out of her waist! There was comfort in the knowledge that there were no cattleguards to tumble into in this lonesome stretch of wild Algoma.

She hurried on, straining her eyes at the barrier of gloom that rose a few yards ahead. And out of it kept springing faint grotesque shapes that changed themselves slowly, resolving into dim rocks and bushes, telegraph poles and high embankments, finally melting away behind her and losing their identity in the gloom from which they came. But through it all, ever the same, the never-ending length of track undulated in slow measure beneath her feet. Overhead the sky was filled with drifting shadow hosts.

The night blackened. The heavens seemed to draw down upon her and fantastic ghost creatures of her disordered fancy crept hungrily in. The warm air hung heavy and still between the flanking forest walls and she might have been lost in some unreal world but for the rough insistence of the roadbed through the thin soles of her shoes.

She stopped. A loud rustle of the bushes a few feet away in the dark set her pulses beating foolishly. Some animal was there, she knew, and breaking into a run, she fled from the spot, halting only when her breath gave out. She found herself walking rapidly, agitated and alert, shuddering with a nameless fear that was getting on her nerves. She caught herself looking over her shoulder, haunted by the idea that she was being followed. There seemed to be stealthy, padded footfalls behind her in the enveloping darkness and numberless eyes that peered as she passed—small, glowing dots in pairs, close together, that were gone when she looked a second time. Was it only imagination or were the soft steps behind her increasing in number? She recalled stories of wolf packs that had tracked down human beings and had torn them to pieces! She stood still and listened. But there was nothing—nothing but blackness and infinite silence.

Very sharply she took herself to task. She must not become nonsensical like this. There had been noises in the underbrush the other night when she and he—"Rabbits," he had said. And who ever heard tell of a rabbit attacking a person? They were given big ears to hear well, so that they could use their long legs for running away from everything. The idea of her being afraid of a rabbit!

She laughed nervously. If only she had a revolver or some weapon. Off the track she was in an instant, groping about in the ballasting for a large stone. She found two and walked on more confidently, carrying one in each hand.

A fine drizzle began to fall intermittently. She hoped it would not rain hard, though after all, what difference did it make whether it did or not? She would be wet through anyway by the time she got there.

How much longer would that be? She must have come quite a distance now, and the thought cheered her. The ankle was beginning to give an occasional twinge and growing a little weak; in fact, it was feeling rather numb. Nothing to be alarmed about, she told herself. What else could she expect? It was sure to be hurting before she reached her destination.

Something struck her knee and she found that it was one of the doughnuts. She went on, munching the food she had brought along. The doughnuts were very dry. The cheese was hard, too; but it was old cheese that nipped the tongue, the kind she liked.

Time dragged. The girl plodded on painfully. There was no use in trying any longer to deceive herself into the belief that the injured ankle was holding out; it was not! She was hobbling now, as she had done the other night; but there was no strong arm to lean on now.

She would get there all right. That station could not be so very much farther on and she simply had to succeed. It was not that the "story" would be a feather in her own cap, nor yet was it the success of her paper which was at stake; not even the restoration of her father to his place in the financial world—not even that was the main result that hung in the balance. But the prevention of a great wrong, the meting out of rogues' deserts, the saving from suffering of the "everyday" people, thousands of them, to whom life meant little more than a grind for bread—these were the things that mattered; for chiefly upon these poor people whose all was entrusted to the keeping of the Interprovincial Loan and Savings would fall the disaster of the company's failure if it were forced to close its doors because of a swindle of trust funds.

Faces began to float about in the darkness—faces of careworn clerks; of factory workers, lined and lean; child faces with great gaunt eyes; old men, old women—she MUST not fail!

The fitful drizzle settled down steadily, blotting them out. The girl dropped the stones she had been carrying and struggled on bravely, fears lessened by discomfort. She was wet through and began to feel chilly, shuddering as she stumbled forward. Perhaps after all it might have been better to wait—but she cried aloud in anger at the thought. This had been the only way and she must do what she had set out to do. Time was everything. She wondered what time it was now. Surely the station could not be much farther away!

Her mind wandered back to this strong, broad shouldered young man who had shared with her all the strange experiences of the last few days. Three days? Four days? Was that all? It seemed as if she had known him for years. And he had had his arm around her the other night! She laughed, forgetful of everything else for the moment, in a funny sense of belated dismay.

He had been very good to her. And he was handsome. Above all, he was manly—a gentleman. She knew that now. Her woman's intuition told her he was a fine, splendid boy, sincere, brave. Now that she had come to know him, she realized that her former suspicions had been based upon a misunderstanding of the situation. He was not to be held responsible for the kind of man his uncle was. How quickly he had taken the right attitude when he found out the truth about the Honorable Milton Waring. He had urged her not to lose a minute, to get away without fail, even when he knew that her success meant a family disgrace which would be very bitter to bear. Oh, but he was a dear!

That kiss, the night of the fog? How angry she had been! Yet who was to blame for it? Hadn't she invited it? Hadn't she dared him to it? Phil would take no dare from anybody! She laughed softly as she thought of it all, her cheeks blush-burning in the dark.

Time passed. She halted suddenly, aware of a huge shadowy something directly opposite, looming out at her unexpectedly. With a cry of delight she recognized it as a water-tank; she could make out the spout overhanging the track, a stick of pallor in the darkness.

And the station? Eagerly she ran forward—then stopped again, perplexed. There ought to be lights of some sort; but where were they? A day station, maybe, with the operator asleep not far away. She would have to waken him. She did not think to look for switch-lights, and when she discerned the dark mass where the station stood she ran to it gladly and began pounding on the door.

The echoes resounded hollowly through the little building. They seemed strangely loud—with emptiness! She started for the nearest window and broken glass crunched beneath her feet.

Her sharp cry of consternation fell upon the unresponsive night and was swallowed up in blackness, solitude, dead heavy silence. The windows were full of broken panes!

Frantically she hobbled around to the side of the building, only to find the doors boarded up! The truth laid a cold hand upon her. This was one of those stations she had heard Phil tell about, built during construction of the road, but afterwards closed up as unnecessary in the depths of the wild country. Not even a flag station! Not even used by section men! Deserted, abandoned!

And there was no operator here!—nobody who could come to her assistance!

Cristy sank upon the rotting boards, trembling and sick at heart. Her long walk had been for nothing. She was still miles and miles and miles from the goal, with no possible chance of making the distance with an ankle which was swollen now and becoming very painful.

Wet and chilled through, miserable and dazed, she crouched in a huddle of fear. She was utterly alone, miles from help of any sort. The silence throbbed, it was so deep. She imagined faces again, grinning at her from the blackness—the leering faces of Nickleby and others; her father's, pleading; the working people's, the disappointed face of Philip Kendrick! The hour was late already and all the issues which hung at stake—?

"Oh, what can I do? Whatever can I do?" she sobbed.

But the night held no answer to her despair.

CHAPTER XXV

EVERY MAN FOR HIMSELF

The little sweet-toned French clock that stood on the mantel above the fireplace in the library chimed the half hour after midnight as the Honorable Milton Waring replenished the decanter and pried the cap from a fresh bottle of plain soda.

"Even if all the servants have been dismissed for the night, that is no reason why we can't have another little drink, gentlemen. J. C., old man, say 'when.' Help yourself to another cigar, Blatch."

As a host few could outshine the Honorable Milton in geniality, and there was little room in any man's system for pessimism in company with four glasses of the Honorable Milt's special brand of Kentucky Bourbon. J. Cuthbert Nickleby's manner was one of open enthusiasm. Elation possessed him. His laugh was frequent and boisterous. Any doubts he may have entertained at midnight that the deal was going through had been dispelled within the half hour during which the meeting had been in progress. Brazen as the whole thing was, its very boldness apparently had captured the imagination of Waring and Ferguson. Nickleby felt a huge satisfaction in his own perspicacity; he had not cultivated these two men during the past few months for nothing. He knew them and he was about to convert that knowledge into cash and bid them farewell.

It was a good time to be moving along. Nickleby had made money during the past year. His temporary control of the Interprovincial Loan & Savings Company had enabled him to manipulate to considerable personal advantage; but he was quite aware of the fact that his methods were liable to be questioned sooner or later, and the next annual meeting of the shareholders was not far away. Besides, the unexpected arrival of Harrington Rives on the scene and his very evident intention of getting on his feet by hanging on to Mr. Nickleby's coat-tails compelled a change of plans and the seeking of pastures new. Friend Rives knew too much and was himself too well known to be a safe companion in their present location. Rives and he could work together to mutual advantage, beyond doubt; but it would have to be in some new territory where the limelight had never played upon either of them in the past.

Accordingly when Nickleby discovered that Rives had some valuable mining concessions in Mexico, it had seemed very desirable for them to become partners and try their fortunes in a country where wealth awaited a pair of up-to-date filibusters like them and where political disturbances held forth untold opportunities for their peculiar abilities. To carry out their plans they needed all the capital they could scrape together. Hence the present proposal to unload all the Nickleby interests as quickly as possible for as much ready cash as might be.

The logical victim was the Honorable Milton Waring. Already Nickleby felt that his cultivation of the honorable gentleman had proceeded far enough to justify some boldness. He had succeeded in getting the Honorable Milt pretty well entangled in speculative investments and under his thumb by way of certain personal loans, protected by personal notes. In addition, there was the little flyer in real-estate which the Honorable Milton and his satellite, Blatchford Ferguson, had put through with Nickleby's assistance. That little transaction would cost the honorable gentleman his portfolio with the Government if it became known. So that, taking everything into consideration, Mr. Nickleby felt quite confident that he could persuade the Honorable Milton Waring and Blatchford Ferguson to fall in with the somewhat ambitious plans which President Nickleby had conceived for disposing of his stock in the Interprovincial Loan & Savings Company at a satisfactory figure.

These plans amounted practically to theft; but this was something which Nickleby would not admit, even to himself. He preferred to call it "high finance," "clever dealing," "sharp practice" perhaps. But he had no intention of overstepping the law. If, after he was safely away, trouble developed as a result of the situation which he left behind him, that would be the least of his worries. The "mismanagement" of his successors in the control of the loan company would be responsible, not J. Cuthbert Nickleby.

The old Abercrombie farm, outside the city limits, had been a happy discovery. The property really was a valuable one and before many years went by it was destined to rise in value rapidly as the city grew. The place had dropped into neglect of late and the old lady who had fallen heir to the estate was a non-resident. Rives had discovered that this spinster, Miss Patience Hollinsworth, was in her dotage and for a man of Rives' ability the rest had been easy. He had secured an option on the farm at a ridiculous price. Nickleby thereupon had had it subdivided into blocks and streets and building lots, and the beautiful new residential suburb of "River Glen" had appeared in blue print.

At the moment these very blueprints, mounted on beaver-board, were propped in convenient position about the library. On the Honorable Milton's desk reposed sundry legal documents pertaining to the transfer of the Abercrombie property and certain other papers awaiting signature.

"I've seen Fawkner, of Suburban Trolleys Ltd., and it will be a simple matter for them to extend their line as soon as you're ready to put 'River Glen' on the market," remarked Nickleby. "Properly advertised, gentlemen, that subdivision will net a clean half million. I'm getting quite excited about it myself and I only wish I was going to be on hand to handle it personally."

"I'm sure you do," commented Ferguson. "With things moving as they are at present, it ought to go, Milt."

"It looks good to me," was the Honorable Milton Waring's ready response.

"The proposition is certainly an exceptional one," went on Nickleby.

"Very exceptional," grinned Ferguson, running his hand up along the bald streak on top of his head. "So much so, J. C., that you've got to convince us that this 'control' of the Interprovincial you are to hand over to us is *bona fide* beyond question. We'd be in a fine mess if we lost out at the annual meeting, wouldn't we?"

"Yes, that is important, J. C.," nodded Waring. "You might just go into that end of it a little more fully. Why not begin at the beginning and tell us exactly how you got yourself elected President and how you propose to cover up?"

And with an easy laugh, Mr. Nickleby did so. Because when

one is talking to "friends" whom one has under thumb and who are about to shoulder heavy responsibilities one can afford to talk freely; because, also, whisky loosens the tongue and enables one to vizualize a flock of poultry out of a basket of eggs! Then, too, there is inspiration in nods of approval and expressions of admiration, and both Honorable Milton Waring and Mr. Blatchford Ferguson were prodigal of these as the recital progressed.

Certainly it was an amazing confession. With considerable gusto did J. Cuthbert Nickleby explain the various moves by which he had dethroned the Lawson interests and usurped control of the Interprovincial Loan & Savings Company. The quiet gathering together of proxies, the appointment of dummy directors, the "purchase" of others, the "personal loans" which silenced others still, the failure of "Old Nat" to produce his authority for voting the Bradford block of stock—all of these factors Mr. Nickleby set forth with a lucidity and frankness which aimed to convince his two auditors that when they and their associates assumed "control" it would be absolute, with no possibility of failure in swinging the annual meeting to suit themselves.

"By heaven, Nickleby, you're a wizard!" cried Ferguson at last, unable longer to restrain his enthusiasm. "You've got the situation tied up in a pretty knot and no mistake. Hasn't he, Milt? Take it from me, J. C., if you'd been cruising the high seas in the days of Captain Kidd, you'd have given him a run for his money! Some buccaneer, believe me!" and he went off into a peal of laughter born of sheer admiration.

"Quit your kidding, Blatch," grinned Mr. Nickleby modestly as he reached for the decanter, quite unconscious of the pun. "But I hope you're now convinced that this proposition is feasible and quite in order."

"I don't know about that," objected the Honorable Milton slowly. "It's clear enough that you've got things in your own hands just now, J. C., and can shove through this deal O.K. But your whole control rests upon the fact that the Bradford stock is side-tracked. Supposing Nat Lawson locates that missing power-of-attorney? What then?"

"I give you my word that he can't do it," chuckled Nickleby.

"That's all very well. But supposing he does? How do you know he can't?"

"Because I do." Nickleby set down his glass triumphantly. "I don't mind letting you into a little secret, gentlemen. That power-of-attorney has been destroyed."

"Are you sure?" gasped Ferguson.

"I ought to be. I burned it myself!"

"No! You're stuffing us, J. C. You may be clever; but you're not as clever as that! Say, will you swear to that?"

"Here's a bible, Blatch. Make him swear to it and the deal's on." The Honorable Milton handed a small bible across the desk as he spoke. "If that's the situation, I guess it's safe to go ahead."

"You son-of-a-gun!" cried Ferguson, when Nickleby had duly taken his oath. "I don't mind admitting that when I first heard your proposition I thought it was impossible to get away with it. You buy a farm, turn it into a subdivision, hand it over to us, then we hand it back to you as collateral for a loan of $250,000, with which we purchase from you the subdivision and all your stock in the company, which gives us control of the transaction—Phew! give me air!"

"You understand, Nickleby, that we've got to be mighty careful how this thing is handled," said Waring gravely. "It's taking chances."

"'Nothing venture, nothing win,'" quoted Nickleby. "But I'll cover it up. Leave that to me."

"Lawson has a lot of friends, remember. There's Ben Wade, for instance—"

"You needn't worry about him, Milt. He hasn't been able to get together more than thirty per cent. of the votes."

"And there's Timothy Drexel—He's a director, isn't he?"

"That old fool! Yes, he's a director; but he's putty! Hand him some taffy and you can pat him into any shape you like. You should have heard his speech when he nominated me for president last year," and Nickleby laughed heartily at the recollection.

The Honorable Milton Waring got up and began to pace the room. It was evident that there were certain aspects of the deal which disturbed him.

"If my connection with this thing ever got out, Blatch," he said, pausing in front of the lawyer, "it would mean—the finish!"

"Oh, hang the political end of it, Milt!" exclaimed Ferguson impatiently. "Between us, J. C. and I will see that you are protected legally. And anyway, what's the use of being in politics if you don't get a share of the loaves and fishes while you've got the chance? All politicians are supposed by the public to be feathering their own nests, and you might as well feather yours when you've got to come under the accusation anyway. It's all in the game. If you've got the sponduliks you can do anything these days. It's every man for himself and the devil take the hindmost!"

"There's a lot of truth in what you say, Blatch. Well, let's get down to business and get it over with," sighed the Honorable Milton Waring.

Abruptly he sat down at his desk and reached for the papers.

CHAPTER XXVI

NIP AND TUCK

Engine No. 810 was running free through the night with a big string of box-cars and gondolas tossing along behind her, dim shadows in the dark. Her powerful electric headlight threw a beam, long and bright, that burrowed into the black void far in front. But for this and the few red-glowing chinks in her firebox and the thunder of the wheels, the freight might have been some phantom reptile rushing through the land with two red eyes in its tail.

Evans, the fireman, kicked impatiently at the slash-bar and hooked the fire. The lurid glare from the white fires that curled and writhed under the crown-sheet flung wide upon flying right-of-way and the woods on either side, and played with the swirling ribbon of steam that was hissing back from the dome. Bathed in the blinding light, the fireman stood for a space, swinging his scoop with pendulum precision from fire-box to coal-tank and back again; then the whole scene went out suddenly.

Engineer Macdonald, leaning out over his armrest, chafed at the delay as he choked her head for the Spruce Valley grade. The line was clear as far as Indian Creek; but up there somewhere they would have to take the siding for the first section of the Limited, eastbound.

With a glance at the indicator and the guages, the fireman jerked a blackened thumb over his shoulder towards the coal-tank. Macdonald shook his head.

"We'll fill her at Number Seven," he shouted.

They were bearing down upon the switch lights opposite Thorlakson. But Macdonald was in a hurry and too anxious to take advantage of the grade to stop for water there. The few scattered lights flicked by and they were off again into the blackness ahead.

On the time-card No. 7 was a "blind" water tank farther on up the line, the loneliest tank on the division. The surrounding country was wild and uninhabited save for the isolated groups of loyal track-men who stuck to their lonely but important posts during the blizzard months with the same persistence that carried them through the fly season. Engine 810 would take water there.

Fifteen minutes' run and Macdonald drew in his head, shut off steam, opened the sander, threw the brakeshoes against the drivers and brought everything to a shuddering standstill with the pilot slipping just past the tank, while his fireman was scrambling back amongst the coal to haul down the overhanging spout. And all of this was quite within the prosaics of the night's work.

What immediately followed was not. There was nothing in the locality to prepare them for it, while the hour was late and the night damp and disagreeable—nothing to account for the flying figure of a girl dashing wildly up the headlight's path, straight for the engine, arms waving frantic signals.

The engineer's wondering profanity scarcely had begun to flow freely before she was on top of them. Panting, wild-eyed, hair in riotous disorder, this beautiful young woman climbed up into the cab with the agility of an overpowering excitement, pouring out upon the astonished enginemen a wonderful stream of incoherent "explanations."

Evans, who never before had seen a girl on the verge of hysteria, swore deep and long under his breath, staring as if in a trance. He came to himself only when the water overflowed the manhole, and he let go of the spout with a carelessness that earned him a wetting as it lifted, dripping, back into place.

No sooner had the girl set foot on the deck than she clambered into the head brakeman's seat, nestling in alongside the boiler-head as far forward as she could get, her feet on the fireman's lunch-pail, her knees drawn up in clasped fingers and her eyes looking straight ahead out of the narrow cab window. That it might be against the rules of the road for strangers to ride on an engine apparently had not occurred to her, for she seemed to take it for granted that she was entirely welcome as long as she did not get in their way.

The fireman stared across at Macdonald and surreptitiously tapped his forehead; the engineer stared back at Evans and winked knowingly. The whole thing had taken but a few moments. A light was swinging out from the top of the cars at the rear and Macdonald opened the throttle. They were moving ahead before either of the two men could think of anything but several variations of the word "damn."

In this manner did Miss Cristy Lawson come to take her first ride on an engine. The night had been crowded with nerve-wracking excitement; but in the elation which she experienced over this unexpected way out of her difficulty, she felt renewed strength and confidence that surely would see her through. Half an hour ago she had been lost in a welter of despair; but she was all right now. Everything was all right now. The story would get through yet; nothing could stop it now. And, protected by the roar of the wheels, she cried a little in relief.

Just a moment of this, however. She was not ordinarily the crying kind. The furnace glare presently filled the whole cab as the fireman shovelled in more coal, and the novelty of her surroundings pressed upon her to the temporary exclusion of everything else.

Wasn't the din something awful? She had no idea that a locomotive was such a noisy place. She soon found herself getting more used to it and watched the engineer with wonder and interest. Her idea of an engineer, she found, had been formed by the illustrations in the magazines; she had pictured him in her mind as a man who sat with hand constantly on the throttle or the levers or whatever it was, bent far forward, peering keenly and steadily from beneath the visor of his greasy cap with eyes riveted unswervingly on every yard of track ahead. She was surprised, therefore, to find that this engineer seemed almost careless of attitude, leaning back in his cushioned seat, body jogging loosely to the motions of the great machine. It was only occasionally that he seemed to arouse enough interest to lean out of the window, and scarcely ever did he touch the levers in front of him. Once he actually got down from his seat and came over to the fireman's side to shout something in that grimy individual's ear, and all the while they were thundering along without any lessening of speed. What if something should appear suddenly on the track in front of them? Her heart leaped at the thought. She was sure he could not get back in time to stop, and it was all very surprising to her.

Curiously her eyes roved over all the levers and queer instruments. Certainly an engineer must have to carry a terrible lot in his head to know how to manage them. There was a little knob, for instance; if she were to give it a pull, something would happen somewhere, an explosion perhaps,—dear knows what! She watched the hand of the indicator on the boilerhead fluttering around the figure 190. She studied the liquid in the glass tubes. A little apparatus, too, that looked like a small whistle. Was it a whistle and when did they blow it? Steam was bubbling out of a joint in a pipe right at her side; the hot water dribbled on her dress once when she leaned too far over and she caught the fireman grinning at her.

She laughed light-heartedly, taking a child-like joy out of this new and thrilling experience. She could not help marvelling at the unconcern with which these men attended to their work; they were perfectly at home on this rolling engine.

Didn't it rock and jerk about, though? It was enough to tear out the rails almost, it seemed to her, and her pulses quickened at the thought that if anything should break! But it did not seem to, somehow.

The fireman's gloved hand seized the chain on the feed-door again and jerked it open. She watched him toiling with his scoop, the white glare beating upon the rugged lines of his face till it was a wonder he could stand that fierce heat. There was a funny black smudge running across his nose, and when he bent his back she saw that a buckle was missing from his overalls and he had substituted a piece of coarse twine. Was he married? If he was, why didn't his wife look after those buckles? He worked hard enough to deserve to have little things like that looked after for him. Why, she'd heard they even shovelled as much as a whole ton of coal on a single trip!

The lurch of the engine as they swung around a curve drew her attention to the track which was sweeping in upon them with dizzy continuity. Out there, ahead of the big black body of the locomotive, the funneled path of the headlight streamed away into the unknown. Far up the track the white mile-boards on the poles caught it, ran toward them, flashed at them and skipped out of sight behind. Tall weeds nodded in it as they swept past. It poured out along the wet rails, which glistened in the bright bath and let go only when the beam plunged away at a curve and went exploring in the woods or rioted across a valley into panorama on the other side.

Once a little rabbit sat in the middle of the track, staring the great light in the eye with a fascination that threatened its life. The tiny creature seemed to be paralyzed by the glare and they almost ran it down before it tore away in sudden fright and its cotton-white tuft vanished in the long grass.

But as the novelty of all this wore off, her mind reverted to the thing that she was trying to do. The speeding engine, the flying track, became merely the accessories which were carrying her nearer and nearer her goal—a telegraph operator.

The fireman's watch hung on a hook alongside and the hands showed twenty-five minutes past midnight. It was standard time both here and in Toronto; so that would be the time at the *Recorder* office also—12.25 a.m. They would be well into the rush of the night's work by now. The boys would be in from assignments and pounding out "copy" in the city room. The wires would be warming up and the "flimsy" arriving at the telegraph editor's desk in bunches, and old man Jeffreys would be reaching in the left bottom drawer of his scarred old desk for his little package of bread and cheese with an apple or a banana to top it off; he always ate that twenty-five minutes after midnight, just before the linotype men and the rest of the composing-room staff, who ate at the all-night restaurant around the corner, straggled back to their work.

Cristy began to go over the things she must do and to arrange them in the order she must do them. The very first thing would be the messages to McAllister and Brennan; there must be no delay in getting the police into action. If they could surprise their quarry over at Waring's house on the Island—catch them in the middle of it—it would provide a dramatic climax to the sensational story. She could trust her editor not to overlook any such opportunity and her eyes sparkled as she pictured the uproar that would follow those messages in the *Recorder* office. The old place would be buzzing and the whole staff on the jump like a bunch of excited kids!

Impatiently she peered out ahead, looked for lights down the track, glanced continually at the hands of the watch. She ran hastily over the strong features of the sensation, marshalling her facts, getting the general scheme of the story into her head in proper newspaper style and planning a strong "lead."

She became so engrossed in this that not until a vibrant shudder passed through the engine did she notice. The engineer was leaning out the window on his side of the cab, one hand on a lever. She threw a quick glance out the narrow window in front of her and saw that they were bowling down a straight stretch of track and that far ahead in the darkness were little specks of light.

A station! It must be the station at last!

Anxiously she watched the far-away dots arrange themselves

Hopkins Moorhouse

slowly into switch lights beside the track. The larger lights on the right—those would be station windows. Another light, a red one—the order board was out against them and the train would have to stop!

She cried out in her excitement and satisfaction. She felt like opening the narrow window, rushing out along the running-board to the front of the engine and cheering!

They were beginning to slow up now. A man came out and stood on the platform, some papers in his hand. She could see him quite plainly in his shirtsleeves in the glare of the powerful headlight. That must be the night operator—the Mecca of all her hopes.

The hands of the fireman's watch indicated 12.30.

They rolled in beside the platform and the long string of freight cars bumped, groaned, squeaked and stopped. A lantern came bobbing along the tops of the cars from the rear. The conductor dropped off the caboose and jogged forward beside his train.

Macdonald drew in his head and looked across the cab. But the seat was empty. The girl had slipped away already and presently he caught sight of her, disappearing into the station.

CHAPTER XXVII

CLOSE QUARTERS

Brennan, Night Editor of the *Recorder*, scribbled a two-column head, folded it in with a sheet of "flimsy," dropped it into the dumb-waiter box and yanked the string that shot it aloft to the composing room. He reached for his long scissors, snipped off a fresh piece of the typewritten C.A.P. report, fastened it with a daub of paste to a sheet of copy paper and marked it for a single-column "box," Page 1. The whistle blew in the speaking-tube at his elbow and he answered the foreman's question while scribbling his initials to the slip which a newly arrived messenger boy from one of the telegraph companies was holding flat for him.

"'Phone, Bren," called Chic White, Sporting Editor.

Brennan took down the receiver as a reporter laid a wad of new "copy" on the desk and hurried out again. Then Brennan opened a drawer in his desk and took another bite out of a ham sandwich before tearing the envelopes from the newly arrived telegrams.

Up until now things had been very quiet all evening, so quiet that the lay-out of a decent front page was a problem. The Chief had gone home early to-night and had paused on his way out to ask Brennan how the news was breaking and instruct him to "boil everything down." If there was anything that McAllister detested it was a thirty-six point head on a twelve-point item.

"Kerr! Jackson! Brock!"

Every typewriter in the city room stopped clacking and the three reporters jumped. They crowded together in the doorway as Brennan snapped his instructions.

"Get the Chief on the 'phone and hold him for me, Jackson. Here, Brock, sit in at the desk and keep everything down to a couple of sticks. Call a taxi, Kerr."

He glanced at his watch as he made for the stairs. It was ten minutes to 1 a.m. Up in the composing-room he went over the forms with the foreman, asking questions, "killing" perfectly good "stories" with rapid decision, clearing space for the biggest "scoop" which the *Recorder* had achieved in many months.

"Chief's not home and they don't know where he is," came Jackson's anxious voice through the speaking tube.

"Find him! Find him!" cried Brennan impatiently. "Try the National Club. Use your head, Jackson!"

But when Brennan hurried downstairs a few minutes later McAllister had not been located yet.

"He went out somewhere with Wade, of the C.L.S., and left no word at the house as to when he'd be back," explained Jackson.

"Call up Wade, then."

"I did, but he's out too, and nobody seems to know where."

Brennan swore.

"Get me Nat Lawson on the 'phone. Say, Chic, where's Pardeau? What? Not back from that assignment? Then see if you can find him for me. The rest of you chop your stuff. Cristy Lawson owns the front page!"

Briefly he answered their eager questions, then turned to listen to Jackson, talking to the Lawson residence. Apparently Nathaniel Lawson was not at home either.

Brennan fiddled with the stem of his watch for a moment. He was in a quandary. He had been taken into McAllister's confidence, of course, regarding this graft exposure story which had been nursed along so carefully. The cuts to illustrate it were locked up in McAllister's desk, he knew. It was unlike the Chief to leave no word of his whereabouts. That it should happen on this of all nights! No doubt they'd locate him after a bit; but in the meantime—? It was nearly one o'clock and Cristy Lawson's wire brooked no delay.

There was only one thing to do—go ahead on his own initiative. Brennan went into McAllister's private office and closed the door while he talked to the Chief of Police on the private line. He came out hurriedly, called Kerr, and went down in the elevator to the waiting taxi. Next to Pardeau, Kerr was the fastest shorthand man on the staff.

They stopped at the Central Police Station to pick up a couple of plainclothes men who were waiting for them and the taxi sped through the almost deserted streets at breakneck pace, heading for the waterfront.

A few minutes later the harbor police launch was streaking

across the quiet waters of the bay. It threw a wake that curled and widened, and in it danced the broken reflections of the harbor lights.

The Honorable Milton Waring ushered them into the library with a smile. He was quite calm as he cleared away the blueprints and invited them to find seats.

"You are just in time, gentlemen, to witness the end of the comedy," and he pressed a button beneath the edge of his desk as he spoke. "Pass around the cigars, Blatch, like a good fellow—Well, upon my word!"

"Arrest that man!" cried Ferguson, springing after J. Cuthbert Nickleby, who had made a dash towards the French doors which opened on the verandah.

"It's all right, sir. I've got him," assured one of the detectives who was waiting without for some such move. As he came through the doorway the click of the handcuffs was quite audible to the startled group within the room.

"What's the meaning of this, Waring?" shouted Nickleby, his face distorted with rage. "Are you trying to frame something on me? Take off these bracelets, damn you!"

"I'd advise you to sit down, Nickleby, and keep quiet. You are under arrest and you'll know all about it in a few minutes. Ah, good evening, gentlemen, I'm afraid there aren't chairs enough to go around; but make yourselves at home please."

From the hallway they filed into the library—McAllister, of the *Recorder*; President Wade, of the Canadian Lake Shores Railway; Nathaniel Lawson, ex-president of the Inter-provincial Loan & Savings Company; Timothy Drexel and another director of the same concern. Detective Sainsbury from Headquarters and Parsons, official court stenographer, brought up the rear with Pardeau, star reporter for the *Recorder*. Their faces were serious and their entry partook of the solemnity of a jury bringing a verdict into court.

A brief whispered colloquy with his editor quickly smoothed the perplexity from Brennan's face. McAllister had picked up Pardeau on the street and had sent a belated message to the office. It was a big "story" that was breaking and he ordered Brennan and Pardeau back to their desks with instructions to hold the galleys till he arrived shortly. Kerr could handle the present end of it. He waved his hand impatiently and focussed his undivided attention upon what was transpiring.

A silence had fallen upon the crowded room and as the Honorable Milton Waring allowed his gaze to rove upon their tense, expectant faces he smiled reassuringly. He began with an explanation of the circumstances leading up to the present situation. It was not merely to adjust Interprovincial Loan Company affairs by the exposure of its official head that he had brought them together. His integrity as a public servant had been questioned and there were certain features that in the interests of clean government required official enquiry. He was prepared to move for the appointment of a royal commission to investigate and report upon conditions vitally affecting financial institutions, election laws and other matters. It was something with which he had concerned himself seriously for several years, and it was partly to prove his theories in this connection that with the assistance of Mr. Blatchford Ferguson he had taken advantage of the situation which had developed in the affairs of the Interprovincial. As a result of their investigations they stood prepared to prove gross mismanagement, falsification of the returns required by the Federal authorities, misuse of trust funds for private ends, attempted corruption of government officials, et cetera.

The Honorable Milton was frank in his admission that during the recent orgy of speculation into which the discovery of new mineral wealth had led the public, he had become personally involved. He was only human and the general excitement had induced him to make several disastrous investments which had left his personal affairs in a precarious tangle for a time. But it was an ill wind that blew nobody good. The financial crisis through which he had passed had brought him in touch with J. C. Nickleby, and it was not long before his eyes had been opened to the unscrupulous methods that were being followed by the president of the Interprovincial Loan & Savings Company. He had called in his learned friend, Mr. Ferguson, and as a result of their consultations it had been decided to make a few experiments in high finance with the object of uncovering the whole system.

To this end they deliberately had cultivated Nickleby's confidence. It was apparent from the first that the man was utterly devoid of common honesty. It was his idea that government graft was an established method of revenue and he seemed to be obsessed with the belief that no Minister of the Crown would allow his oath of office to interfere with the acquisition of personal wealth. As their relations had ripened he had grown bolder and had organized a construction company with the object of using his "connection" to swing certain tenders for public works into the graft column. Nickleby had felt so sure of himself by this time that he even had proposed a contribution of $50,000 to the party campaign funds in return for "privileges." He had been told quite plainly that he would make such a contribution at his own risk. Nevertheless he had gone ahead with it on his own initiative. The money had mysteriously disappeared between the office of the construction company and its destination; it had never reached the party exchequer.

Which brought the Honorable Milton Waring to the point of paying high compliment to the editor of the *Recorder*. He bowed to McAllister. He had never before quite realized, he said, what a debt all lovers of clean government owed to the press. No man with designs upon the public treasury could go very far without some journalistic watch-dog being on his trail, and it was so in the present instance.

The Alderson Construction Company had aroused the suspicions of Mr. McAllister shortly after it became active. In some way he had learned of the proposed campaign fund contribution and, as it turned out, it was due to the zeal of a *Recorder* reporter that Nickleby's contribution had been intercepted and photographed. It had then fallen into the hands of Mr. Benjamin Wade by accident and Mr. Wade had deposited the $50,000 in trust, pending proof of ownership.

A few days ago Mr. Wade had come to him with these facts and also to warn him that the *Recorder* was preparing to accuse him of being implicated with Nickleby and Blatchford Ferguson in a certain doubtful real-estate transaction. Not until then had he realized the risk which Mr. Ferguson and he had assumed in attempting to follow their own line of investigation in secret. The possibility that the hunter might in turn be hunted—and quite legitimately hunted on the face of it—had not occurred to them. They had taken Mr. McAllister into their confidence as soon as they realized the extent of his knowledge, and only his patience and co-operation had enabled them to carry their investigations to fruition.

The real-estate transaction in question had been planned by Mr. Ferguson for the purpose of quieting suspicion in the mind of Nickleby. It was a case of fighting the devil with fire; for had Nickleby not believed that he was dealing with men who were as greedy as himself they would never have succeeded in uncovering the evidence they were after.

As part of their plan, therefore, they had gone to Nickleby with the proposal that the three of them—Nickleby, Ferguson and himself—form a little syndicate on the quiet to buy up a tract of land on which the Government had its eye as a prospective location for the new Deaf & Dumb Institute. The land had a market value of $100,000 and this sum the Government was quite ready to pay. Nickleby had advanced the loan to negotiate the deal and Ferguson had bought up the land in small lots at sacrifice prices from individual owners for a total of $50,000. The Honorable Milton had told Nickleby that he was acting for the Government; but the cheque with which he had "purchased" the land from the syndicate of three had been his personal cheque. The amount was $200,000. The syndicate's profit, therefore, was $150,000 and this sum they had divided in three, $50,000 each. But Nickleby did not know—nor McAllister, either—that the whole thing had been juggled for a purpose, with the sanction of the Attorney General, and that the "profits" which had gone to Mr. Ferguson and himself had been thrown back into the deal when the site had been turned over to the Government, which therefore obtained the land at its legitimate market value, $100,000.

No doubt the whole thing had been indiscreet; but by this time both Ferguson and himself had got so interested in the little game they were playing with the salvation of the loan company as the stakes that they had overlooked the surface appearances. The discovery that every move they had made had been watched by the lynx-eyed McAllister had instilled in them a profound respect.

To bring things to a head and to justify their actions Ferguson and he had undertaken to prove their case against Nickleby by exposing him and his methods to the gentlemen who had last entered the room. These gentlemen had been placed where they could listen to the evidence for themselves and, to make doubly sure, a dictaphone had been installed and an official court stenographer had taken down the whole thing. It was almost incredible that a criminal of this man's type had been able to engineer himself into a place of trust in an institution of such influence as the Interprovincial Loan & Savings Company, to play fast and loose with its credit as he had done, and to bamboozle its directorate. The fact that he had been made to convict himself must plead excuse for the subterfuge in which they had been forced to indulge. It had been a most disagreeable experience and the Honorable Milton Waring was glad that it was over.

"I have only this to say, further, gentlemen," he concluded. "It is no sinecure to hold public office and administer a public trust and I am moved to protest most earnestly against the public tendency to discredit politics and the men who are devoting their energies—frequently at great personal inconvenience and loss—to the government of the country. There are those who cannot seem to admit that it is possible for a man to enter the political arena and remain as honest and sincere in public life as he has been as a private citizen. Such a condition of the public mind is to be deplored, even as the past events upon which the condition is based are to be deplored. If the people look upon government as a joke, the joke is on them; for their government is what they make of it or permit it to be.

"It is my belief that below all government, like the sure-rock foundation of a worth-while edifice, must lie the spirit of fair dealing and a law-abiding citizenship. Let the people determine that corruption in politics will spell political ruin instead of personal aggrandizement and see how swiftly every political yacht will trim its sails. The cry that politics are so rotten that the men who count most in their

communities will have nothing to do with active participation in government will then cease and we will have
genuine public service.

"I did not intend to make a political speech; but many times
of late I have felt like resigning. As long as party success and
corporation support dictate our political standards, so long
will we have men like Nickleby there attempting corruption,
so long will political leadership be forced to dance for its
balance upon shifting platforms.

"I thank you, gentlemen, for your attention. The facts I have
given you can be substantiated readily by Mr. Ferguson, Mr.
Wade and Mr. McAllister; but no doubt the demonstration of
the attempt to misuse the loan company's funds to the extent
of a quarter of a million dollars—the interview that has taken
place in this room tonight—is sufficiently conclusive in
itself."

"Conclusive?" piped old Timothy Drexel, unable longer to
contain himself. He elbowed his way towards the prisoner
and shook a bony finger in front of his nose. "You miserable
scoundrel!" he exploded. "Old fool, eh? Putty, eh? You hand
me taffy and pat me into any shape you like, eh? You
confounded thief! You—you—!"

"Aw, you shut up!" snarled Nickleby, who had sat through it
all with that cynical sneer of his. He knew when he was
beaten. With no further word he followed the detectives from
the room.

They crowded about the Honorable Milton Waring and
Blatchford Ferguson with congratulations. Nathaniel Lawson
could not say much; but his grip was tight when he shook
hands and his gratitude was evident. McAllister was not
given to expressions of sentiment, but as he bade adieu there

was an unaccustomed enthusiasm in his keen eyes. His editorial in the morning paper would be strong, very strong; he would call it "The Mantle of Disraeli," or something like that.

Ben Wade stood to one side, watching them take their leave, and his tanned face was alight with satisfaction. There would be a tremendous sensation when the *Recorder* came out. It would be a bully spread—not one of graft charges, as originally planned by Mac, but even a better story of the fight which an honest politician had been forced to put up in order to remain honest, of the Honorable Milt's investigations and his announcement regarding a royal commission to probe conditions, the escape of the Interprovincial from the criminal activities of its president, the dramatic arrest of Nickleby, the work of Cristy Lawson. Trust Mac not to miss any of it.

And Ben Wade, whose faith in the Honorable Milton Waring had remained unshaken when things looked blackest, smiled as he watched. His advice to McAllister, his faith in Waring, had been vindicated; but he was not thinking of this. He was thinking of another's steadfast faith that had been sorely tried. It would be a happy morrow for Dolly Waring.

"So long, Milt," he said heartily. "We're proud of you, old man."

CHAPTER XXVIII

SOUVENIRS

Because the world is such a very big place and there are so many people busy with so many different things, life goes on as usual with little time for more than a brief pause of wonder at the experiences of others. The metal which casts the page of to-day's events goes back into the melting-pot of the stereotyper to appear to-morrow with new announcements.

During the weeks that followed the *Recorder's* sensation routine resumed its sway and only among those directly concerned did memory linger. There was a very lively meeting of irate shareholders in the offices of the Interprovincial Loan & Savings Company and a unanimous demand for the return of Nathaniel Lawson to the government of its affairs. Upon Old Nat's recommendation the new secretary appointed was a reliable and loyal young man by the name of James Stiles.

Nickleby's attempt to secure bail was unsuccessful, and while awaiting trial upon several charges he had plenty of time to philosophize. Thanks to the work of Bob Cranston, Chief of the Special Service Department of the Canadian Lake Shores Railway, Nickleby's past record stood revealed and there was talk of extradition.

After a conference between Wade and the Honorable Milton Waring it was decided to prefer no charges against Harrington Rives, who pleaded to be allowed to carry out his plan of going to Mexico to look after his interests there. He departed for the south, where he could bestride a burro and lose himself among the Mexican hills.

Ben Wade had nodded his approval. Rives had learned his lesson and was not fool enough to come back. Knowing the calibre of the man, he had regarded Rives as a dangerous breeder of mischief and when Mrs. Waring had confided her fears that the Honorable Milton was in difficulties, Wade had been afraid that Rives would seek some revenge on his old-time enemy through Aunt Dolly. That he was preparing for something of the kind in sending Weiler to Sparrow Lake was apparent. Placing McCorquodale at the summer resort had seemed a Quixotic thing to do; but Benjamin Wade was not given to over-looking bets. He was glad to see the last of Rives.

And McCorquodale? The "Iron Man" had scored official notice when he brought the notorious "Red" McIvor to trial. He had had several flattering offers as a result of it; but all of these he had refused at the request of President Wade. Bob Cranston had decided to accept a place with another railroad, and McCorquodale took over his duties as Chief of the Special Service Department for the C. L. S.

Another promotion that took place about the same time affected a "gude smart mans," named Svenson, who became foreman of an important section of the line, with a shanty of his own and six-foot Olga Olafson as his brand new bride. The couple went on a wonderful honeymoon trip to Niagara Falls, all expenses paid by President Wade no less, and when they got back to their new home they found certain bulky packages and boxes piled on the big deal table that Svenson had made. Cristy Lawson's gift was a complete set of beautiful dishes and a bolt or two of dress goods and curtain material; there was a brand new, latest model repeating rifle from Phil and a gold watch, monogramed; McCorquodale sent a case of assorted tobaccos and a fine hunting-knife in a leather sheath, while from Jimmy Stiles came a big box of groceries. When everything lay open before them Mr. and Mrs. Svenson stared at the array, speechless.

"Yumpin' Yudas!" yelled the big fellow at last. He grabbed his six-foot smiling wife and kissed her with a loud smack.

The selection of these gifts had been the outcome of many consultations between Mr. Philip Kendrick and Miss Cristy Lawson. It was surprising how much serious thought was necessary in order to decide on the weight and pattern of a set of dishes or the color scheme of window drapes. Almost every evening in the week Kendrick had found it necessary to go up to the Lawson home to discuss something or other and they had gone shopping together for two whole afternoons—excursions which had extended to motor spins into the country and dinners down town and so on. And when the Svenson wedding presents no longer furnished excuses, for the very good reason that they had been shipped to their destination, there was always something else that needed consultation, such as President Wade's flattering offer to Phil to join the executive of the Canadian Lake Shores Railway or the very exceptional investment opportunity that presented itself in connection with a certain choice suburban villa with a wonderful lake frontage.

It was surprising, too, the way the gasoline consumption of the Waring motor launch increased. The Honorable Milton even took occasion to mention the matter to Aunt Dolly in Phil's presence at dinner one night; he thought there must be something wrong with the engine, but there was a twinkle in his eye that betrayed him.

"Here's a clipping that I got to-day from Billy Thorpe," said Phil, quite irrelevantly. "It's from the North Bay paper and concerns our friend, Hughey Podmore."

He read it aloud. It cited the particulars of a strange case which had reached the hospital at North Bay some weeks ago—a man who had been found wandering in the woods with bits of what appeared to be bank-notes sticking to his skin. His skin had been scratched and bleeding in many places and the man when taken in hand had been delirious. Later, when he had become rational apparently and his condition had improved, he had refused positively to reveal his identity or to make any statement as to the circumstances which had led to his condition; so that he had been discharged as a "mystery." He had expressed an intention to go West, take up a homestead and eventually go in for pure-bred stock. It was presumed, therefore, that he was a young farmer who had been working in some lumber camp and on his way out to civilization had got lost in the woods and had become temporarily deranged by the experience.

Having successfully sidetracked the conversation, Phil excused himself from the table and hurried to his room. Here he dressed with scrupulous care. He unfolded a small cambric handkerchief and a dollar bill to make sure that the little hand-painted pin was quite safe; then he folded the articles together again and placed them in an inside pocket with a care befitting the important part they were about to play.

He now unlocked a drawer in the cheffonier and took out a very small square box, morocco leather, velvet-lined. The stone was a beautiful white one and he stood off a pace or two and admired it. It certainly made that other solitaire she had been wearing on her engagement finger look like thirty cents! And to think that the "engagement" had been merely a detail of her masquerade in Fergey's office! To-night—?

With a sigh of satisfaction he pocketed the little leather box. Then he slipped out the back way, taking a latch-key with him. They were going canoeing to-night and he knew that it would be late, very late, when he returned.

Choose from Thousands of 1stWorldLibrary Classics By

A. M. Barnard
Ada Leverson
Adolphus William Ward
Aesop
Agatha Christie
Alexander Aaronsohn
Alexander Kielland
Alexandre Dumas
Alfred Gatty
Alfred Ollivant
Alice Duer Miller
Alice Turner Curtis
Alice Dunbar
Allen Chapman
Alleyne Ireland
Ambrose Bierce
Amelia E. Barr
Amory H. Bradford
Andrew Lang
Andrew McFarland Davis
Andy Adams
Angela Brazil
Anna Alice Chapin
Anna Sewell
Annie Besant
Annie Hamilton Donnell
Annie Payson Call
Annie Roe Carr
Annonaymous
Anton Chekhov
Archibald Lee Fletcher
Arnold Bennett
Arthur C. Benson
Arthur Conan Doyle
Arthur M. Winfield
Arthur Ransome
Arthur Schnitzler
Arthur Train
Atticus
B.H. Baden-Powell
B. M. Bower
B. C. Chatterjee
Baroness Emmuska Orczy
Baroness Orczy
Basil King
Bayard Taylor
Ben Macomber
Bertha Muzzy Bower
Bjornstjerne Bjornson

Booth Tarkington
Boyd Cable
Bram Stoker
C. Collodi
C. E. Orr
C. M. Ingleby
Carolyn Wells
Catherine Parr Traill
Charles A. Eastman
Charles Amory Beach
Charles Dickens
Charles Dudley Warner
Charles Farrar Browne
Charles Ives
Charles Kingsley
Charles Klein
Charles Hanson Towne
Charles Lathrop Pack
Charles Romyn Dake
Charles Whibley
Charles Willing Beale
Charlotte M. Braeme
Charlotte M. Yonge
Charlotte Perkins Stetson
Clair W. Hayes
Clarence Day Jr.
Clarence E. Mulford
Clemence Housman
Confucius
Coningsby Dawson
Cornelis DeWitt Wilcox
Cyril Burleigh
D. H. Lawrence
Daniel Defoe
David Garnett
Dinah Craik
Don Carlos Janes
Donald Keyhoe
Dorothy Kilner
Dougan Clark
Douglas Fairbanks
E. Nesbit
E. P. Roe
E. Phillips Oppenheim
E. S. Brooks
Earl Barnes
Edgar Rice Burroughs
Edith Van Dyne
Edith Wharton

Edward Everett Hale
Edward J. O'Biren
Edward S. Ellis
Edwin L. Arnold
Eleanor Atkins
Eleanor Hallowell Abbott
Eliot Gregory
Elizabeth Gaskell
Elizabeth McCracken
Elizabeth Von Arnim
Ellem Key
Emerson Hough
Emilie F. Carlen
Emily Bronte
Emily Dickinson
Enid Bagnold
Enilor Macartney Lane
Erasmus W. Jones
Ernie Howard Pie
Ethel May Dell
Ethel Turner
Ethel Watts Mumford
Eugene Sue
Eugenie Foa
Eugene Wood
Eustace Hale Ball
Evelyn Everett-green
Everard Cotes
F. H. Cheley
F. J. Cross
F. Marion Crawford
Fannie E. Newberry
Federick Austin Ogg
Ferdinand Ossendowski
Fergus Hume
Florence A. Kilpatrick
Fremont B. Deering
Francis Bacon
Francis Darwin
Frances Hodgson Burnett
Frances Parkinson Keyes
Frank Gee Patchin
Frank Harris
Frank Jewett Mather
Frank L. Packard
Frank V. Webster
Frederic Stewart Isham
Frederick Trevor Hill
Frederick Winslow Taylor

Friedrich Kerst
Friedrich Nietzsche
Fyodor Dostoyevsky
G.A. Henty
G.K. Chesterton
Gabrielle E. Jackson
Garrett P. Serviss
Gaston Leroux
George A. Warren
George Ade
Geroge Bernard Shaw
George Cary Eggleston
George Durston
George Ebers
George Eliot
George Gissing
George MacDonald
George Meredith
George Orwell
George Sylvester Viereck
George Tucker
George W. Cable
George Wharton James
Gertrude Atherton
Gordon Casserly
Grace E. King
Grace Gallatin
Grace Greenwood
Grant Allen
Guillermo A. Sherwell
Gulielma Zollinger
Gustav Flaubert
H. A. Cody
H. B. Irving
H.C. Bailey
H. G. Wells
H. H. Munro
H. Irving Hancock
H. R. Naylor
H. Rider Haggard
H. W. C. Davis
Haldeman Julius
Hall Caine
Hamilton Wright Mabie
Hans Christian Andersen
Harold Avery
Harold McGrath
Harriet Beecher Stowe
Harry Castlemon
Harry Coghill
Harry Houidini

Hayden Carruth
Helent Hunt Jackson
Helen Nicolay
Hendrik Conscience
Hendy David Thoreau
Henri Barbusse
Henrik Ibsen
Henry Adams
Henry Ford
Henry Frost
Henry James
Henry Jones Ford
Henry Seton Merriman
Henry W Longfellow
Herbert A. Giles
Herbert Carter
Herbert N. Casson
Herman Hesse
Hildegard G. Frey
Homer
Honore De Balzac
Horace B. Day
Horace Walpole
Horatio Alger Jr.
Howard Pyle
Howard R. Garis
Hugh Lofting
Hugh Walpole
Humphry Ward
Ian Maclaren
Inez Haynes Gillmore
Irving Bacheller
Isabel Cecilia Williams
Isabel Hornibrook
Israel Abrahams
Ivan Turgenev
J.G.Austin
J. Henri Fabre
J. M. Barrie
J. M. Walsh
J. Macdonald Oxley
J. R. Miller
J. S. Fletcher
J. S. Knowles
J. Storer Clouston
J. W. Duffield
Jack London
Jacob Abbott
James Allen
James Andrews
James Baldwin

James Branch Cabell
James DeMille
James Joyce
James Lane Allen
James Lane Allen
James Oliver Curwood
James Oppenheim
James Otis
James R. Driscoll
Jane Abbott
Jane Austen
Jane L. Stewart
Janet Aldridge
Jens Peter Jacobsen
Jerome K. Jerome
Jessie Graham Flower
John Buchan
John Burroughs
John Cournos
John F. Kennedy
John Gay
John Glasworthy
John Habberton
John Joy Bell
John Kendrick Bangs
John Milton
John Philip Sousa
John Taintor Foote
Jonas Lauritz Idemil Lie
Jonathan Swift
Joseph A. Altsheler
Joseph Carey
Joseph Conrad
Joseph E. Badger Jr
Joseph Hergesheimer
Joseph Jacobs
Jules Vernes
Julian Hawthrone
Julie A Lippmann
Justin Huntly McCarthy
Kakuzo Okakura
Karle Wilson Baker
Kate Chopin
Kenneth Grahame
Kenneth McGaffey
Kate Langley Bosher
Kate Langley Bosher
Katherine Cecil Thurston
Katherine Stokes
L. A. Abbot
L. T. Meade

L. Frank Baum
Latta Griswold
Laura Dent Crane
Laura Lee Hope
Laurence Housman
Lawrence Beasley
Leo Tolstoy
Leonid Andreyev
Lewis Carroll
Lewis Sperry Chafer
Lilian Bell
Lloyd Osbourne
Louis Hughes
Louis Joseph Vance
Louis Tracy
Louisa May Alcott
Lucy Fitch Perkins
Lucy Maud Montgomery
Luther Benson
Lydia Miller Middleton
Lyndon Orr
M. Corvus
M. H. Adams
Margaret E. Sangster
Margret Howth
Margaret Vandercook
Margaret W. Hungerford
Margret Penrose
Maria Edgeworth
Maria Thompson Daviess
Mariano Azuela
Marion Polk Angellotti
Mark Overton
Mark Twain
Mary Austin
Mary Catherine Crowley
Mary Cole
Mary Hastings Bradley
Mary Roberts Rinehart
Mary Rowlandson
M. Wollstonecraft Shelley
Maud Lindsay
Max Beerbohm
Myra Kelly
Nathaniel Hawthrone
Nicolo Machiavelli
O. F. Walton
Oscar Wilde

Owen Johnson
P.G. Wodehouse
Paul and Mabel Thorne
Paul G. Tomlinson
Paul Severing
Percy Brebner
Percy Keese Fitzhugh
Peter B. Kyne
Plato
Quincy Allen
R. Derby Holmes
R. L. Stevenson
R. S. Ball
Rabindranath Tagore
Rahul Alvares
Ralph Bonehill
Ralph Henry Barbour
Ralph Victor
Ralph Waldo Emmerson
Rene Descartes
Ray Cummings
Rex Beach
Rex E. Beach
Richard Harding Davis
Richard Jefferies
Richard Le Gallienne
Robert Barr
Robert Frost
Robert Gordon Anderson
Robert L. Drake
Robert Lansing
Robert Lynd
Robert Michael Ballantyne
Robert W. Chambers
Rosa Nouchette Carey
Rudyard Kipling
Saint Augustine
Samuel B. Allison
Samuel Hopkins Adams
Sarah Bernhardt
Sarah C. Hallowell
Selma Lagerlof
Sherwood Anderson
Sigmund Freud
Standish O'Grady
Stanley Weyman
Stella Benson
Stella M. Francis

Stephen Crane
Stewart Edward White
Stijn Streuvels
Swami Abhedananda
Swami Parmananda
T. S. Ackland
T. S. Arthur
The Princess Der Ling
Thomas A. Janvier
Thomas A Kempis
Thomas Anderton
Thomas Bailey Aldrich
Thomas Bulfinch
Thomas De Quincey
Thomas Dixon
Thomas H. Huxley
Thomas Hardy
Thomas More
Thornton W. Burgess
U. S. Grant
Upton Sinclair
Valentine Williams
Various Authors
Vaughan Kester
Victor Appleton
Victor G. Durham
Victoria Cross
Virginia Woolf
Wadsworth Camp
Walter Camp
Walter Scott
Washington Irving
Wilbur Lawton
Wilkie Collins
Willa Cather
Willard F. Baker
William Dean Howells
William le Queux
W. Makepeace Thackeray
William W. Walter
William Shakespeare
Winston Churchill
Yei Theodora Ozaki
Yogi Ramacharaka
Young E. Allison
Zane Grey